The Poetics of Description

DE DESCRIPTIONE, QUÆ
Græcè ἔκφρασις dicta.

CAP. XII.

Descriptio est oratio expositiva, qua narratione id, quod propositum est, diligenter vel ut oculis subjicit: *Descriptionis summa est virtus, inquit Qu. l. 8. c. 3. Facillimè enim id accipiunt animi, quod agnoscũt. Historici simplici appellatione, Thucydidem intelligunt.*

Describuntur autem
- Personæ,
- Res,
- Tempora,
- Loci,
- Bruta animalia,
- Plantæ.

Personæ: ut Homerus in Odyssea ad Eurybaten. Latus erat humeris, ore ater, crineque crispus.

Res: ut navales pedestresque pugnæ; quemadmodum Historicus fecit.

Tempora: ut ver, aut æstas, disserendo, quod multi proferant in hisce flores.

Loci: ut idem Thucydides portum Thesprotarum χειμέριον, id est, hyemalem, quamque teneat formam, dixit.

Describentes verò personas, à summis ad ima usque ire oportebit, id est, à capite ad pedes.

Res verò ab antecedentibus, & eis quæ insunt ipsis, quæque ex ipsis solent provenire.

Lem-

Detail from a Latin redaction of the *Progymnasmata* of Aphthonius edited by R. Agricola and annotated by R. Lorich, published in Amsterdam in 1649. (Reproduced by permission of the Rare Book and Manuscript Library, Columbia University).

The Poetics of Description
Imagined Places in European Literature

Janice Hewlett Koelb

THE POETICS OF DESCRIPTION

Copyright © Janice Hewlett Koelb, 2006
All rights reserved. No part of this book may be used or reproduced in any manner whatsoever without written permission except in the case of brief quotations embodied in critical articles or reviews.
Permission has been generously granted by the William Blake Archive to reprint a selection from William Blake, *The Marriage of Heaven and Hell*, Copy C, plate 6.

First published in 2006 by
PALGRAVE MACMILLAN™
175 Fifth Avenue, New York, N.Y. 10010 and
Houndmills, Basingstoke, Hampshire, England RG21 6XS.
Companies and representatives throughout the world.

PALGRAVE MACMILLAN is the global academic imprint of the Palgrave Macmillan division of St. Martin's Press, LLC and of Palgrave Macmillan Ltd. Macmillan® is a registered trademark in the United States, United Kingdom and other countries. Palgrave is a registered trademark in the European Union and other countries.

ISBN-10: 1-4039-7489-6   hardcover
ISBN-13: 978-1-4039-7489-1 hardcover

Library of Congress Cataloging-in-Publication Data is available from the Library of Congress.

Koelb, Janice Hewlett.
   The poetics of description : imagined places in European literature / Janice Hewlett Koelb.
     p. cm.
   Includes bibliographical references and index.
   ISBN 1-4039-7489-6 (cloth)
   1. Imaginary places in literature. 2. European literature—History and criticism. I. Title.

PN56.I44K64 2006
809'.93372–dc22
                                                2006043424

A catalogue record for this book is available from the British Library.

Design by Macmillan India Ltd.

First edition: December 2006

10 9 8 7 6 5 4 3 2 1

Printed in the United States of America.

For T.G.P.

Thus the theory of description matters most.
It is the theory of the word for those

For whom the word is the making of the world,
The buzzing world and lisping firmament.

—Wallace Stevens
"Description without Place"

Contents

Acknowledgments	ix
Preface	xi
Introduction: Ecphrasis, Description, and the Imagined Place	1
1 As if Present: Classical Ecphrasis	19
2 Unity, Form, and Figuration	43
3 A Sylvan Scene	69
4 The Universe Dead or Alive: Gilpin, Wordsworth, and the Picturesque	97
5 The Visionary Eye: Wordsworth's Antipicturesque *Excursion*	125
6 "Till the Place Became Religion": Byron's Coliseum	155
Epilogue: Immediacy	189
Notes	199
Works Cited	207
Index	221

Acknowledgments

It is a pleasure to thank the Graduate School of the University of North Carolina, Chapel Hill, for a generous one-year fellowship that enabled me to write full-time; Thomas J. Nixon, Humanities Reference Librarian at Carolina's Davis Library, for his instant solutions to all my research problems and queries; Eric S. Downing for mentoring the teaching experiences that stimulated this project; Farideh Koohi-Kamali and Julia Cohen of Palgrave Macmillan and the staff of Macmillan India for unfailing courtesy and efficiency in handling my manuscript; and the expert readers engaged by Palgrave to evaluate the manuscript. Their comments and criticism provided the spur for many important changes and improvements. Many others have helped me in many ways, but I would like especially to acknowledge Dino S. Cervigni, Gareth Cook, Carl Harris, Jerzy Linderski, Townsend Ludington, and Tram Kim Nguyen.

Special thanks are due to Lilian R. Furst, under whose direction my project began to take shape as a dissertation, for giving me the freedom to find my own way even as she sheltered and nurtured my work at every step; to Joseph S. Viscomi, whose 1997 lectures and 1999 seminar, Revolutions in Romantic Art and Literature, inspired many writings that eventually grew into chapters 4–6, William H. Race for generously translating passages from the Greek that have not previously been available in English; to Paul Piehler and Karl Kroeber for graciously responding to a stranger's work with enthusiasm and constructive suggestions; and above all to Alexander C. Cook and Clayton Koelb for supporting the project in countless ways, large and small, throughout its long gestation. Without their wisdom and encouragement there would have been no book.

Preface

This project began in a moment of distress. While teaching the first book of the *Aeneid*, I had quickly advanced, as usual, to the celebrated episode in which Aeneas, having washed ashore in Carthage, wanders onto one of the great imagined places of European literature. He visits the construction site of a temple to Juno, whose walls depict scenes from the destruction of Troy, Aeneas's home. The Greeks had a word for such an episode, I told my class: *ekphrasis*, "the description of a work of art." Writing on the board the syllables of this word, which literally means only "speaking out," I began to have doubts, though I never expressed them to my students. I suspected that the received wisdom I had just imparted was—most likely—egregiously inaccurate. For as every student of aesthetics knows, the ancient Greeks and Romans did not have the modern notion of "art" as a special category containing painting, sculpture, and the like, elevated above other products of human craft; so I could not really believe that they would have a rhetorical term naming a specialized discourse about these kinds of things. The authoritative dictionaries and lexicons I consulted gave no account of how or when "description of art" evolved out of "speaking out."

A brilliant essay by Ruth Webb in *Word & Image* clarified my immediate confusion. Webb established that ecphrasis, defined as description of art, is a twentieth-century invention and that in classical *ekphrasis*, "a speech which leads one around (*periegematikos*) bringing the subject matter vividly (*enargos*) before the eyes" (11), works of art had no special status at all.

Oddly enough Webb's meticulous scholarship has been largely ignored (or grudgingly acknowledged, even by classicists), and its implications for scholars of more modern literature remain completely unexamined.

But what of any importance, the reader will ask, could possibly be at stake here? Why bother with pedantic reminders about a word that has changed its meaning over the course of a couple thousand years? Nearly every word in any living language has suffered a similar fate, and an ancient definition is surely no more right or wrong than a woolly mammoth is the right or wrong version of an elephant. An animal, ancient or modern, is as adapted to its synchronic environment as a definition is to its cultural milieu. But just as the historical forms and functions of animals have coevolved with a living environment to which the fossilized mammoth or the living elephant bears witness, so too have the historical forms and meanings of words coevolved within a much broader context to which evolving definitions themselves bear witness at each synchronic moment. Definitions that reflect actual usage are specimens of cultural history. Owen Barfield, to whom I owe this notion, points out in *History in English Words* that ancient definitions are quite unlike extinct creatures in one important respect: ancient definitions, accurately recovered and dated, are valuable documents in the history of ideas, or even consciousness itself. They can play an important role in the living world of today by allowing us to communicate in a particularly intimate fashion with the minds of the people for whom they served a vital function (18–19).

I would like therefore to reassure readers who are committed to art ecphrasis that, although I reflect upon the cultural climate that produced the extinction of the old definition and the flourishing of the new, my project does not entail expunging a modern definition of an ancient Greek word. A living definition is a stubborn creature, a vital organ of perception, a psychological fact. Few taboos are more difficult to transgress than a useful definition; "ecphrasis" now names a certain indispensable concept that its speakers think with. But when a definition enables sharp attention to one phenomenon, the acuity often comes at the expense of obscuring other important things. What the successes of late-twentieth-century critics of art ecphrasis have obscured is the actual history of ecphrasis as it developed in antiquity and flourished until at least the Romantic period. Romantic poets assimilated and transformed a particularly vigorous form of classical ecphrasis: the depiction of places that are, like Virgil's temple, imbued with human significance. This study brings to light a few of the richest episodes in that much larger story.

Introduction: Ecphrasis, Description, and the Imagined Place

> It is not down in any map; true places never are.
> —Melville, *Moby-Dick*

The frontispiece to this volume, a chapter title page from a widely distributed seventeenth-century textbook, summarizes the understanding of ecphrasis[1] from Latin antiquity until at least the eighteenth century: "*De descriptione, quae Graecè* ekphrasis *dicta*" ("On description, which in Greek is called *ekphrasis*"). It is with ancient Greek commentary on *ekphrasis* that the poetics of description begins. But today the term *description* has little cachet, while *ekphrasis* arouses a clear and entirely appealing expectation: that soon the discussion will turn to the vivid scenes depicted on Homer's shield of Achilles, on the walls of Virgil's Carthaginian temple, or on Keats's Grecian urn—that is, to verbal descriptions of visual art. That description—the term and concept—should languish in the stagnant backwaters of literary theory long after one of its subgenres, the description of works of art, has come into prominence is an odd historical fact that is certainly worth careful scrutiny.

The first sustained treatment of ecphrasis in a widely read work of twentieth-century scholarship was Leo Spitzer's 1955 essay on Keats's "Ode on a Grecian Urn." Ruth Webb has proposed that Spitzer's essay marks the moment when the Greek word "catapulted" out of the recondite world of late- classical and Byzantine studies into English and Comparative Literature and thence into the literary theory of the late twentieth century (16–17). Spitzer asserted with complete confidence that Keats's "Ode"

> belongs to the genre, known to Occidental literature from Homer and Theocritus to the Parnassians and Rilke, of the *ekphrasis,* the poetic description of a pictorial or sculptural work of art, which description implies, in the words of Theophile Gautier, "une transposition d'art," a reproduction through the medium of words of sensuously perceptible *objets d'art* ("ut pictura poesis"). (72)

In the wake of Spitzer's article, discussions of ecphrasis began to proliferate in scholarly studies of European literature of all periods. By the last decade of the twentieth century, numerous books on the subject were being produced by some of the most prominent literary critics and published by the most distinguished presses.[2] Spitzer's analysis of the "Urn" as an ecphrasis thus spawned a minor industry and established firmly the notion that "the poetic description of a pictorial or sculptural work of art" was what the Greeks had meant with their word *ekphrasis*.

Unfortunately, Spitzer had not got it quite right.

The source of Spitzer's misinformation appears to have been John Dewar Denniston's entry in the 1949 *Oxford Classical Dictionary*, the earliest version of the modern English definition of *ekphrasis* that I have been able to find:

> The rhetorical description of a work of art, one of the types of progymnasmata (rhetorical exercise, q.v.) [. . .]. The efflorescence of the representational arts in the second century A.D. gave an impetus to this type of writing, which Nicostratus of Macedonia (second century A.D., author of an *Eikones*) is perhaps the first exponent. (310)

Indeed, scholars have revealed that the Greek word *ekphrasis* is not extant before the first century A.D. and does not come into regular usage before its treatment in the Early Empire progymnasmata (elementary rhetorical manuals). But Denniston's definition differs quite a bit from Theon's first-century definition of *ekphrasis:* "A speech which leads one around (*periegematikos*) bringing the subject matter vividly (*enargos*) before the eyes" (Webb 11). All the manuals list general subject-matter for this exercise in vivid presentation: people, places, things, times, events. Works of art have no special status at all. They are among the many "things" (*pragmata*) that may be described. When the Romans encountered this material in the Greek manuals, they translated *ekphrasis* as *descriptio*. All postclassical European discussions of "description" thus ultimately derive from the broad notion of ecphrasis found in the progymnasmata and in subsequent Latin interpretations of that notion.

The modern English restrictive application of the term solely to works of art has no classical precedent; it is entirely a twentieth-century innovation, authorized initially by Denniston and taken up by Spitzer. Like Spitzer, Denniston curiously cites no classical authority for his definition of ecphrasis; or rather, he misattributes it to J. W. H. Atkins's article titled "Progymnasmata" in the same volume. Atkins translates ecphrasis—correctly—as "description," not description of art in particular (734). It is Denniston, in stark contrast to Atkins, who declares that the object of ecphrasis is exclusively art. Guided by his limited definition, Denniston finds that second-century Nicostratus is "perhaps the first exponent" of "this type of writing," the genre we have come to know as ecphrasis, so baptized by Denniston's misreading of the progymnasmata. The misreading was understandable enough. The efflorescence of the arts in the second century A.D. did indeed stimulate ecphrases of art objects, but other subject matter did not suffer a decline. As Shadi Bartsch has reminded us, all progymnasmatic topics flourished in Greek romances throughout the period. Even Achilles Tatius's *Leucippe and Clitophon*, a romance that opens with a description of a painting and contains more art ecphrasis than any other extant romance, contains only 6 art ecphrases among the 30 or so major set pieces that include treatments of the crocodile, the hippopotamus, the elephant, the phoenix, the Egyptian ox, the peacock, the viper, and the lamprey (Bartsch 12–13 and n. 12). The animals far outnumber the art objects. Had twentieth-century literary theorists been more fascinated by natural history than they were by art, they would have given us a different modern definition of ecphrasis. Just how fruitful such a development might have been is illustrated by several useful discussions in Gaston Bachelard's works, including especially his *Lautréamont* and his reading of d'Annunzio's hare in *The Poetics of Space* (208–209).

So skewed was Denniston's attention to art, however, that he concluded his article with a bibliography of only one entry, and it is not classical: Paul Friedländer's 1912 *Johannes von Gaza und Paulus Silentiarius*. Friedländer's treatise about certain Greek descriptions of works of art, found in all bibliographies on modern ecphrasis, contains an explanation of ecphrasis (which I have never seen quoted in English translation) that goes much against the grain of those who, like Denniston, cite Friedländer as authorizing the modern definition. "According to Theon and Hermogenes," writes Friedländer,

> one can describe persons and things, places and times, to which Aphthonius in the fourth century adds animals and plants. There is still not a single word here about works of art, and Nicolaus in the fifth century appears to be the first to cite statues and pictures among the proper objects of description. In practice some such thing had evidently occurred earlier, since there is a fulsome rendering of two paintings among the paradigmatic examples, ascribed to Libanius, of such progymnasmata.
>
> One must, however, finally be quite clear about the fact that there is no justification for considering ecphrasis as a completely distinctive artistic genre. What is focused upon is first and foremost the activity of describing. (85)[3]

In what may be an attempt to counter the dubious usage of classicists such as Bougot and Bertrand (whom I discuss a bit later in this chapter), Friedländer felt it necessary to remind his readers that there is "not a single word here about works of art" until Nicolaus.

But Denniston's misreading was brilliant in its way, and it stuck. For critics of modern literature and for modern classicists, the new definition forged a link with the distant past. It named an authentic nineteenth- and twentieth-century desire to give the "illusion of antiquity" to its own aesthetic preoccupations and achieved this aim by a kind of inconspicuous synecdoche (Webb 17–18). By substituting a genuine and compelling subgenre of ecphrasis for the whole, the definition has obscured all other ancient ecphrasis and given us a distorted filter through which to perceive the ecphrases in earlier literature and the relations among the ecphrases of a single work. When for example modern critics claim that the decoration of Dido's temple is the "initial use of ekphrasis in the *Aeneid* [. . .] and serves to educate the reader in many of the imaginative patterns the poet will follow in subsequent descriptions" (Putnam 23); or that "*ekphrasis* has no place in *Paradise Lost*" (Du Bois 93), both the premises and the conclusions of such critics invite revision.

The modern definitions of ecphrasis, besides restricting the subject matter to art, narrow the ancient definitions in another way: modern ecphrasis (like modern description in the wake of G. E. Lessing's critique) tends to be formally distinguished from, or even opposed to, narrative. Ancient ecphrasis embraces narrative, but only in its most vivid forms. All the progymnasmata mention battle as a subject of ecphrasis; all cite or allude to Thucydides.[4] An ordinary narrative, explains fifth-century Nicolaus, "gives a plain exposition of actions," while ecphrasis "tries to make the hearers into spectators" (Kennedy 127). Hermogenes advises that ecphrasis of action "proceed from what went before, from what happened at the time, and from what followed" (Webb 36). The action, moreover, might be quite brief. Modern readers would be surprised to learn, for example, that the account in *Iliad* 23.232, when Achilles sinks exhausted into sleep beside the funeral pyre of Patroclus, was named an ecphrasis in an ancient scholion to Homer (Erbse 404). What matters to the ancients is that the presentation, whether long or short, have a heightened and credible immediacy. Writers of later periods have made extensive use of ecphrasis in the ancient manner—as vivid description, with or without elements of narrativity—although they and their contemporaries may not have named it so.

A measure of the profound obscurity from which the term *ekphrasis* has only recently emerged is its treatment in standard English dictionaries. Neither *ekphrasis* nor ecphrasis appears at all in Webster's *Third;* and "description of art" or the like does not appear under ecphrasis in the *Oxford English Dictionary*.[5] Unlike such Greek terms as *hyperbaton* and *anaphora* that are well attested in English since the sixteenth century, *ekphrasis* remains a foreign word without a settled English meaning, despite its currency among literary scholars and theorists.

Webb attributes the modern coinage to the French classicists Bertrand and Bougot, each of whom uses the term in 1881 in separate studies of the rhetorician Philostratus (16). Bertrand posits an ancient and cumulative tradition of competing describers of art, including Catullus, Virgil, Statius, and Philostratus, who were moved by a certain anxiety of influence—"This taste spreads; all the poets compete," writes Bertrand. The result was "a fashionable genre with a particular name"—ecphrasis (48–49; my trans.); but, as Webb points out, "Bertrand was curiously reluctant to display his find. He relegated it, untransliterated, to a footnote, as if he were not wholly confident in his new use of the term" (16). In the text, however, Bertrand consistently uses the word "description"—which for centuries had been the French translation of Greek *ekphrasis*.[6]

The new French usage was slow in gaining ground; but in 1955 in America, as Webb explains, "Spitzer's article fell on fertile ground, already prepared by the New Critics' interest in the poem as artifact, an idea in search of a name" (17). Strangely enough, the new ecphrastic poem-as-artifact was imagined as recursively *representational* art, and at a historical moment when representational art had lost its theoretical cachet. Stranger still, this new ecphrasis with its emphasis on obviously mediated subject matter is not just narrower but in its most basic character exactly the opposite of ancient Greek *ekphrasis,* whose aim is immediacy. The idea that ecphrasis pertains primarily or entirely to representations of representations is thus not only postclassical—it is nearly postmodern.

In chapter 1, I give a historical synopsis of classical ecphrasis, the *descriptio* of Latin Europe, that shows how the continuity of classical ecphrasis was assured not so much by art descriptions as by descriptions of significant places. Because the Romans translated the Greek *ekphrasis* by the Latin *descriptio*, speakers of English and the Romance languages had no need, until the late nineteenth or twentieth century, to reach back for a Greek term. The semantic turnabout in *ekphrasis* certainly suggests that the proper starting point for a discussion of ecphrasis in European literature might be an investigation of the theory and practice of literary description. But, remarkably enough, two-and-a-half millennia of Western literary criticism have produced very few inquiries into literary description, notwithstanding the fact that poets and novelists often obsess about getting it right. Compared with narrative, to which it is usually opposed, and which has an "ology" and technical vocabulary of its own, description has not fared well among twentieth-century critical theorists, as Michel Beaujour shrewdly observes:

> Description, which opens (or should in principle open) windows in the reader's imagination, which expands worlds and multiplies quasi-perceptions, ought to

be considered a life force, the ever-available key to inexhaustible treasures. It is, on the contrary, scorned, skipped, or else praised for the paradoxical reason that it has nothing to do with the real world. Within our high culture, the history of description and its appreciation is that of a continuous and seemingly undeserved misfortune. (47)

The "humiliations suffered by description" (49) outlined by Beaujour are perhaps best summed up in Philippe Hamon's account of its downward drift, "la dérive descriptive." Excluded from poetry by Mallarmé "by its prosaic attachment to reality" and from theater by Valéry on the opposite charge of insufficient naturalness, description has ended up associated with the novel, the "genre boulimique," in Hamon's colorful formulation (Introduction 11). These compulsively disorderly eaters cram themselves with the stuff of description: words, words, words.

Examples of disdain for description abound in late-twentieth-century criticism, even and perhaps especially in those instances where the ubiquity of descriptive material is acknowledged. Roland Barthes, accepting the premise that novels are full of useless descriptive detail, attempts to rescue all this uselessness and put it (as Hamon correctly points out) into the service of another mimesis, "l'effet du réel," or "the reality effect" as it is usually translated (Introduction 9). "It is the category of the 'real,' and not its various contents, which is being signified" by superfluous detail (Barthes 140). More than that, the reality effect is in Barthes's view the "true signifier of realism, [. . .] the basis of all that unavowed 'vraisemblance' which forms the aesthetic of all the standard works of modernity" (140). Since what Barthes means by "unavowed vraisemblance" is all the detail that cannot be assigned another essential function—and he does allow broad latitude for functional detail— a critic who wishes to distinguish the reality effect in a modern or any other text from other effects has to decide whether or not a particular detail is essential for characterization or atmosphere, whether or not it is symbolic or allegorical, and so forth.

The difficulties of doing this can be illustrated by one of Barthes's examples, : "When Flaubert, describing the room occupied by Madame Aubain, Félicité's mistress, tells us that 'on an old piano, under a barometer, there was a pyramid of boxes and cartons,'" Flaubert produces, explains Barthes:

> *notations* (data, descriptive details) which structural analysis, occupied as it is with separating out and systematising the main articulations of narrative, ordinarily, and up to the present, has left out, either by excluding from its inventory (by simply failing to mention them) all those details which are "superfluous" (as far as structure is concerned), or else by treating these same details (as the present author has himself attempted to do) as fillers, padding

(catalyses), assigned indirect functional value in that, cumulatively, they constitute an indication of characterisation or atmosphere, and so can finally be salvaged as part of the structure. (135)

And as he further explains, "we will inevitably be confronted with *notations* which no function (not even the most indirect) will allow us to justify" (135). Such details

> seem to be allied with a kind of narrative *luxury,* profligate to the extent of throwing up "useless" details and increasing the cost of narrative information. So, although it may be possible just to regard the detail of the piano as a sign of the bourgeois status of its owner, and that of the boxes as a sign of disorder and something like a reverse or fall in status, appropriately evocative of the Aubain household, there seems to be no such end in view to justify the reference to the barometer, an object which is neither incongruous nor significant, and which, therefore, at first sight seems not to belong to the domain of the *notable.* (135–136)

Flaubert's barometer, and other such details, "say, in the last analysis, only this: we are the real" (140).

We might well ask: What authorizes even such a distinguished reader as Barthes to dismiss the barometer in this rather cavalier fashion? When the rhetorically self-conscious Flaubert places a barometer at the apex of a pyramid of boxes atop a piano in the opening description of the short story might he not mean it to function figuratively, just as the boxes and the piano do? After all, the barometer signifies the occupant's bourgeois status as much as the piano; both are standard but not inexpensive furnishings. The more important point, though, is that the pyramidal still life of piano, boxes, and barometer, composed within the musty room, has a thematic and imagistic importance that far exceeds the barometer's usefulness as either status symbol or indicator of the tale's reality. The tale's opening pyramid prefigures the Corpus Christi pyramid that appears out-of-doors at the end of the tale in conjunction with Félicité's death from pneumonia. Flaubert places Félicité's idolized parrot at the apex of the closing pyramid; he puts the barometer at the apex of the opening one. This meteorological instrument, bringing indoors a predictive indication of as yet invisible weather conditions outside, was also in the nineteenth century considered a medical predictor of as yet unseen bodily conditions. It thus serves as a particularly apt and concrete emblem of exactly the kind of complex internal-external relation Flaubert is attempting to explore in the human world. Indeed, if we agree with Barthes that the pile of boxes suggests "disorder and something like a reversal or fall in status"—and I think we should—the barometer, which predicts changes in weather and in health, only adds to the sense that Mme. Aubain's musty parlor is a pathogenic place and that the pyramid is a proleptic tomb.[7]

Such quasi-symmetrical framing is moreover characteristic of Flaubert's style. It is one of the ways that he modulates descriptions of the most ordinary objects into figurations that can only be fully understood as such in retrospect. Because such descriptions lack a stated tenor and thus are not explicitly metaphorical, a reader such as Barthes may fail to notice that they are nonetheless figurative. Such a figurative reading is justified, however, not by a specific tenor provided by the text, but by the work as a whole, especially when the whole is supplemented by what the reader has already experienced in Flaubert's writing and in the cultural models that formally orient it. When viewed in these terms, even apparently "irrelevant" descriptive passages in Flaubert, and indeed in many authors of all periods, are readily understood as participating in a larger structure of figuration holding together an entire work. Chapter 2 shows that these formal and reader response issues cannot be reduced to mere subjectivity or indeterminacy, on the one hand, or to mere convention or ideology on the other. I argue that a firmer understanding of descriptive practice needs to be reestablished, but on a different basis than the anti-Horatian, quasi-Aristotelian position staked out by Lessing and elaborated by twentieth-century narratologists.

The motivation for Barthes's project in "The Reality Effect," to find a theoretical justification for Flaubert's descriptive practice, starts from the assumption that a great deal of the descriptive material has no thematic or poetic role in the structure of the work beyond "increasing the cost of narrative information" (135). It has been precisely that assumption, we may reasonably suppose, that has motived both the "dérive descriptive" noted by Hamon and the stunning success of Spitzer's spurious definition of ecphrasis. Though "description" (understood in Barthes's limited way) might have no figurative function, "ecphrasis" (understood in Spitzer's equally limited way) not only has a figurative function, it has the status of an officially named figure. The Greek term names an ancient but misunderstood figure of thought that attracts theoretical speculation precisely because it "speaks out"—somehow or other—from ordinary language. All these assumptions and limited understandings need to be reexamined. Even a relatively brief analysis of Flaubert's text reveals that Barthes's assumption about the emptiness of Flaubert's descriptive material was entirely unwarranted. One line of argument I begin to develop in chapters 1 and 2 and carry forward throughout this study is that such assumptions about description have often been unwarranted; that there has been a powerful and consistent tradition in European literature in which description (especially place description) is both essential to human characterization and integral to the design of the entire work (as it is in Flaubert's story); and that Romantic poetry exploited and renovated that tradition as one of its most characteristic strategies.

The example from Flaubert is in fact quite directly relevant to Romantic poetics. Flaubert was the immediate inheritor of the Romantic method of incorporating descriptive elements into a larger figurative pattern. He had learned from the Romantic poets, particularly from Byron whom he idolized, how to trim the fat and leave the telling naturalistic detail in high relief, and he elevated this trimming of superfluous detail to an aesthetic program for the modern novel. This much was clear to early admirers such as Henry James, whose remarks about bad novels, those "large loose baggy monsters" (*Art* 84), are in the same spirit as Flaubert's dictum "Il y en a toujours trop dans les romans."

Hamon cites Flaubert's dictum; but Hamon, like Barthes, argues against the grain of Flaubert's theory and practice. Hamon deconstructs description-as-victim, valorizing the corpulence that Flaubert condemns, to serve the higher aims of the linguistic fundamentalism to which he is committed. Thus Hamon calls fat description the "lexicographical conscience" that reminds fiction of what it tends (sinfully, it seems) to forget: "That all literature is in the first place made from 'words'" ("Rhetorical Status" 11–12). Beaujour finds in despised description the positive generative power of language, but since this power (for Beaujour as well as Hamon) can only exert itself within language imagined as a closed system, Beaujour ascribes to description the bland indeterminacy that is the fate of all thoroughly deconstructed terms. Description, writes Beaujour, "may turn out to be a mirage that keeps receding and disappearing before our attempts to locate and analyze it" (51). Description's metamorphoses from words into figurative foodstuffs and back again into words—or even further back into receding mirage—would seem only to confirm and extend the humiliations of description and to extinguish from theoretical discourse the sort of textual element that Beaujour—whether ruefully or ironically—calls that "which opens (or should in principle open) windows in the reader's imagination, [. . .] expands worlds and multiplies quasi-perceptions" and "ought to be considered a life force."

Indeed description had once had this "life force" status in French criticism. Eighteenth-century French theory, which preserved classical thinking on ecphrasis, shines through Beaujour's deconstruction of its paradoxes. In 1751 Denis Diderot, for example, read the "descriptions" of the ode and epic as privileged sites where "a spirit passes into the speech of the poet" and "moves and animates all its syllables" (*Lettre* 70, qtd. in Porter 496). Although the notion of that which "moves and animates" would turn out to be inimical to Lessing's far more influential theory of description that appeared at almost the same time, the French *philosophe*'s high valuation of description as a life-giving spirit is as much a window into a genuine classical tradition of ecphrasis as it is onto the future poetics of the generative "symbol" that Romantic theorists insisted on distinguishing from an enclosing code that can be cast aside once we discover the limited meaning inside.

But—to illustrate yet another humiliation suffered by description—Diderot's views on description are not well known to speakers of English, even though they appear in Jourdain's widely available translation of his essays, because Diderot's French *descriptions* is translated out as English *grand style* (194), as if it were necessary to purge Diderot's text of a term that now sounds too paltry to mean what it did in fact mean to Diderot and generations of Europeans: Latin descriptio or Greek *ekphrasis*.

Much of the energy behind the radical devaluation of description that made such a translation seem reasonable came from a twentieth- century revival of Lessing's *Laocoön* in the non-German-speaking world. Lessing's authority obscures a long line of critical thinking about description that is behind (for example) Paul Piehler's assessment of medieval visionary landscape: certain descriptions evoke "a feeling that through the specific description shines some great human desire or fear that can never be fully elucidated" (*Visionary* 70). But twentieth-century theorists do not contextualize such descriptions as ecphrasis. To feel the full force of these animated descriptions, according to Diderot, the reader must almost share its creator's state of mind (*Lettre* 70).

Diderot illustrates his own intersubjective participation with many brief and vivid passages from French and classical literature, but the English reader would never guess that Diderot's topic is "description," not "grand style." Diderot's descriptions, precisely those textual moments that would open "windows in the reader's imagination" in the manner of the "life force" lamented by Beaujour, are precisely the moments that analytic procedures like Beaujour's or Barthes's are not designed to find. It is perhaps not surprising, then, that Barthes fails completely to notice such a moment in Flaubert's "A Simple Heart" when it is staring him in the face. If we are attentive to such matters, in the participatory spirit of eighteenth-century Diderot or twentieth-century Piehler, we find many descriptions that open the "windows" that have become all but opaque. These moments are sometimes among the most famous passages in the canonical literature of the West, sometimes among the most ignored and skipped; and sometimes, over the centuries, both. They are central to a proper understanding of the role of description in European literature, ancient and modern.

Particularly instructive among the examples from classical literature are Virgil's highly patterned and psychologically sensitive descriptions in the

Aeneid, which treat matters that often depart substantially from the frequently cited ecphrases of Aeneas's armor and Dido's murals. The classical scholar Michael C. J. Putnam, though primarily interested in art in *Virgil's Epic Designs,* does go further by undertaking a discussion of an animal ecphrasis. (It is symptomatic of the current state of scholarship that this entirely proper effort struck some of his reviewers as an *extension* of the concept.)[8] Putnam clearly understands Virgil's ecphrases to be digressive in that they are "outside" and detachable from the main stream of the story, a quality stressed by Hamon:

> The term ecphrasis [. . .] designates the literary description [. . .] of a real or imaginary work of art [. . . ,] a decorative development that is "detachable" (*ek*), the part of a text that describes artistically an object already constituted as a work of art. (Introduction 8; my trans.)

But even though he assumes that Virgil's ecphrases are detachable in this way, Putnam also shows that they always relate thematically to the central issues of his poem. The narrative thus may take a detour, sometimes into another narrative, but on that detour one learns much about how to manage the main road when it reappears.

Such descriptive or digressive material, though it undoubtedly adds to the vividness and texture of the invented world presented in the text, does far more than simply produce a "reality effect" in the mind of the reader: it provides an opportunity to elaborate matters important to the thematic, though not necessarily the (main) narrative structure of the work.

That is, it may not be so important to the story of the founding of Rome that we learn all about the background of a pet deer killed in *Aeneid* 7; but the biographical description (and destruction) of Sylvia's domesticated beast prefigures the long biography of Camilla, a feral human being who grew up in the forest, and provokes the reader's consideration of the relation of the animal to the human, the forest to the city—at exactly that point in the story where the humans are taking a distinctly more beastly turn in their behavior (Putnam 97–118). Examples of this sort of ecphrastic patterning abound in the "skippable" pages and scenes of later plays, narrative poems, and prose fiction both ancient and modern, from *Leucippe and Clitophon* to *Moby-Dick* and "A Simple Heart."

The example from Flaubert cited by Barthes points us toward another important feature of Romantic (and post-Romantic) descriptive practice: Flaubert's text focuses the reader's attention on a *place,* Mme. Aubain's parlor, and it proposes a figurative connection between that place and the people and events connected to it. Romantic poetry is full of place descriptions that do not simply enumerate features; the descriptions function as figurative nodes. This is such a well-recognized characteristic of Romantic imagery that we generally simply accept it as something those poets created out of their inherent genius or out of an ideology specific to their historic moment. We can, however, trace legitimate sources of this compositional practice and show how Romantic place description participates in a long and quite distinguished tradition that interfuses the character of mind and place.

That places can function as emblems of mind is a notion inherent in the Greek and Latin meanings of their words for *place*. Like Greek *topos*, which gives us both *topic* and *topography*, the Latin word *locus* has a wide range of both physical and intellectual meanings; *locus* can mean a physical place or an intellectual position or outlook (both *position* and *outlook* of course being spatial metaphors). In American slang, we say we are "in a good place" when we are psychologically at ease. There is no "getting away" from such spatial figurations of mental states: "The mind is its own place," as Milton puts it in *Paradise Lost* (1.254). "Her green mind made the world around her green," writes Wallace Stevens ("Description" 339). Bachelard recalls that Thoreau "had the map of his fields engraved in his soul" (11) and insists that all of us "cover the universe with drawings we have lived," drawings "tonalized on the mode of our inner space" (12). The mind's phenomenological attunement with place is of course Bachelard's entire project in *The Poetics of Space:* topos and psyche are the twin terms. He explicitly proposes "topoanalysis," the "systematic study of the sites of our intimate lives," as the essential "auxilliary of psychoanalysis" (8). It is easy to imagine how descriptions of places might have developed out of primitive homeopathy with the world into Romantic figurations of the individual mind's reflection or creation of the outer world. Much Romantic poetry, characterized as it is by extended descriptions of landscapes both natural and manmade—and by meditations on just what the difference might be—recapitulates, usually in a secularized form, classical depictions of places as suffused with a kind of divine magic that is intelligible to humans and that speaks to the deepest human concerns. It is this classical heritage of places possessing animate, recognizable personalities that prompts Romantic poets to understand even remote places as versions of "home" and to find the numinous quality of home in every significant place. "The unconscious abides," writes Bachelard, and it "is housed." "The normal unconscious knows how to make itself at home everywhere" (*Poetics* 10). Space, given value by the psychic image, becomes the most fitting abode.

Wordsworth acts out his own homecoming gestures time and again, but in his case a description of "home" always turns out to delineate a certain nontranscendent imaginative participation in a self-transforming natural world, where the individual human is at home (or, tragically not at home) and "fully existent only in relation to other selves" who share that home

(Krober, *Ecological* 5, 38). Romantic spiritual homecomings reenact a mythic motif that is as old as European literature. The Greek word for "homecoming," *nostos,* the root of "nostalgia" (a word not attested in English before 1780), is essentially the entire plot of the *Odyssey.* In that poem, as nearly always in the tradition of homecoming tales, the various true and false arrivals serve as the occasion for place descriptions that reveal human character and identity. Virgil quite consciously follows this tradition in depicting several haunting depictions of false and true homecomings in the *Aeneid.* In chapter 3 I turn to one of Virgil's most influential false homecoming scenes, Aeneas's arrival at Carthage.

One of Virgil's models for the arrival at Carthage is Hermes arrival at Kalypso's island in *Odyssey* 5. Homer presents the place under the banner of "home," though it turned out to be only a temporary and involuntary home for shipwrecked Odysseus. The description of the area outside Kalypso's cave evokes a scene of apparent charm:

> He came to a great cave, wherein dwelt the fair-tressed nymph; and he found her within. A great fire was burning on the hearth, and far over the isle spread the fragrance of split cedar and citronwood, as they burned; but she within was singing with a sweet voice as she went to and fro before the loom, weaving with a golden shuttle. Round about the cave grew a luxuriant wood, alder and poplar and sweet-smelling cypress, in which long-winged birds made their nests, owls and falcons and sea crows with chattering tongues, who ply their business on the sea. And right there about the hollow cave ran trailing a garden vine, in pride of its prime, richly laden with clusters. And four springs in a row were flowing with bright water close by one another, turned one this way, one that, and round about soft meadows of violets and celery were blooming. (5.57–5.73; Murray trans.)

Here we find all the "six charms of landscape" enumerated several centuries later by the Greek rhetorician Libanius (A D 314–c. 393), the "springs and plantations and gardens and soft breezes and flowers and bird-voices" that define the late antique topic of the *locus amoenus,* the "lovely place" (qtd. in Curtius 197). Curtius's notion of the locus amoenus is useful as a point of departure for the complicated function of place description in European literature, but only as a point of departure. As early as his 1949 review, Spitzer found that Curtius's locus amoenus and other *topoi* tended to be static and reductive. I align myself with Spitzer when he warns that finding "a *topos* in a poem may blind the student to what the individual poet has done with it and how he has transcended it" (429–430).

With Spitzer's admonition in mind, it is instructive to note that, already in Homer, the "six charms" are deployed in ways that will become more important in the later, more elaborate rhetorical development of the locus amoenus. For the place is not entirely lovely, and its charms are not entirely innocent. In the role of Libanius's "soft breezes," scented smoke infuses the air from the enchantress's hearth. All the named birds are birds of prey, and predatory Kalypso (not the birds) does all the sweet singing. The poet concludes the description with a comment: "There even an immortal, who chanced to come, might gaze and marvel, and delight his soul" (5.73–5.74; Murray trans.). In fact, at this point in Homer's tale, the god Hermes has arrived to free Odysseus from the delightful place that has become the hero's prison. Kalypso may indeed love him, but her behavior is more like that of a capturing bird of prey than of a lover—whence the somewhat disturbing nuances in the description of an otherwise irresistibly attractive place.

A locus amoenus such as Kalypso's island home is typically the abode of a powerful or numinous figure like the divine Kalypso herself. In the most successful examples of this genre, the topographical elements are attuned to the character of its powerful inhabitant, giving the description as a whole a figurative or allegorical potential. Throughout this study I call a place description that is interfused with (human or divine) character or feeling an "ethical" description for short, after Greek *ethos*, "character" (simply because "characteristic description" often raises the question, characteristic of what? This is the only piece of idiosyncratic terminology I introduce). The ethical place description survives in much later literature, from the gardens of troubadour love poetry and medieval visionary allegory to Spenser's Bower of Bliss and Milton's Eden, to Tolkein's descriptions of Rivendell and Mordor in *The Lord of the Rings,* and even on to historicist readings of Wordsworth's Alps that find the mountains deeply inscribed with traces of Napoleon.[9]

Wordsworth himself gives numerous nods to this tradition, often transforming Virgilian landscape in ways that both respect the ancient topos and go far beyond mere copying. Nicola Trott and Duncan Wu have shown, for example, how Wordsworth modeled a description of London after a Virgilian cave, and Bruce Graver has shown how Wordsworth worked fragments of his own translations of Virgilian descriptions into his original poetry. Graver in fact goes so far as to say that the *Georgics* provided Wordsworth "a vocabulary for expressing what became his most important subject," the fit between the human mind and the external world ("Wordsworth's" 156). When reading Wordsworth, it is well to remember that the poet of the *Aeneid* was also the poet of the *Eclogues* and the *Georgics*. Virgil had made his name as a poet of rural places long before he got into the business of creating a Roman national epic, and what he learned about place description from this earlier work informed the design of the *Aeneid*. In chapter 3, I examine Virgil's harbor first as part of the Aeneid's ecphrastic program. Then I turn to Milton's and

Dryden's use of the description and to how Wordsworth tried his hand at translating it in a way that might recover a more authentic Virgil from what he considered to be Dryden's depredations. At the same time, in chapters 3 and 4, I try to show the underlying historical continuity among Virgil's harbor landscape, Milton's Eden, the picturesque quest for the protoartificial in nature, and the twentieth-century fascination with descriptions of obviously mediated and constructed objects.

More than any other subgenre of description, the powerful example of classical place description had a profound impact on the poetic landscapes of painters such as Claude, whose work became firmly associated with eighteenth-century doctrines of the picturesque. Chapter 4 focuses on how Wordsworth exploited the British fascination with "picturesque" travel, setting its values against equally compelling eighteenth-century speculation about the true nature of the physical world. The goal of picturesque travel, as promoted by Gilpin, was to transform nature's appearance into pictures that satisfied schematic notions of picturesque composition. Nature itself was understood to be, very often, a weak composer who needed a lot of help. Wordsworth, a travel writer himself who promoted the beauty of British scenery, felt that such a quest for the picturesque, guided as it was by quick visual appraisal grounded in expectations of disappointment, was an alienating and pathogenic desire, an indulgence in Fancy at the expense of the essential imaginative work of patiently developing a connection to the world's living forms and power. For Wordsworth, unlike the picturesque traveler, the task of reenvisioning places did not concern visual aesthetics; it was an emotional and imaginative matter. The poetic sensibility of a Wordsworth, like that of Blake before him, was always prepared to find a spiritual Jerusalem in England's green and pleasant land.

In chapters 5 and 6 I have chosen to study in detail a few Romantic texts that seem to me salient and representative of how Romantic poets developed and transformed classical place description. Chapter 5 provides a close reading of "The Wanderer," the introductory book to *The Excursion,* Wordsworth's bold and controversial experiment in dramatizing how a skilled poet might communicate to a receptive audience a vision of humankind fully at home in a mutable world. Chapter 6 takes a close look at Byron's complex response to (and ultimate rejection of) the metaphysics of *The Excursion.* In *Manfred* and in *Childe Harold's Pilgrimage,* Byron provided his own distinctive contribution to the Romantic poetics of place description.

Byron exclaims in *Childe Harold,* "O Rome, my country, city of the soul,! / The orphans of the heart must turn to thee, / Lone mother of dead empires!" (4.694–96). Of course Rome is neither his country nor his mother, but he frames his visit to Rome as a homecoming, and not simply because he is returning to the origins of his professional identity as a poet. The maternal city provides spiritual nourishment to orphans of the heart like Byron, much as a maternal nature nurses Wordsworth. In chapter 6, I examine Byron's special, intimate relationship with the Coliseum, perhaps the most characteristically Roman of all places. When the place speaks both for and through the poet, whose personal genius temporarily merges with the *genius loci,* the place becomes characteristically Byronic as well.

Some propose that it is no longer possible to argue that Romantic places represent personal "genius" or any other emblem of mind, because it has been shown that Romantic poetry serves other purposes; it expresses "false consciousness"; it displaces representations of repressed "history" (however defined); or one way or another it evades painful realities. When closely examined, however, these other purposes turn out to be special cases of psychological activity. Alan Liu, for example, boldly asserts that there is "no self or mind" (39). But he resorts again and again to notions of "repression" (563–64 and elsewhere) and "displacement" (319–20 and elsewhere) to justify his readings of Wordsworth's poetry. What sort of process, one wonders, could repression and displacement be, if they are not mental acts? Where could they happen, if not in someone's mind? Liu cannot have it both ways. If there really is no self or mind, there can be no meaning to notions such as displacement and repression, which are inherently and indubitably psychological. Liu's interpretations, whether we find them persuasive or not, still leave us with emblems of mind; but his are emblems of a mind engaged in complex feats of evasion and self-delusion. It does not help to locate these delusions in "ideology" defined as "false consciousness" as Jerome McGann does (*Romantic* 12). "Consciousness," true or false, inevitably brings us back to the mind and to the modern depth psychology that developed out of Romantic thinking about the sometimes demonically pathogenic energies of creative perception and cognition. Neither Engels, when he coined the useful phrase "false consciousness" in his letter to Mehring of 14 July, 1893, nor any subsequent commentator has been able to show where such false consciousness would reside if not in individual human minds. The works studied in chapters 5 and 6 show how urgent such matters were for Wordsworth and Byron and how place ecphrasis—the vivid description of locations—figured forth their meditation on the disintegration and integration of mind and world.

For students of the Romantic colloquy with nature, place ecphrasis as developed from antiquity onward is unquestionably of central historical importance. Nearly all recent treatments of ecphrasis have, however, lost sight of the concept as understood and practiced by writers of earlier periods. Instead, a self-consciously post-Romantic theoretical climate, privileging artifice and representation over the alleged "real thing," variously redefined and restricted ecphrasis to fit particular notions of representation. Echoing dominant trends in contemporary literary and cultural studies, late-twentieth-century scholars foregrounded the notion of ecphrasis as double representation—the verbal representation of visual representation. Such concerns do not, however, break entirely with classical tradition. The postmodern preoccupation with representation has deep roots in Western philosophy and aesthetics and carries forward, often unconsciously, old debates about the vivid mimetic evocation of life.

This study traces how the tradition of classical ecphrasis continued past antiquity and into the modern world; how its transformation after antiquity was particularly vigorous in the form of place description; and how the poetry of Wordsworth and Byron was among the most successful and historically important offspring of that tradition.

Wordsworth, in the Preface to *Poems* (1815), situates himself in a long line of critical thinking when he embraces description as the poet's sine qua non:

> The powers requisite for the production of poetry are: first, those of Observation and Description,—i.e. the ability to observe with accuracy things as they are in themselves, and with fidelity to describe them, unmodified by any passion or feeling existing in the mind of the describer; whether the things depicted be actually present to senses, or have a place only in the memory. (372)

It is not likely that anyone other than an expert Wordsworthian would correctly attribute these remarks to the Romantic poet who held that poetry has its origins in "emotion recollected in tranquility" (Preface to *Lyrical Ballads* 297). Indeed Wordsworth qualifies his high valuation of description in a way that we more comfortably place as Romantic when he writes that description is never an end in itself: "This power, though indispensable to a Poet, is one which he employs only in submission to necessity" (Preface to *Poems* 372). What is most remarkable about Wordsworth's total assessment is its great antiquity; both the high valuation and the concern about excess, and the double commitment to emotion and to verisimilitude. Horace and Quintilian expressed their own misgivings about these very same double-edged swords.

CHAPTER 1

As If Present: Classical Ecphrasis

> I'm trying in all my stories to get the feeling of the actual life across—not to just depict life—or criticize it—but to actually make it alive. So that when you have read something by me you actually experience the thing.
> —Hemingway, 20 March 1925

"He had rehearsed / Her homely Tale with such familiar power," writes Wordsworth in the 1814 *Excursion*, "that the things of which he spake / Seemed present" (33).[1] The "as if present" motif, as modern as it is classical, has a venerable history and still enjoys a long afterlife among poets and novelists. Wordsworth's praise of the speaker's almost magical conjuring—Hemingway's ideal—might have been drawn from Homer, Quintilian, or Longinus, or from ancient textbooks that prescribe the virtues of *ekphrasis*. Classical ecphrasis is neither Scott's "topos of stillness" (*Sculpted* xii) nor Hollander's "mimesis of mimesis" (*Gazer's* 6); nor is it preoccupied with enabling "silent figures of graphic art to speak," as Heffernan suggests ("Ecphrasis" 304). Ecphrasis in antiquity had to do with a notion of vividness that makes imaginative eyewitnesses of the audience. But from the late nineteenth-century French classicists to the American New Critics to the literary theorists of the late twentieth century, the impulse to define ecphrasis as the description of works of art (however "art" is defined) has tended to efface the well-attested defining properties of classical ecphrasis, and even of its sequelae in much later European literature. Those sequelae were far more vigorous than our heritage from twentieth-century theory would lead us to expect. Even in the late eighteenth century the classical idea of vivid description, the "as if present" notion, was still as alive and well among influential rhetoricians as it was among poets. Hugh Blair, whose work remained popular well into the nineteenth century, wrote in 1783 that description is "the great test of a poet's imagination" and that "a true poet makes us imagine that we see it [the subject] before our eyes [. . .]; he gives it the colours of life and reality" (404). The difficult question about the strange fate of vivid description in European literary theory is: Just what does this "vividness" entail and why has it been at times so highly valued and at others so severely disparaged? In this chapter I would like to focus on the earliest extant usages of the term *ekphrasis* (Latin *descriptio*) and related terms, such as *enargeia* and *phantasia* in Greek and *evidentia* and *repraesentatio* in Latin. I will also briefly examine the ecphrases of some ancient authors who apply the notion as set forth in the progymnasmata. The ecphrastic practice of Ovid, for example, who scarcely figures in the twentieth-century theory, was deeply and continuously influential on medieval and modern European literature. I will forgo detailed discussion of one ancient writer who might be expected to receive substantial attention: Philostratus, whose descriptions of paintings (perhaps imaginary) are associated primarily with the emergence of the twentieth-century notion of ecphrasis and have received ample attention from other commentators.

The stable notion of ecphrasis that persisted long after the fall of the Roman Empire, throughout the Middle Ages and the Renaissance, and into the recent past was secured in part—like so much else in our high canonical culture—by the stubborn persistence of antique textbooks that were readily at hand to be widely copied and disseminated after the advent of printing. So successful was the Renaissance distribution of such basic teaching materials that Milton's grammar school education at St. Paul's in London was almost identical to Ovid's in Rome. "Milton read the same school authors, practiced the same imitative exercises of translation and paraphrase, and wrote and spoke themes on the same sort of assignments" (Clark, *John Milton* 4). Their first lessons in rhetoric followed a curriculum set forth in the progymnasmata, four Greek versions of which are extant from the imperial period: those of Theon (first century A.D.), pseudo-Hermogenes (possibly second century A.D.), Aphthonius (fourth century A.D.), and Nicolaus (fifth century A.D.). The set of exercises appears to have been more or less settled by the time Quintilian discussed them near the end of the first century. Several Greek and Latin versions of all these progymnasmata were available in Europe throughout the Middle Ages and were widely disseminated in the schools of sixteenth- and seventeenth-century Europe (Clark, *Rhetoric* 180). They owe their phenomenal success to the sound pedagogical principle of proceeding from the known to the unknown through a series of graded exercises, each building on what has been learned in the last (Clark, *Rhetoric* 181). All the exercises are imagined as "parts of a speech and not [. . .] complete speeches," as John of Sardis (possibly ninth century A.D.) explains in a commentary on Aphthonius:

> Progymnasmata are miniature rhetoric. Just as in learning handicrafts there are things to learn before getting a complete understanding of the art—in the case of metal workers, for example, how to light the coal and work the bellows [. . .]—so in the progymnasmata one should begin first from the easier ones, and this is the fable. (Kennedy 176)

The prerequisite for the fable is only that the child know his letters and how to read. The literary form of the fable, a popular genre, would have been effortlessly absorbed at home. *Ekphrasis,* far more difficult than the fable, is an advanced exercise for older boys of perhaps 12–15, but a discrete exercise all the same. At this stage in the boys' education the emphasis is still on learning how to light the coal and work the bellows, not on how to deploy each skill in fashioning the complete work. What recommended Aphthonius above all other authors of progymnasmata were the model themes that he included to demonstrate the sort of writing to be expected at each stage from the boys. Aphthonius's first theme retells "The Grasshopper and the Ant" with age-appropriate simplicity.

The *Progymnasmata* of Aphthonius was endorsed by Erasmus, recommended in the major seventeenth-century English treatises on education, and prescribed in the statutes for various English grammar schools, including St. Paul's (Clark, *John Milton* 230; F. R. Johnson xix). Milton's Aphthonius was a Latin translation that had been edited by Reinhold Lorich, a professor of rhetoric at the Protestant university at Marburg during the 1530s and 1540s (F. R. Johnson xiii). The Lorich editions, based on earlier translations by Agricola and Cataneo, contained an extensive commentary, additional model themes, updated illustrative examples taken primarily from Latin literature, and selections from pseudo-Hermogenes that elaborated on matters neglected by Aphthonius. Lorich's greatly augmented edition, running to 219 leaves instead of the 40 occupied by Aphthonius proper, enjoyed hundreds of reprintings over a period of a century and a half. Editions from Frankfurt, Cologne, Lyons, Paris, Rouen, Geneva, London, Cambridge, Amsterdam, Breslau, and Venice are still extant in the world's university libraries (F. R. Johnson xii–xiii). Such a widely circulated textbook, with all its accretions and commentary, gives an accurate idea of ecphrasis as it was handed down to modern writers and particularly to Wordsworth's "divine Milton." Especially instructive for students of Milton and his Romantic heirs is how privileged place ecphrasis had become by the sixteenth-century Lorich editions; I examine this phenomenon later on in the chapter.

As indispensable as the progymnasmata may be for a proper understanding of classical ecphrasis, a caveat is in order. Their virtues as textbooks for the young do limit their value as literary theory. Shadi Bartsch, who has written a learned study of how progymnasmatic description functions in the ancient novel, cautions that the

> theory, if it deserves the name, stays within bounds too narrow to reveal how [descriptive] passages might be manipulated for broader aims. Nevertheless they do demonstrate several important points: the general interest of the epoch in the descriptive; its treatment as a component of rhetorical and compositional technique, and its relatively early use, in this simple guise, in the schools of rhetoric at a time when education *was* rhetorical training. Even the more sophisticated employers of rhetoric must have started here. (9)

Milton and Ovid started here. La Fontaine probably wrote his first grasshopper-and-ant fable here. It should go without saying that the best evidence of how sophisticated writers applied their education is found in their mature writing, not in their school books. Because a fable is still a fable after 2000 years, we have no difficulty recognizing La Fontaine's participation in an ancient enterprise and do not need an Aphthonius to explain it to us. This is not at all the case with ecphrasis, for without the ancient schoolmasters we neither know what to look for when looking for an ecphrasis in literature before the twentieth century; nor do we recognize the persistence of ancient critical ideas and descriptive practices when they occur in modern literature. If we insist on always imagining ecphrasis as art description, we risk filtering out much of the phenomena we are trying to identify and study, even when those phenomena are primarily art description. For the literary interactions among whatever is sorted into art and not art—among descriptions of the natural and the man-made, among the obviously mediated and the less obviously mediated subject matter, and so forth—must surely be a focus of inquiry for the theory of art in literature. The implications of a more holistic approach to classical description remain largely unexplored; but Bartsch, for example, gives a rare glimpse of what can be achieved when she illuminates the paintings of gardens and girls in *Leucippe and Clitophon* by focusing with equal intensity on the descriptions of actual gardens and girls in Achilles Tatius's fictional world, a world largely constructed of progymnasmatic ecphrasis (40–79). Our inquiry properly begins with the progymnasmata, the only ancient texts that both define *ekphrasis* and provide examples of its literary application.

Description in the Ancient Progymnasmata

The definitions of ecphrasis in the *Progymnasmata* of the first through fifth centuries remain in remarkable accord with the earliest one, first-century

Theon's: "A speech which leads one around (*periegematikos*) bringing the subject matter vividly (*enargos*) before the eyes" (trans. and qtd. in Webb 11). That the subject matter might be anything at all was still quite well understood in the eighteenth century, when Alexander Pope picked out the most vivid descriptions of the *Iliad* and cataloged them into the same four general categories that are standard in the progymnasmata: personages (*prosopa*), places (*topoi*), times (*chronoi*), and things done or made (*pragmata*) (Poetical Index 1170–1174). Following another pattern established by the progymnasmata, Pope also added two special categories of his own: military description and description of emotions. Theon had added customs; Hermogenes, crises; Aphthonius, animals and plants; Nicolaus, festivals or assemblies. Nobody added paintings or statues. Despite these minor taxonomic differences, the authors of the progymnasmata do not contradict each other concerning what is suitable subject matter for ecphrasis; they only differ slightly as to how to categorize it. One author's apparently supplementary topic usually figures as another's subtopic, specific literary citation, or suggested student exercise. So, for example, while Theon's "customs" include how Achilles' shield was made, Hermogenes cites the shield story as "object or event." Festivals, which Nicolaus introduces as a special topic, had been included by Theon as examples of "times." Theon, who unlike Aphthonius has no special category for animals, calls Herodotus's descriptions of the Egyptian ibis, hippopotamus, and crocodile ecphrases of "personages." Hermogenes points out that ecphrastic subject matter may be mixed: "Ecphrasis may combine these [topics], as in Thucydides the battle by night; for night is a time and battle is an action" (trans. and qtd. in Webb 35). What distinguishes one kind of subject matter from another is not important. The point of enumerating the topics is not to limit the subject matter but to show just how general it is.

Curiously, however, paintings and statues are mentioned only by fifth-century Nicolaus, the latest author, and only in passing. This should not, of course, be taken as evidence that descriptions of paintings or statues would have been unacceptable subjects to the earlier rhetoricians. These artifacts are certainly pragmata. Descriptions of paintings and sculpture would logically be included in a description of the spoils of war—a common suggested topic in the progymnasmata. The sequelae of war are, moreover, a typical context for finding paintings and statues described in ancient Greek literature. But literary attention to "works of art" as objects detached from some broader narrative, cultural, educational, historical, or geographical program is arguably rare if not entirely absent from classical literature before the Hellenistic period. Bartsch points out that even the set-piece descriptions of Philostratus, while at first glance just one picture after another, are united by the speaker's programmatic commitment to the moral and cultural edification of his young audience (16).

Another feature of classical ecphrasis that is consistent with the progymnasmata, although counterintuitive to us, is that ecphrases may describe *actions* as well as objects; ecphrases may be stories or narratives. The modern antinomy of narrative versus description that was so successfully promulgated by Lessing—and all that such an opposition entails for our interpretation of ancient and modern literary structure—simply does not operate, as becomes quite clear when Hermogenes explains ecphrasis of action to the schoolboys, in an influential passage that the Renaissance humanists added to their editions of Aphthonius:

> Ecphrasis of actions will proceed from what went before, from what happened at the time, and from what followed. Thus if we make an ecphrasis on war, first we shall tell what happened before the war, the levy, the expenditures, the fears; then the engagements, the slaughter, the deaths; then the monument of victory, then the pæans of the victors and, of the others, the tears, the slavery. (Trans. and qtd. in Webb 36)

Moreover, since "narrative" has been a previous exercise that Hermogenes wishes the boys to build upon, he explains that ecphrases of "places, seasons, or persons will draw also from narrative and from the beautiful, the useful, or their contraries" (Kennedy 36). Hermogenes feels the need to comment on how difficult it actually is to separate ecphrasis from the other components of rhetoric. Even an intuitively well-done fable performed on the first day of school could also be a good ecphrasis. Hermogenes admits, in another passage favored by the Renaissance editors of Aphthonius,

> that some of the more exact teachers do not make ecphrasis an exercise, on the ground that it has already been included in fable and narrative and commonplace and encomium; for there too, they say, we describe places and rivers and actions and persons. Nevertheless, since some writers of no small authority number ecphrasis among the exercises, we have followed them to avoid any criticism of carelessness. (Kennedy 86)

Although Hermogenes' catalog of appropriate subjects of ecphrasis explicitly cites "places and rivers and actions and persons," twentieth-century scholars, including Grant F. Scott and many others, ignore classical precedent and insist that three descriptions of shields epitomize the classical conception of ecphrasis: Homer's shield of Achilles, the pseudo-Hesiodic "Shield of Heracles," and Virgil's shield of Aeneas. According to Scott—whose account echoes Bertrand's 1881 ecphrastic anxiety-of-influence (48)—"Achilles' shield establishes the character of classical *ekphrasis* and becomes the blueprint from which all later ekphrases derive and against which they must contend" (*Sculpted* 2). It "appears to be the first imaginary or 'notional' ekphrasis"; that is, the first description of an imaginary work of art (3). It is only because Scott restricts ecphrasis to artifacts that he can make this claim about the shield. All sorts of imaginary persons, places, and things are described by Homer. Descriptions of magical weapons, armor, warhorses, and other preparations for battle are typical of war epics in all traditions. What distinguishes Homer's shield from the other two is its narrativity, a feature that appears as a *problem* for Scott and others since Lessing, though it clearly was not a problem for the ancients. Scott finds that "we must work hard to remind ourselves of the object's iconicity, its hypothetical existence as a static object [. . .]. References to its artistry or its material are rare" (2). Speaking of the description of the ambush scene in particular, Scott finds that "every detail [. . .] conspires to persuade us that we are listening to a story rather than viewing a static artwork," as if the text is really—underneath its deceptive narrative appearance—a description of a static artwork. The reason we must work so hard to "remind" ourselves of its iconicity is, of course, that Homer does not present a static icon. Homer manifestly presents an ongoing activity, a shield in the process of being made; and such a narrative ecphrasis was entirely normal in the view of the ancients. Indeed, the ancient Greeks referred to the episode with a verbal noun that names the action: *hoplopoiia,* the arms-making (Patillon 67).

Nevertheless, Achilles's shield has been so consistently read in the twentieth century as a "verbal representation of a work of art" that Jean Hagstrum anachronistically takes Lessing to task for understanding the episode as ancient Greeks did: as a story about making a shield (*Sister* 19). Lessing, however, is in good classical company when he reads the episode as narrative. Theon considered the shield episode an ecphrasis of the *manner* in which something is made (Kennedy 46). Aphthonius, whose progymnasmata were by far the most successful in modern Europe, does not mention the shield at all in his discussion of ecphrasis; he mentions it as a poetic analog to narrative (*diegema*), "exposition of an action that has happened or as though it had happened" (Kennedy 96). There is no contradiction here. Homer's account of the shield keeps process and product fused in a single *pragma,* a "thing done or made," by presenting the images *as* they are made. No modern reader would actually deny this feature of the text; but an objectifying habit of mind, strangely attentive to the shield as static artifact, suppresses the dynamic narrative that attracted the attention of the ancients. The same biased attention translates Greek pragmata as "objects" when it is clear from the progymnasmata that the authors mean "things done or made—events or objects." This "or" is moreover not necessarily exclusive, as the shield episode shows. The sharp distinction between process and product does not operate. Pope shows the same flexibility that the Greek language permitted the ancients when he classifies the shield under "Descriptions of Things," among other such vividly described pragmata as "dancing," "fires by night," and a "woodman's dinner" (Poetical Index 1171–72).

Quintilian's preliminary exercises cover much the same ground as the Greek, but the arrangement is somewhat different. One variation is that Quintilian is evidently one of the "more exact teachers" that Hermogenes alludes to, a teacher who does not "make ecphrasis an exercise, on the ground that it has already been included in fable and narrative." Quintilian discusses *descriptio* not as an exercise in its own right but in a long digression from *narratio*, giving more ink, however, to the digression than to the main topic. Quintilian is ambivalent. In his view, description is a fertile element of narration that encourages the young to develop their incipient speaking skills. On the other hand, description often clutters adult speech. Quintilian's counsel of perfection is that the child's narratives should neither be dry nor "tortuous and reveling in those irrelevant descriptions to which many are tempted by their wish to imitate the license of the poets" (*Institutio Oratoria* 283; 2.4.3). Nevertheless it is better that children err on the side of rhetorical excess: "In boys, a perfect style is neither to be demanded nor expected; but there is a better prospect in a fertile mind, ambitious effort, and a spirit that sometimes has too many bold ideas" (283; 2.4.4—5).

Descriptive excess is milk for the tender mind, according to Quintilian; he likens teachers to gentle nurses who understand the value of baby fat to an active youngster:

> let [boys] have their fill of the milk [. . .]. That will put flesh on them for a time, but growing up will in due course slim them down [. . .]. The baby whose limbs are all distinctly visible from the start threatens to be skinny and weak later on. The young should be more daring and inventive, and take pleasure in their inventions, even if for the time being they are not sober and correct enough. Exuberance is easily remedied; no effort can overcome barrenness. [. . .] I like the raw material at the start to be over-abundant, poured out more generously even than it ought to be. The passing years will reduce it greatly. (283; 2.4.5–7)

This digression continues with more admonitions to the teacher, all in a similar vein: correct the child without hurting his feelings and stunting his growth: "Farmers know this; they do not believe in applying the pruning hook to the tender leaves, because they seem to be afraid of the knife and not yet able to bear a scar" (283; 2.4.5–7). The teacher "must praise some things, tolerate others, suggest changes (always giving reasons for them), and brighten up passages by putting in something of his own" (283; 2.4.5–7). Quintilian returns from this digression to offer a few practical teaching tips for narration. But most of his treatment of narration as a preliminary exercise articulates a teaching philosophy that tellingly incorporates, through figurative wet-nurses and farmers, an exuberant ecphrastic defense of description in the elementary education of the future lively adult. Quintilian's figurative wet-nurse is a play on *ubertas* (exuberance), whose root is *uber* (breast or teat). Exuberance is free-flowing milk.

Much later on when Quintilian undertakes a more advanced discussion of *narratio*—as a statement of facts in forensic oratory—the audience is the older student, now ready for the pruning hook. Quintilian advises him to introduce the relevant persons, places, and times in a straightforward manner, rather than introduce "Marcus Lollius Palicanus, a Picentine of humble birth, a man gifted with loquacity rather than eloquence"; to state the season rather than copy Virgil's "early spring, when on the mountains hoar / The snows dissolve" (52; 4.2.2). Less is more, in Quintilian's view: "It is sometimes sufficient and expedient to summarise a case in one sentence such as 'I say that Horatius killed his sister'" (53; 4.2.7). Quintilian's last example fully restrains the impulse toward ecphrasis of the mechanically formulaic sort.

Vividness

Quintilian was hardly the first to have misgivings about school ecphrasis—the "early spring, when on the mountains hoar" syndrome. At least several decades earlier, Dionysius of Halicarnassus (late first century B.C.) had censured irrelevant and showy ecphrasis in legal oratory:

> Some make a fault of the so-called ecphrases [*ekphraseis*] by describing [*graphein*] on every occasion a storm or plagues or famines or battle formations or heroic actions, for it is not in this that the decision of a lawsuit lies, namely in describing in detail [*diagrapsai*] a storm. Rather, these are a vain display [*epideixis*] and a waste of words. This fault comes in exercises/declamations [*meletais*] in imitation of history and poems, for we forget that it is appropriate [*eoiken*] that prose history and poetry bring in graphic depictions [*graphicas opseis*] of things necessary for the listeners, but that a law case is adjusted with respect to the issue [*chreian*]. Poets and historians stamp [*ektypousin*] events with certain places and characters [*prosopois*], for they actually happened, but orators in training, not having any agreed-upon or specific [*idian*] notion [*idean*] of what has happened, invent [*anaplattousin*] for themselves scenes [*opseis*] of plagues and famines and storms and wars, when all these did not happen in the way that they themselves say. At least then, it is possible for the legal adversary to

say these things differently than the opponent says them. As I said then, these things make speeches uselessly long. That is the mistake of people who do not realize that in the relevant details of lawsuits there is ample motivation for depiction [*phantasias*], and there is no need to pile up extraneous depictions [*phantasias*] in speeches. (*Rhetoric* 272–73, ch. 17; Race trans.)

Dionysius's remarks merit further attention because they contain the earliest extant use of the word *ekphrasis*. Dionysius says nothing here at all about art; his central concern is quite otherwise: how easy it is to insert emotive topics where they do not belong, "plagues and famines and storms and wars"—standard ecphrastic fare in the centuries to follow. This offhand catalog of schoolboy topics, and Dionysius's dry understatement that cases are not won by "describing in detail a storm," suggest how hackneyed such descriptions had already become. Like Quintilian, Dionysius locates the problem in the bits and pieces of description picked up at school from history and poetry and imported willy-nilly into any speech.

There is still more to be learned from Dionysius's critique. His elegant variation of terms amplifying the meaning of *ekphrasis* shows just how deep he and Quintilian are in the same stream of ancient thought about literary description. Dionysius's variations include *diagrapsai* ("describing in detail") and *graphicas opseis* ("graphic depictions"), terms consistent with progymnasmatic definition, as well as *phantasias*. Dionysius concludes his brief against the irrelevant by insisting that the particulars of the case give "ample motivation" for *phantasias* without bringing in extraneous bits of literary description.

Phantasia, a synonym (here) for *ekphrasis* that is as pointedly psychological as it is rhetorical, intersects both Quintilian's theory of emotion and description and Longinus's entirely congruent theory of pathos and the sublime. "The rhetorical theory about emotions is becoming the core not only of rhetoric but of poetics," according to Dockhorn, when "Longinus establishes pathos as the actual and essential characteristic of the elevated, at about the same time Quintilian establishes the theory about emotions as the core of rhetorics" (268).

According to Longinus, "Weight, grandeur and urgency in writing," the properties of the elevated or sublime, "are very largely produced by *phantasiai*" (215–17; 15.1). Longinus explains that the word has a general meaning as well as a newer and more particular one that he would like to emphasize:

> For the term *phantasia* is applied in general to an idea which enters the mind from any source and engenders speech, *but the word has now come to be used predominantly of passages where, inspired by strong emotion, you seem to see what you describe and bring it vividly before the eyes of your audience.* (215–17; 15.1–2; my italics)

Longinus documents a shift in meaning, which identifies a kind of depiction whose impetus is, at least in part, internal; at some point it became necessary for Greek to make a distinction between an idea that enters the mind "from any source" and one that is engendered from within (Barfield, *History* 213). Longinus further distinguishes the most emotive *phantasia,* which aims at astonishment (*ekplexis*) and is found in poetry, from the *phantasia* of prose, which aims "to present things vividly"; but the difference is only one of degree: "Both indeed aim at the emotional and the excited" (217; 15.2). The new meaning Longinus attests for *phantasia* is congruent with the phenomenon that the imperial schoolteachers named *ekphrasis*—a speech that brings the subject matter vividly before the eyes—whence Dionysius's synonymous usage of *ekphrasis* and *phantasia*. Longinus's newer emotive meaning is supported by the context of Dionysius's critique and implies another and more psychological dimension to what Dionysius might be getting at when he contrasts extraneous literary *phantasia* with the *phantasia* appropriate to the case: the only ecphrases (i.e., emotionally engaging depictions) that belong in lawsuits are those motivated by the case—meaning not just by the facts of the case but the by speaker's emotional engagement with and amplification of his client's plight. If this interpretation is correct, Dionysius's point would be fully consistent not only with Longinus's gloss on *phantasia* but with Quintilian's (and Cicero's) theory of the necessary role of vivid description in legal speech.

Just how to bring the facts of the case before the judge with credible immediacy and emotional urgency is for Quintilian a subtle problem whose solution evades the rules and precepts: "If I thought it sufficient to follow traditional rules," writes Quintilian in his most romantic mood,

> I should regard it as adequate treatment for this topic to omit nothing that I have read or been taught, provided that it be reasonably sound. But my design is to bring to light the secret principles of this art, and to open up the inmost recesses of the subject, giving the result not of teaching received from others, but of my own experience and the guidance of nature herself. (431; 6.2.25)

His method, then, will be subjective confession. Quintilian's rhetoric of privilege and intimacy— *quae latent, penetralia loci,* the "secret principles," the "inmost recesses"—draws readers sharply closer to this matter of personal concern to him. Our own experience of Quintilian's rhetoric at this moment of heightened attention shows that an effective appeal to emotion actually entails producing a kind of contagion between speaker and audience: "Fire alone can kindle, and moisture alone can wet" (433; 6.2.28). The speaker's own feelings need to prevail in the judge, according to Quintilian; but this is easier said than done, especially since an advocate needs first to generate the right affect in himself. "But how are we to generate these emotions in ourselves, since emotion is not in our own power?" asks Quintilian. He answers, "I will try to explain as best I can" (433; 6.2.29). The false modesty with which he introduces his forthcoming explanation further ingratiates the reader and reinforces the larger point that no authority (not even Quintilian) can write a recipe for creating and transmitting emotion. He proceeds as follows:

> There are certain experiences which the Greeks call *phantasiai,* and the Romans visions [*visiones*], whereby things absent are presented to our imagination with such extreme vividness that they seem actually to be before our very eyes. It is the man who is really sensitive to such impressions who will have the greatest power over the emotions. (433–35; 6.2.29–30)

From such mental states, "when we seem to ourselves not to be dreaming but acting," (435; 6.2.30) there arises enargeia —"vividness," a defining property of ecphrasis. According to Quintilian, Cicero translates *enargeia* both as *illustratio,* (illumination) and as *evidentia* (actuality) qualities "which make us seem not so much to narrate as to exhibit the actual scene, while our emotions will be no less actively stirred than if we were present at the actual occurrence" (435–37; 6.2.32).[2] In discussions of enargeia, evidentia, and phantasia, the "as if present" motif regularly recurs throughout the period to distinguish an ordinary account from what the progymnasmata call ecphrasis. The authors of the progymnasmata "speak freely of the psychological impact of the word and the imaginative contribution of the listener" (Webb 18). They distinguish between "a simple account of what happened" and an ecphrasis—a vivid, imaginatively engaging account—telling "*how* it happened, how it looked [. . .] how it sounded and felt" (Webb 13).

"The 'as if present' motif (implying an imaginative 'eyewitness' role for the viewer-audience of art)" appears in the *Odyssey,* as Steven J. Halliwell points out, "and later becomes a commonplace for narrative-dramatic vividness" in the mimetic theory of antiquity (*Aesthetics* 20, n. 48). Consider, for example, how Odysseus praises the bard Demodocus for truly singing the fate of the Achaeans, "as perhaps one who had [. . .] been present, or had heard the tale from another" (8.491; Murray trans.). Such credible immediacy is the divine gift of the Muse, according to Odysseus. The proof of the Muse's gift to the bard is that his next story (the sack of Troy) moves Odysseus to tears, a point that Homer dramatizes with shrewd dramatic irony; for the bard who was not literally present at the battle conjures up a story that features Odysseus, who actually had been there. But the victor is made to reexperience the siege of Troy with even greater intensity, and now from the perspective of a vanquished woman:

> And as a woman wails and throws herself upon her dear husband, who has fallen in front of his city and his people, seeking to ward off from his city and his children the pitiless day; and as she beholds him dying and gasping for breath, she clings to him and shrieks aloud, while the foe behind her beat her back and shoulders with their spears, and lead her away to captivity to bear toil and woe, while with most pitiful grief her cheeks are wasted—so did Odysseus let fall pitiful tears from beneath his brows. (8.523–31; Murray trans.)[3]

Odysseus (whom Homer has placed in the role of the ideal, discerning audience) had wanted his war story told, true-to-life as an eyewitness would tell it, but Odysseus (and Homer's audience) get more uncomfortable truths than they had bargained for. The effect is so intense that Odysseus's host asks the storyteller to stop. Enchantment like this, entailing a mediated experience of image and emotion that unites speaker and audience, in the way that Demodocus enchants Odysseus with words, may well be the oldest aesthetic principle we have. It is in any case a variously problematic point of departure for Plato and Aristotle and finds itself once again at the center of rhetorical theory during the period of the Roman Empire.

Quintilian's most complete account of the phenomenon is actually in 8.3, an influential text that Lorich cites in marginal glosses on Aphthonius's treatment of descriptio: "The power of description is of the highest order, according to Quintilian at 8.3; to be sure, our minds most easily entertain that which they recognize" (Lorich in Aphthonius 307; my trans.). The sixteenth-century scholiast correctly understands that vividness is the core of descriptio; "some call it evidentia, others repraesentatio" (Lorich in Aphthonius 311; my trans.), he remarks, paraphrasing Quintilian. At 8.3 Quintilian places vividness under the head of *ornatus,* which we are more or less forced to translate as "the ornate." Since enargeia is a species of the ornate, it is crucial to understand that *ornatus,* for the Romans, lacks modern negative connotations of the superficial or meretricious. It is rather a highly desirable quality that

> goes beyond what is merely lucid and acceptable. It consists firstly in forming a clear conception of what we wish to say, secondly in giving this adequate expression, and thirdly in lending it additional brilliance [*nitidiora . . . faciat*]. (245; 8.3.61)

Ornate speech—the most effective speech—is "nitidiora," or quite radiant and polished. Consequently Quintilian places enargeia, whose Greek root is *arges,* "bright" foremost among the ornaments because, as he explains in yet another reformulation that is congruent with progymnasmatic ecphrasis:

> vivid illustration [*evidentia*], or as some prefer to call it, representation [*repraesentatio*], is something more than mere clearness, since the latter merely lets itself be seen, whereas the former thrusts itself upon our notice. It is a great gift to be able to set forth the facts on which we are speaking clearly and vividly. (245; 8.3.61)

The translator's English "vividly" renders Quintilian's "ut cerni videantur," literally "they seem as if perceived"—the emotionally engaging quality that Odysseus had praised in the bard. Pope made a similar observation about Homer: "What he writes is of the most animated nature imaginable; [. . .]. [T]he reader is hurried out of himself by the force of the Poet's imagination, and turns in one place to a hearer, in another to a spectator" (Preface 4).

We should take special note of the fact that Quintilian's three-part hierarchy of clarity and adequate expression that is somehow made "nitidiora" persisted well into modernity. We can hear the echo of Quintilian behind Diderot's three-part analysis of the virtues of description in the epic and the ode:

> If the thought is rendered with clarity, purity and precision it suffices for familiar conversation; join with these qualities careful word choice and the rhythm and harmony of the period and you will have the style appropriate to the pulpit; but you will still be far from poetry, especially the kind of poetry that the ode and the epic poem display in their descriptions. There a spirit passes into the speech of the poet which moves and animates all its syllables." (Diderot, *Lettre* 70; trans. and qtd. in Porter 496).

When Diderot advances to the position that this spirit is not available to readers unless they almost share the state of mind of the poet, he fully recapitulates Quintilian's overarching point that there can be no permanent canon of vividness for all occasions. Creating a vividly shareable experience: *hoc opus, hic labor est,* "this is the task, this is the toil," writes Quintilian, quoting from the Sybil's incantatory warning to Aeneas before his descent into the underworld (*Aeneid* 6.125 ff.). Returning from the underworld is all but impossible, but the imaginative-affective task of oratory is just as difficult, according to Quintilian, as "the soul and spirit of this work is in the emotions" (420; 6.2.7; my trans.).

Quintilian complains about how "certain writers" have tried to approach the difficulties merely by setting forth an overly detailed taxonomy of enargeia. He himself outlines a basic but wide-ranging anatomy of vividness that gives as much insight into the many rhetorical possibilities—from word-painting and similes to emphasis and well-placed terseness—as into the futility of reducing the orator's choices to rules. In the even more wide-ranging discussion that follows all this, Quintilian embraces the Aristotelian concept of *energeia* ("liveliness") as kindred to the almost identical word *enargeia* (261; 8.3.89). He has often been scolded for encouraging readers to conflate the two terms,[4] but Aristotle himself had long before invited the practice when he advised writers to become imaginative eyewitnesses to their fictions; to

> construct plots, and work them out in diction, with the material as much as possible in the mind's eye. In this way, by seeing things most vividly [*enargestata*], as if present at the actual events, one will discover what is apposite. (*Poetics* 87–89; 1455a)

He treated the same phenomenon of imaginative eyewitnessing at *Rhetoric* 1411b, equating "bringing-before-the-eyes" with energeia and distinguishing its effect from that of simple metaphor: "a good man is foursquare" is metaphor without energeia; "having his prime of life in full-bloom" is energeia. *Energeia* (cognate to "energy") and *enargeia* ("vividness"), distinct Greek words that are by no means synonymous in all contexts, do overlap as rhetorical "bringing-before-the-eyes." The kinship is borne out by their English translations. According to Webster's, *vivid* means "having the appearance of vigorous life or freshness: animated [. . .] lively." And *lively* means "animated [. . .] vivid." Quintilian, who was fluent in Greek and more conversant with Aristotle than we are, does not split hairs.

In this connection, however, it is well to recall that ecphrasis has not one but two virtues —vividness and clarity. An apparently paradoxical entry "ecphrasis" in the *Oxford English Dictionary* does not define the term but seems to set clarity and vividness against each other with two dated citations: (1) "1715 Kersey, *Ecphrasis* (in Rhet.) a plain declaration or interpretation of a thing";[5] (2) "1814 Edin. Rev. XXIV.65. The same florid effeminacies of style . . . in . . . an ecphrasis of Libanius, are harmless." The apparent contradiction between "plain declaration" and "florid effeminacies" can be illuminated if we take a closer look at one ecphrastic virtue: clarity. In light of the first definition, "a plain declaration or interpretation of a thing," consider the description of an ibis that Theon cites as an ecphrasis of a personage: "Here is a description of the ibis,"[6] writes Herodotus in his *Histories*.

> It is pitch-black all over, and it has the legs of a crane and a very hooked beak. It is about the size of a corncrake. That is what the black ibises are like, which are the ones that fight the snakes, but there are two kinds of ibis and the other kind,

which one is more likely to come across in places inhabited by human beings, is different. It has no feathers anywhere on its head and neck, and its plumage is completely white, except for its head, neck, and the tips of its wings, and the very end of its tail, all of which are pitch-black. Its legs and beak are like those of the other kind. (124; bk. 2, para. 76)[7]

Herodotus is describing an exotic animal to an audience that has never seen such things. A straightforward and concise exposition of the important particulars of this strange semibald bird quite does the job. Theon, in citing this text, evidently does not consider an elaborate style essential to a vivid description. In fact, for Greek critics, "the plainer styles were more likely than the more elaborate ones to excel in lucidity [. . .]. In this respect, a Herodotus or a Lysias might be expected to surpass a Thucydides" (Roberts 16). Neither vividness nor even ornament in general is a matter of rhetorical elaboration: "Absolute and unaffected simplicity [. . .] has in it a certain chaste ornateness," writes Quintilian, "while a minute accuracy in securing propriety and precision in our words likewise produces an impression of neatness and delicacy" (261; 8.3.87). At the other end of the spectrum, and without contradiction, Thucydides's more elaborate descriptions of battle are frequently cited in the progymnasmata. Hermogenes teaches that the style, whether plain or elaborate, should fit the subject matter:

> Virtues (*aretai*) of an ecphrasis are, most of all, clarity (*sapheneia*) and vividness (*enargeia*); for the expression should almost create seeing through the hearing. Moreover, of course, the word choice ought to correspond to the subject. If the subject is flowery, let the style be so too; if the subject is dry, let the style be similar. (Kennedy 86)

The virtues of description, vividness and clarity, may actually be undermined by excess: by ornament that is inappropriate to the subject, or by irrelevant detail. Theon stresses the importance of not extending into useless detail (Patillon 69). When Lorich repeats Hermogenes' advice about thoroughly describing the course of a siege, from its outset to the cries of the enslaved victims, the scholion ends with a reservation: "Although this catastrophe encompasses everything, to say less than everything is nevertheless to tell all" (Lorich in Aphthonius 313; my trans.). Ecphrasis, "speaking out," is not necessarily expatiation. In many ecphrases, terseness only adds to the plangency.

An especially moving example of ecphrastic terseness can be found in book 23 of the *Iliad*, where Homer describes the final moments in Patroclus's cremation:

> Then the pyre died down, and the flames ceased. And the winds went back again to return to their home over the Thracian sea, and it roared with surging

flood. Then the son of Peleus drew away from the burning pyre, and lay down wearied; and sweet sleep leapt on him. (23.228–32; Murray trans.)

Readers from antiquity onward testify to the emotional impact of these lines. A scholion to 23.232 picks up the root of *ekphrasis,* and deploys the concept as a verb: "He has described ["ecphrased"] him lying down in sleep after being awake for a long time" (Erbse 404; Race trans.). Greek has many words for "describe." In reaching for a term that would register the emotionally persuasive vividness with which Homer presents this simple gesture, the scholiast chooses the uncommon "to ecphrase."

Homer's treatment of Achilles' gesture exemplifies how poets use ecphrasis to "stamp events with certain places and characters," as Dionysius puts it. Marmontel was thinking along the same lines when in the eighteenth century he suggested that the powerful effect the lines have exercised on audiences over more than two millennia has to do with the

> analogy between the landscape and the action that should take place there. It is by no means a pleasant canopy that Achilles should seek for mourning the death of Patroclus, but a solitary and arid seashore that is either silent or heaving in response to his grief. ("Description" 448; my trans.)

The passage describes an event, the collapse of Achilles, with primary focus on his emotional state rather than on something about Achilles proper that is more available to the senses, such as exactly how Achilles might have looked or what he might have said under these painful circumstances. For, as the accompanying scholion suggests, the possibilities of ecphrasis extend well beyond enumerating the literal features of persons when we want to describe them with the deepest complexity or intensity. Halliwell explains that "the combination of, or interplay between, a standard of verisimilitude (ostensible conformity to the known conditions of lived experience) and the power of vivid, credible immediacy (mimesis as the simulation of life) underpins many of the Homeric scholia's comments on mimesis" (*Aesthetic*s 304–305). Halliwell does not discuss ecphrasis as such, but his discussion of mimesis in this period suggests that ecphrasis was a concept waiting for a name. That concept was "the strong evocation of reality, practically synonymous with 'vividness,' *enargeia*" (293—294, n. 23). Halliwell's gloss on "the mimetic" in this context might serve just as well as a gloss on "the ecphrastic."

The subject of Homer's ecphrasis is *apoklinanta,* "him-lying-down"; the scholiast's participle, a single word, names not merely a person or an action but the inclusive event as the subject matter. Here Homer "speaks out," not in a lengthy discourse about Achilles' collapse, but with a grave emotional amplitude that is supported by the powerfully and literally down-and-outward "moving" wind and waves. Homer "stamps" or inscribes the event on a place that communicates its emotional character, and at the same time deepens the reader's developing understanding of Achilles' depressed and angry soul. The seascape description is the figure that fully describes him-lying-down. Its heaving swells and changing winds are more ethically attuned to Achilles than any signs the poet might have picked out merely by observing Achilles' person. Although Ruskin claimed that Homer did not indulge in what he called the "pathetic fallacy," Homer's emotionally charged seascape would appear to be an almost paradigmatic example of the practice Ruskin was denouncing. One of the tasks of this book will be to demonstrate just how misguided was Ruskin's low opinion of this mode of figuration—and how wrong he was to have assumed that it was "always the sign of a morbid state of mind, and comparatively of a weak one" (79).[8]

Literary Topography

Homer's seascape in *Iliad* 23 may be properly understood as an ethical place description, in that the character of the place described is made congruent with the psychic state of a character in the poem. This sort of ecphrasis was extremely common in antiquity, and the tradition it inaugurates has had a powerful influence on postclassical European literary practice, including notably, British Romanticism. We can get an idea of just how widespread this sort of figurative topography was in ancient writing by noting its prominent appearance in a canonical text of Greek philosophy, the *Phaedrus*. Plato did more than just make casual use of ethical place description by situating his dialogue in a thematically resonant locus amoenus; he made his own distinctive contribution to the development of this mode of figuration by creating productive tensions between the marked rural character of the place and the equally marked urban character of the dialogue engaged in by its visitors. Plato establishes the setting by giving Socrates a decidedly "sophistical" speech, as Adam Parry has shown, in praise of the grove of the Ilyssian nymphs (16–19), where the ensuing dialogue on love and rhetoric takes place. Here Plato develops a locus of the Kalypso type, deploying the landscape description in new rhetorical-cum-psychological ways that will become more important in the later development of figurative landscape description, from the medieval visionary landscape to the dramatic dialogue of Wordsworth's *Excursion*. In Homer as in Plato, the locus amoenus is the abode of powerful or numinous figure(s). Plato's topographical elements suit the character of its chaste and lovely nymphs, giving the description as a whole a figurative or allegorical function that, as in Homer, reaches beyond the description proper to create a certain dramatic irony. In Homer, however, the irony is more or less local: Odysseus may have thought he was safe when the nymph kindly welcomed him to her abode, but Kalypso's violets and parsley line a tender trap from which only divine intervention can rescue him. To an even greater extent, Plato's locus amoenus—allusive and urbanely spoken by a man normally given to distrusting such speech—prefigures the ironies of the *Phaedrus.*

The allusion to Homer would, of course, be obvious to a Greek audience; and precisely for that reason Socrates' description can introduce Homer's same broad themes of love, seduction, and deceptive appearance, while Socrates' specific detail and context can express quite firm distinctions between the quality of the experience to be expected in the Ilyssian grove and the entrapment Odysseus experienced on Kalypso's isle. The same traditional motifs are found in both descriptions, "springs and plantations and gardens and soft breezes and flowers and bird-voices" (Curtius 197), but the way Plato particularizes these motifs to the nymphs, the river god Achelous, and to the dramatic situation gives the ecphrasis a subtle figurative function that merges Socrates (and his teaching and learning) with the tutelary spirits who inform the dialogue in their grove.[9] The grove is fragrant with the blossoms of the chaste tree (Greek *agnos,* which sounds like *hagnos,* "chaste"). The ground conforms perfectly to the body, as Socrates notes with pleasure and ironic seductiveness:

> The most exquisite thing of all, of course, is the grassy slope: it rises so gently that you can rest your head perfectly when you lie down on it. You've really been the most marvelous guide, my dear Phaedrus. (6; 230C)

Socrates' description begins to reach more deeply into the entire dialogue, figuring forth the experience the two men will have. The reader probably begins to sense the ethical function of the grove already at the point when Phaedrus observes that Socrates, the one who had suggested they wade through the river to get to the grove and is now evidently eager to stretch out on the grass in the posture of a river-god, looks "out of place." Socrates replies, "places and trees"—*choria kai dendra*—"have nothing to teach me: for that I must look to the men in town" (6; 230D). Then he lies down and invites Phaedrus likewise to choose a comfortable position and begin reading a speech about love that he has brought from town. Just how much Socratic irony the reader ultimately finds in the way Socrates domesticates the grove, merges with its contour, and sets the terms of engagement will condition the interpretation of the entire dialogue. It ends quite pointedly, as everyone remembers, with Socrates' prayer, "O dear Pan and all the other gods of this place, grant that I may be beautiful inside" (86; 279B). What the gods of this place (not the men of the town) have to give is precisely the goal of Socrates' urban discourse.[10] The closing prayer invites the reader to return full circle to the opening place ecphrasis, and read it now as the true praise it becomes in the course of the dialogue.

In contrast to the figuratively embedded locus amoenus of Homer or Plato, the "Amnis ibat" of Tiberianus (fl. A.D. 335; cited in full by Curtius [196]) presents a late antique Latin example of the locus amoenus as a stand-alone poem. It is impossible to overestimate how much the tone and diction of later European lyric poetry was influenced by this genre of late classical ecphrasis, which carefully exploits all "six charms" of the pleasant landscape. Curtius points out that the "surging wealth of sensual perceptions" is strictly "ordered by conceptual and formal means. The finest fruit ripens on espaliers." The number of lines is 20, an attractive "round number" in antiquity and the Middle Ages (197). The poem develops by alternating attention, above and below. The movement is from river and meadow to the trees above; back to the meadow, then to the fragrant air and back down to the rose; tall trees among grass, rivulets, and grottoes, and back to the canopy with birdsong. A vestige of the ancient goddess/enchantress living in such abodes survives here as epithets characterizing the rose: "The queen of all fragrances, and of all colors the light-bringer, / The golden-flowered [*auriflora*] torch of Dione," Aphrodite's mother (9–10; my trans.). The poet's neologism *auriflora* imitates and evokes Homer. The poet engages and blends the pleasures of all the senses: fragrance and taste, sight, hearing, and the soft tactile comfort of breeze and grass. A speaking river joined in song with the leaves, at the Zephyr-muse's direction, gives a satisfying sense of closure, unity, and harmony.[11]

The locus amoenus is but one type of place description that passed without hiatus into the vernacular literature of the later Middle Ages, whence into more modern European poetry. The ethical landscape found *in parvo* in Homer, and that Plato made more psychologically and rhetorically complex by adding dialogue, is just the sort of merged description of person and place that will give all the great visionary landscapes of the medieval dream vision the psychological credibility and quasi-objective authority they evidently have for the displaced and troubled dreamers who enter them. At a historical moment when the dreamworld can be experienced as liminal—as a subjective place that speaks to one's innermost concerns, as well as an objective abode with its characteristic inhabitants—Dante will develop personal anguish-as-displacement into a coherent rhetorical program for the soul's journey into objective visionary landscapes, the dozens of finely differentiated habitations of hell, purgatory, and paradise.

When we recall that Latin *locus* and Greek *topos* have a wide range of both physical and intellectual meanings, it is easy to see how, in the Middle

Ages, descriptions of places could become emblems of mind with, as Paul Piehler shows, a free combination of pagan and Christian themes and motifs. Piehler discusses some already well-developed hybrids from early Christian visionary allegory written in Greek, in which it is not difficult to discern the imagistic background of later masters of literary topography such as Dante:

> The vision of the ninth similitude of the Pastor of Hermas (second century) includes a detailed description and interpretation of the contrasted topographies of twelve mountains, representing twelve contrasted spiritual states. In the *Symposium* of Methodias (late third century?) the garden in which the banquet takes place is reached by an allegorical journey over a rough and arduous path endangered by reptiles and precipices. The symposium itself is held in the garden of *Arete,* a locus both *amoenus* and *conclusus* [enclosed], abounding with flowers and fruits, irrigated by fountains and rivulets, and cooled by soft breezes, a fittingly remote and exalted place for ten maidens to discourse and allegorize on the topic of virginity, the main substance of the work. (*Visionary* 80)

For the Latin Middle Ages, Ovid's place descriptions provided the most widely available models of "the abode of the *potentia* [powerful one]" (Piehler, *Visionary* 81). All such allegorical places anticipate the ethical house descriptions of more modern indomitable personages such as Charles Dickens's Miss Havisham in *Great Expectations* or Henry James's Osmond in *Portrait of a Lady*.[12] In ancient poetry as in the modern novel, the *potentia* need not be a pleasant person dwelling in a pleasant place. Ovid created (among many others) the abodes of Envy, "filthy with black gore [. . .] hidden away in a deep valley, where no sun shines and no breeze blows; a gruesome place and full of a numbing chill" (113; 2.760–63); of Famine, "on the farthest border of icy Scythia, a gloomy and barren soil, a land without corn, without trees" (461; 8.788–89); and Sleep, "a deep recess within a hollow mountain" where vapors "breathe forth from the earth [. . .] (163; 11.592–96).

> Before the cavern's entrance abundant poppies bloom, and countless herbs, from whose juices dewy night distills sleep and spreads its influence over the darkened lands. There is no door in all the house, lest some turning hinge should creak; no guardian on the threshold. But in the cavern's central space there is high couch of ebony, downy-soft, black-hued, spread with a dusky coverlet. There lies the god himself, his limbs relaxed in languorous repose. Around him on all sides lie empty dream-shapes. (163; 11.605–14)

These three descriptions, Envy, Famine, and Sleep, are among the 14 or so new examples that Lorich adds to his sixteenth-century Aphthonius.

Lorich's list also contains the sudden storm in *Aeneid* 1; Cleopatra's luxurious and decadent ship, the abode into which Cleopatra lures Antony in Plutarch's life of Antony; the flood from Ovid's creation story; Florus's battle at Cyzicus, where Lucullus ingeniously defeated Mithridates VI; Gellius's account of how Justice *ought* to be depicted, whether by painters or orators; but no works of art as such. Most of the examples of ecphrasis are vividly evocative places: besides Envy, Famine, and Sleep, we have the monster Cacus's bloody house, as King Evander describes it to Aeneas; Diodorus's Temple of Ammon; the magical palace of Love as Psyche encounters it in Apuleius's Neoplatonic prose allegory; and Gellius's curious account of how Favorinus compared Pindar's description of Mt. Aetna erupting with Virgil's, to the detriment of Virgil's groaning monster-volcano on Cyclops's island.[13]

Favorinus quotes from both poets, praises Pindar for telling the truth about what really happens when a volcano erupts, and censures Virgil for sacrificing visual verisimilitude to harsh and showy sound effects that produce "the most monstrous of all monstrous descriptions" (Gellius 3:245; 17.10). (Evidently Favorinus notes a certain decorum in Virgil's description of a monster but disapproves of it.) The merits of the veridical Aetna favored by Favorinus against those of Virgil's gut-ruptured, rock-vomiting, star-licking monster may well have been discussed and debated in the adolescent classroom, and with eager partisans pro Virgil. The fact that Lorich cites a bit of second-century literary criticism that pits one famous author against another over canons of naturalism, and also offers Gellius's account of concretizing Justice in words or painting, shows how committed Lorich was to setting forth a flexible notion of ecphrasis whose possibilities cover a wide range of mimetic-expressive significance. The sheer variety and prominence of place description among the examples, from the most culturally evocative battlegrounds and temples to the ethical abodes created by Ovid, Virgil, and (most elaborately and allegorically) by Apuleius, manifest a preoccupation with place description as a flexible topos for representing realities that include and also extend far beyond establishing plausible settings and perusing the surface of things. Such matters were important enough to touch upon (at some level) in school.

Lorich supplements his literary citations with two new model themes as well as a Latin adaptation of Aphthonius's original. Aphthonius's theme, a place ecphrasis, treated the acropolis at Alexandria, better known today as the Serapeum, the monumental shrine built there in honor of the syncretic Greek-Egyptian god Serapis. After some six centuries of incremental development and adornment, the shrine was destroyed by Christians in A.D. 389 during the reign of Theodosius. A modern audience any temple ecphrasis worth the name to hold forth on its statues or carvings or paintings.

But such artifacts receive scant attention here. The subject matter of the temple's painting or relief sculpture (we cannot tell which) is mentioned just once, when Aphthonius notes in passing that an open court is decorated with the battles of Perseus (Kennedy 119). Aphthonius's model ecphrasis does not demonstrate how to describe art, but rather how to establish a sense of place; his focus is the architecture and the site, not the details of the representational sculpture or painting that embellish it. Aphthonius shows what a student might be expected to describe after moving continuously toward and then through a monumental urban space without stopping to take in many recondite details. He describes, for example, the many footpaths and roads leading to small flights of steps rising to larger, more monumental steps, "not ceasing until there have been a hundred steps; for the limit of a number is the end that reaches perfect measure" (Kennedy 119). This is the sort of philosophical reflection that students might have heard from an arithmetic teacher. More copious reflections of this sort are common in professional ecphrases of the period; a youth might have been expected to enliven his ecphrasis with only one or two. Another observation: "The roof of the building rises in a dome, and around the dome is fixed a great memorial of things that are" (Kennedy 119). As to the ornament or the content of the "great memorial of things that are," our modern art ecphrastic curiosity is not satisfied by this piece of model schoolwork.

Lorich, too, would categorize such a speech as place description; for, as he reminds students in the scolia, places run the full gamut of the natural and the man-made, or (as he sorts them) the actual (*topographia*) and the fictive (*topothesia*): cities, mountains, palaces, rivers, regions, ports, villas, gardens, springs, caves, temples, groves (314). One might expect Lorich to supplement Aphthonius's ancient place description with models of different kinds of subject matter; but, following the pattern established by the disproportionate number of places in his examples of description, Lorich adds three new descriptions, and two of them are of places. One, a description of his own school in Hadamard, gives boys a quite modern model for "writing what you know." The other is an unprepossessing description of the residence of St. Anthony from Hieronymous. Anthony's secluded mountain home, with its falling water, streams, tree-lined banks, and minimally intrusive architecture, is a rhetorical humble abode where the saint would sing psalms, pray, rest, and tend his garden:

> He planted vines and little trees. By his own hands he set out a garden plot. With much sweat he built himself a fishpond to irrigate the little garden. But there was also a little room, not very long, where a sleeping man could stretch out. Besides that, on a lofty peak of the mountain, there were two little rooms

[carved out of the living rock, where the saint retired,] escaping the crowd of visitors and the society of his own students. (318–319; my trans.)

The many diminutives—*arbusculos,* "little trees," *hortulum,* "little garden," *cellulae,* "little rooms"—reflect the saint's humility. He toils honorably, and he rests *amoenitatis et commodi,* in "comfort and loveliness" under the palms. Such humble abodes, in harmony with their surroundings and reflecting the virtue and industry of their inhabitants, are among the stock properties of later poetry and prose. How Wordsworth deepens the topos will be demonstrated in later chapters.

Lorich's remaining theme is an animal description, Lucan's snakes of Lybia in *Civil Wars* (9.696–733). But even the snakes do not escape the informing power of the place that created them. Lorich's excerpt begins as follows:

> Though that land is barren and those fields give increase to no good seed, yet they drank in poison from the gore of the dripping Medusa head—drank in from that savage blood a ghastly dew, which was made more potent by the heat and burnt into the crumbling sand. (Lucan 9.696–99)

And that is only part of the story of how Lybia could make snakes, many species of which are then described in a long ecphrastic digression from the matter at hand (Cato's desert campaign). But are we really justified in calling this material on snakes a digression? How are we to decide what counts as relevant or irrelevant in a complex text such as Lucan's *Civil Wars?* Such questions have been explored since antiquity, and they are the topic of the next chapter.

CHAPTER 2

Unity, Form, and Figuration

> Everything we say must surely be mimesis and image making.
> —Plato, *Critias*

Unity of one kind or another is a critical dogma at least as old as Aristotle; but vividness—the "as if present" prescription—is older still. When Odysseus asks Demodocus to tell a story "as perhaps one who had yourself been present, or had heard the tale from another" (*Odyssey* 8.491; Murray trans.), he does *not* add: "And be sure to have a single action and no irrelevancies cluttering the plot." For Homer, centuries away from Aristotle's theory of unity, the storyteller's imaginative participation in what the Muses know, and nothing else, secures the audience's participation and shows that "the god has with a ready heart granted you the gift of divine song" (*Odyssey* 8.498; Murray trans.). Because the Muses are present everywhere, they make obscure things vivid for the gifted storyteller and his audience. The invocation that introduces the catalog of ships at *Iliad* 2 attests to the great antiquity of this idea: "Tell me now, ye Muses [. . .]—for ye are goddesses and are at hand and know all things, whereas we hear but a rumor and know not anything" (2.484–86; Murray trans.).

Vividness and unity can work at cross-purposes or in tandem, as when the opening ecphrasis of *Ars Poetica* serves to illustrate the importance of unity itself. Horace invites his readers into his topic by making them imaginative eyewitnesses to a memorably curious painting. "Imagine a painter," writes Horace,

> who wanted to combine a horse's neck with a human head, and then clothe a miscellaneous collection of limbs with various kinds of feathers, so that what started out at the top as a beautiful woman ended in a hideously ugly fish. If you were invited, as frends, to the private view, could you help laughing? Let me tell you, my Piso friends, a book whose different features are made up at random like a sick man's dreams, with no unified form [. . .], is exactly like that picture. (1–9)

Horace's painting ecphrasis—vivid, original, and pointedly melded with his argument—establishes his credentials to speak with some authority about the use and abuse of description. A few lines later Horace ridicules irrelevant descriptions by invoking three ecphrastic clichés: descriptions of the Rhine, the rainbow, and a set-piece locus amoenus:

> Serious and ambitious designs often have a purple patch or two sewn on to them just to make a good show at a distance—a description of a grove and altar of Diana, the meanderings of a stream running through pleasant meads, the River Rhine, the rainbow: but the trouble is, it's not the place for them.
> Maybe you know how to make a picture of a cypress tree? [. . .]. Let it be what you will, but let it be simple and unified. (14–23)

The passage gives us the English idiom *purple prose,* "a brilliant or ornate passage." The word for "patch," *pannus,* refers to the brightly colored shirts worn by charioteers to identify themselves, whence the metaphor of a show at a distance. Horace puns on "place," *locus*—at once textual, graphical, and topographical—to point up the misplaced, patched-in place that is disrupting the unity of the visual or literary work of art.

Horace freely compares poetry with other arts, not only painting, and not only to illustrate the importance of the unity of the individual work. The explicit formula *ut pictura poesis,* "painting is like poetry," found later on in *Ars Poetica* 361, introduces an explanation of some particular likenesses that have to do less with the work itself than with how the audience responds to it:

> Poetry is like painting. Some attracts you more if you stand near, some if you're further off. One picture likes a dark place, one will need to be seen in the light, because it's not afraid of the critic's sharp judgment. One gives pleasure once, one will please if you look it over ten times. (361–365)

Here in the *locus classicus* of Horace's motto, spatial and temporal metaphors—standing near or further off, pleasing once or ten times over—apply to how *both* poetry and painting might be encountered and experienced. A single perspective is not necessarily the best one; a single encounter does not necessarily exhaust the potential experience. The implication is clear that for Horace the form and duration of attention merited by either a poem or a picture depends significantly on something other than either the medium or the temporal or spatial qualities of what is depicted.

Horace's "ut pictura poesis" is rooted in not one but two fundamental principles of aesthetic unity: the unity of the individual work of art, and the much more ancient generic unity of *all* mimetic arts. In antiquity, a wide range of activities and their products, including poetry, painting, sculpture, dance, music, vocal mimicry, and theatrical acting, shared "a representative-cum-expressive character that made it legitimate to regard them as a coherent group of mimetic arts" (Halliwell, *Aesthetics* 7). Comparisons between poetry and painting were already commonplace by the time Horace wrote "ut pictura poesis." Toward the end of the sixth century B.C., the poet Simonides described poetry as "speaking painting" or "painting with a voice," and painting as "silent poetry." Simonides' speaking picture/silent poetry is the sort of fluid interart comparison that reflects the shared intellectual background against which both Plato and Aristotle developed their theories of mimesis (Halliwell, *Aesthetics* 118). Horace takes for granted that the arts form a coherent group.

"Ut pictura poesis" (however read or misread) has been felt (rightly or wrongly) to encapsulate classical aesthetics. Removed from the immediate context of *Ars Poetica,* and enriched by whatever has been understood as the broader context informing Horace's aesthetics, the motto inspired the neoclassical aesthetics of the fifteenth, sixteenth, and seventeenth centuries, and most of the eighteenth century, including the modern tradition of debate about "sister arts" and interart transactions in general: the problems and possibilities of describing, representing, or illuminating one art in terms of another.[1] In G. E. Lessing's *Laocoön,* however, the doctrines that had accumulated around "ut pictura poesis" were repudiated and the notion of description itself was delegitimized.

Lessing, Mimesis, and Ethical Form

The *Laocoön* effaced Aristotle's generic conception of a unified mimesis and sharpened specific differences among the arts into binary oppositions that, when rediscovered in the late twentieth century, meshed well with certain contemporary trends in literary theory and cultural studies. Lessing's argument set poetry against visual arts,[2] posited a sequential conception of narrative as the only appropriate poetic mode, and "firmly sent description back to where it belonged: the servile, inanimate, inferior paradigm" (Beaujour 48–49). Though Lessing was hardly the first to cast a critical theoretical gaze toward the notion of description (Horace obviously had his own doubts), he established himself as the foremost among the antagonists. For that reason his arguments necessarily receive considerable attention here. Perhaps the most salient feature of his treatment of description is the challenge it poses to notions of artistic unity. Because he assumes that literature is a sequential art that can only be properly apprehended progressively, he leaves no room for literary structures that require retrospective as well as progressive reading.[3] His famous opposition of a statue of Laocoön to the epic treatment of the same theme in Virgil's *Aeneid* depends on this notion of the purely progressive character of literary form. If we look at the classical precedent for Lessing's comparison, however, we begin to understand some of the limitations of this view.

Lessing's comparison of a statue and an epic description actually follows very closely Dio Chrysostom's comparison of Homer's and Phidias's treatment of Zeus in his twelfth discourse (also called the Olympic Discourse). W. G. Howard's edition of *Laocoön*, published in 1910 and no longer widely available, showed how Dio had outlined the essence of *Laocoön* (xiv):

> Dio institutes a real comparison between poet and sculptor in the treatment of one and the same subject [. . .]. Phidias, defending his method of production, declares that he has rivaled and vanquished Homer; for after the creation of his Olympian Zeus it became impossible for anyone to conceive the god in any other form. (xxv)

Howard goes on to outline Dio's comparison and stresses its many similarities to Lessing's treatment. But the differences are equally telling.[4] What marks Dio's treatment of the subject, and distinguishes it from Lessing's, is a classical commitment to the generic unity of the arts that sets their specific differences against some stronger mimetic force that governs their various means of expression. Dio, for example, asks whether there is "some sort of influence which in some way actually molds and gives expression to man's conception of the deity," whether realized by poets or sculptors (29; 12.26). He concludes that Homer and Phidias alike depend on the same conception of deity, "a conception that is inevitable and innate in every creature endowed with reason, arising in the course of nature without the aid of human teacher and free from the deceit of any expounding priest" (27; 12.27).[5] In Dio's view, there is a divine mimetic force molding and shaping human mimetic activity into conformity to its patterns. The complete title of Dio's work is *The Olympic Discourse: or, on Man's First Conception of God*.

Pre-Platonic notions of mimesis included not only what we would call representational art and behavioral emulation but also "metaphysical conformity, as in the Pythagorean belief, reported by Aristotle, that the material world is a mimesis of the immaterial domain of numbers" (Halliwell, *Aesthetics* 15). It is clear from *Republic* 3 that Socrates takes for granted this broad understanding of mimesis when he asserts that buildings and music inform human character by their grace or gracelessness and that "the natural bodies of animals and plants" are full of the same qualities (646; 401a). In *Republic* 3, Socrates articulates

> a general principle of "ethical form" applicable to mimetic and other products of human culture and, by doing so, enunciates in embryo a theory of mimesis as expression, linking the form and beauty of artworks to their ethical content (their "character," *ethos*). (Halliwell, *Aesthetics* 62)

When Socrates speaks freely about the ethical kinship among living things and cultural forms, he appeals to a notion of communicable form and pattern: that is, the same kinds of (possibly mutable) characters pervade the human and the nonhuman world. This ancient line of mimetic thinking underpins Dio's discussion of depictions of Zeus, and indeed all ethical place descriptions, as well as Socrates' speculations about the ideal environment for human beings. The communicability of ethical form accounts for why the activities and artifacts to be allowed into Plato's ideal city matter so much. Since things, including every cultural product, may possess good or bad "character," and since character is in some way contagious, it is essential to keep all things possessing bad character away from the citizenry.

Socrates makes this point by describing the city of luxury as a foil for the ideal city. This city with a fever, modeled after a sick person, needs prostitutes, nurses, and specialists of all kinds—including mimetic artists (619; 2.373b). The story of Plato's banishment of poets is a familiar one—for both poets and painters are defective imitators of ideal beauty, which is both ontologically real and metaphysically prior to material nature; but Socrates' painful ambivalence as he comes to this conclusion is not usually stressed in the retelling (Nuttall 4–5). Socrates' ambivalence illustrates the importance in classical semiotic thinking of the power of representations to arouse affect, induce behavior, and thereby permanently shape character. Despite their diluted reality, representations are potent and deeply informing for good or for ill. When Socrates says that the "battles of gods and giants, and all the various stories of the gods hating their families or friends, should neither be told nor even woven in embroideries," the reason he offers is that since "the opinions [the young] absorb at that age are hard to erase and apt to become unalterable," educators "should take the utmost care that the first stories they hear about virtue are the best ones for them to hear" (625; 2.378c–e). Every modern critic of violence on television or in video games, and every feminist who is concerned to show that pornography and mass sexist advertising inscribe in the mind the worst possible attitudes toward women, repeats Socrates' argument in some form. By the same token, Socrates points out at 3.400e that the best possible character can be trained by emulating the harmony, grace, and rhythm found in a wide range of mimetic products and activities, including weaving and embroidery, architecture, and other crafts. Socrates further acknowledges the positive side of the emulation argument when he welcomes "hymns to the gods and the praises of good men" into the ideal city (832; 10.607a). At *Republic* 10, Socrates would shower upon those who can make such potent and ethically informing artifacts the divine honors due to them and send them on their way, lest their mimetic activities establish the wrong psychological patterns in the audience. But Socrates leaves the door open: "If poetic mimesis designed for pleasure could put an argument to show that she ought to have a place in the well governed city, we would gladly welcome her back, since we are conscious of being enchanted by her ourselves" (69–71; 10.607c; Halliwell trans.). Although Socrates wants to keep the poets at bay, he unequivocally allows into the city poetry's

> representatives—men who do not practice the art, but are lovers of poetry—to offer a prose defense on her behalf, showing that she provides not only pleasure but also benefit to the communities and to the life of man. And we shall listen graciously; for it will be our gain, I think, if poetry should be shown to be not just pleasurable but also beneficial. (71; 607d; Halliwell trans.)

The reference to political communities and to the life of man reminds us that the "city" under discussion in the *Republic* is the inner city of the soul as well as the outer city. Indeed, *Republic* 10 contains Socrates' confession that he is not about to banish poetry from the city of his own personal soul because he considers himself one of the few who have figured out how to manage the potentially damaging effects:

> But so long as she is unable to vindicate herself, we shall, *as we listen to her*, repeat our present argument as a charm to protect ourselves, taking care not to slip back into the puerile love from which most people suffer. So, we shall repeat as a charm that no serious interest should be shown in such poetry, as though it had a serious grasp of the truth; but anyone who listens to it should protect himself against it, out of concern for the city within him [. . .]. (71; 608a–b; Halliwell trans.; my italics)

Socrates' deepest semiotic concern is with defending his soul against the stamp of polluting representations. He actively protects the city within himself by repeatedly stamping himself with one kind of discourse—argument—as a charm against another that he continues to embrace. And of course Aristotle will rise to Socrates' open challenge and offer a prose defense on behalf of poetry, and mimesis in general, in the *Poetics*. Lessing's semiotic theory (unlike Aristotle's) does not engage the psychology of the *Republic:* the ancient and still controversial aesthetic problem of ethical form in cultural products, living things, and the cosmos in general. Romantic poets did, and this is one reason that Lessing's new rules had so little saliency for the creative generation to follow.

Lessing's conception of words (or pictures, or statues) as mere signs is countered by classical philosophy and by the Romantic conception of *logos* as a force of nature, both of which rely on a sense of communicable ethical form. Wordsworth expresses the Romantic view concisely:

> Words are too awful an instrument for good and evil to be trifled with: they hold above all other external powers a dominion over thoughts. If words be not [. . .] an incarnation of the thought but only a clothing for it, then surely will they prove an ill gift; [. . .]. Language, if it do not uphold, and feed, and leave in quiet, like the power of gravitation or the air we breathe, is a counter-spirit, unremittingly and noiselessly at work to derange, to subvert, to lay waste, to vitiate, and to dissolve. ("Essays upon Epitaphs" 361)

He reiterates this idea in a letter to William Rowan Hamilton of 23 December 1829: "Words are not a mere *vehicle*, but they are *powers* either to kill or to animate" (*Letters* 5:185; Wordsworth's italics). Wordsworth, proposing that linguistic representations are powerful either for good or for ill, takes a position essentially similar to that of Socrates in the *Republic*. It is a position essential to his poetic project, which depends upon the "metaphysical conformity" of the natural world with the human mind.

Serial Form and Configural Understanding

Lessing's argument depends absolutely on his notion of the way in which signification works. He assumes a "natural" correspondence between the mode of representation and the thing represented when he argues that objects in space are best represented by other objects (sculpture and painting) and sequences of events by other sequences of events (narratives).

> I reason thus: if it is true that in its imitations painting uses completely different means or signs than does poetry, namely figures and colors in space rather than articulated sounds in time, and if these signs must indisputably bear a suitable relation to the thing signified, then signs existing in space can express only objects whose wholes or parts coexist, while signs that follow one another can express only objects whose wholes or parts are consecutive.

> Objects or parts of objects which exist in space are called bodies. Accordingly, bodies with their visible properties are the true subjects of painting. Objects or parts of objects which follow on another are called actions. Accordingly, actions are the true subjects of poetry. (78)

This correspondence is not necessarily as natural as Lessing assumes, nor has it been taken to be so by other theorists of art. Indeed, it has not always been assumed that a "natural" sign even exists, or that "natural" likeness can be taken for granted.

Gestalt psychology provides one of the most serious critiques of Lessing's notions of semiotic appropriateness. Rudolf Arnheim cautions against confusing the temporal and spatial constraints of the artistic medium with the temporal and spatial constraints on the audience's understanding of the work. Arnheim is particularly interested in the idea of the whole, in how relationships among the elements of any pattern are comprehended, and argues that they cannot be fully comprehended all at once:

> In a spatial manifold, causal relations are not limited to a linear sequence but occur simultaneously in the many directions offered by a two-dimensional or three-dimensional medium. The attractions and repulsions that obtain between the components of a painting create an interplay that must be understood synoptically. Only when the scanning eye has collected and related them all does an adequate conception of the total dynamics emerge [. . .]. Symmetry, balance, and other spatial characteristics can become apparent upon sequential observation, but they can never be experienced linearly. (70)

Arnheim explains a perceptual constraint that unites the experience of all the arts: "The composition of a painting, piece of sculpture, or work of architecture is perceived only when the crisscross of relations between the elements is apprehended synoptically. The same is true [. . .] for the temporal media" (70). It is crucial to distinguish how a work is communicated from how it is experienced and understood:

> [M]usic dispenses chord after chord and a verbal description word after word, but these materials simply form the channel of communication. The aesthetic structure they transmit—the piece of music, the poetic image, is not limited to a one-way sequence. While listening to music, the hearer weaves relations back and forth and even coordinates phrases as matched pendants, e. g. the return of the minuet after the trio, although in the performance they are delivered one after the other. The ample use of repetition in the temporal arts serves to create correspondences between parts following one another in time and thereby to compensate for the one-way structure of the performance. (71)

The principle applies in particular to literary description, as Arnheim explains and illustrates with a fine example that shows how the understanding of even one single literary description can vie "with the spatial complexity of an actual perceptual experience. Even so, the sequence in which a temporal work discloses aspects of the intended structure exerts a decisive influence on the result" (71–72). His example is from Emily Dickinson:

> An everywhere of silver,
> With ropes of sand
> To keep it from effacing
> The track called land. (*Complete Poems,* Part Two, XXII)

Arnheim notes that Dickinson "closes in on the island concentrically, from the outside—a dynamics not prescribed by the image but imposed upon it by the sequence and, to be sure, by the wording" (72). Since this island does not do anything or contain any actors, Lessing and his adherents would find Emily Dickinson guilty of transgressing the bounds of poetry. Her poem, however, demonstrates how problematic such a notion of transgression is; for she actually works within a well-understood constraint of her medium, the sequential delivery of the words, to create a structure that culminates in the surprising but nonnarrative revelation of the island. The last word "land" makes instant sense of the enigmatic "everywhere of silver" and the progressively less enigmatic "ropes of sand" as the terms finally cohere in a single image for the reader. This poetic image could not be presented better—if at all—in a painting. Precisely because she can give us one word, one partial image, at a time, the poet carefully controls our attention to the developing image in ways that are not available to painters. (Of course, visual artists have other means of controlling or directing our attention to their images.) We can be grateful that poets and artists have not in general followed Lessing's rules, that Blake did not feel hounded by the aesthetic police when he merged painting and poetry, and that Emily Dickinson did not feel constrained to narrate a little sequential tour of the island with simple attributive epithets characterizing its features.[6]

The one-wayness of a linear mode of communication is indeed an important aesthetic structure in poetry and music; but it is a structure that can be and often is aesthetically manipulated, made to loop back on itself and interlace itself into structures comprehended as nonlinear and "substantive" by the audience. Just as we learn to understand music as we listen to it and then listen again, so also we learn to understand a highly patterned poem or novel—or any complex structure that offers itself to the imagination. Lessing's close matching of the "sequential" sign with the "sequential" signified commits him to an impoverished theory of the temporal arts that does not even apply to the *more purely* temporal art of music. Lessing limits the possibilities of serial form to the simplest kind of progressive form, the sense of a forward-moving action completed in time. (The musical analogy would be the melodic line or phrase.) He gives no account of what is experientially far more important for the comprehension of serial art: its *retrospective* form, that other sense of the work's coherence that emerges only after the work has been completely heard or read, or heard and read again. Proper descriptions, by Lessing's explicit standards, contribute only to the work's progressive form; they help to motivate and clarify the action in the forward-moving direction only. Like the gestalt psychologists, Karl Kroeber has argued that reading is not at all a one-way process, that "story demands we exercise our capacity for *configural* comprehension, grasping a number of things as elements in a single and concrete complex of elements" (*Retelling* 55; Kroeber's italics). "To comprehend temporal succession means to think of it in both directions at once" (Mink qtd. in Kroeber 55).

While there is no place in Lessing's theory for thematically significant descriptions that control the reader's sense of retrospective form and meaning, Lessing is too thoughtful a reader to not exhibit occasionally a retrospective reading that goes against the grain of his theory. His account of Agamemnon's scepter at *Iliad* 2 and of Achilles' scepter at *Iliad* 1 illustrates the way in which retrospective reading forces its way into and then undermines his argument. Lessing himself feels some pressure to account for Homer's eight hexameters on Agamemnon's scepter, but at the same time he registers discomfort with efforts of others to explain it. He notes with approval that Homer does not describe the scepter as if it "were intended for a handbook of heraldic art, so that at some later time an exact duplicate could be made" (81). But after he entertains us with this red herring, he still needs somehow to account for the presence of this descriptive passage in a poem that he has claimed, has few, if any, descriptive passages. ("Homer represents nothing but progressive actions. He depicts bodies and single objects only when they contribute toward these actions, and then only by a single trait" [79].) Lessing's solution is both to attend to the details and to mock attending to the details by calling such attention "allegory," making it clear as he does so that for him, allegory is a term of abuse:

> I should not be surprised if I found that one of the ancient commentators on Homer had praised this passage as being the most perfect allegory of the origin, development, strengthening, and ultimately hereditary succession of royal power among men. I should smile, to be sure [. . .]. (81–82)

He continues in this vein for about a page and concludes:

> But this is not my present concern, and I am regarding the history of the scepter *merely as an artistic device, by means of which the poet causes us to linger over a single object* without entering into a tiring description of its parts. (82; my italics)

Now, every great classical ecphrasis of an object "causes us to linger [...] without entering into a tiring description of its parts"; Lessing's remark would be at home in any of the progymnasmata.

The problem that Lessing's discussion elides is the nature and function of this mere "artistic device." Why indeed should masters of ecphrasis cause Lessing and the rest of us to linger so? After opening and shutting the door onto the theoretical heart of the matter, Lessing immediately advances to a discussion of another scepter, the scepter of Achilles he remembers from *Iliad* 1: "We see it verdant on the hills; the iron divides it from the trunk, deprives it of its leaves and bark and renders it suitable to serve the judges of the people as a symbol of their godlike dignity" (82). Lessing's own figurative reading alludes to the scepter as a serious "symbol," not part of an "allegory" to be smiled at; but it becomes clear that he is engaging in the same enterprise of figurative interpretation that he has just ridiculed in his discussion of Agamemnon's scepter. He explains the significance of the two scepters now as

> a clear image of the difference in power which the two staffs symbolized. The one the work of Vulcan; the other, cut from the mountain-side by some unknown hand. The one an ancient possession of a noble house; the other destined to fit the hand of any who might chance to grasp it. [...]. This was the real difference between Agamemnon and Achilles; a difference which Achilles himself, in spite of all his blind rage, could not help but acknowledge. (83)

The repetition of the scepters, first Achilles' and then Agamemnon's, suggests to Lessing an analogy and a contrast not only between the objects but between the two warriors. Lessing's retrospective reading of Achilles' scepter, in light of Agamemnon's, stimulates an ethical interpretation of both objects that gives each scepter a deeper thematic significance than would be possible had each scepter been read in the way that Lessing's rules require: merely as implements enfolded locally into the action. In spite of himself, his retrospective reading of Agamemnon's scepter is just as detailed and not so very far from the "allegory" of "royal power among men" that he had rejected with high disdain.

Tenorless Vehicles: Metaphor, Allegory, and Description

By Lessing's time, allegory was well on its way toward becoming a term of abuse, the mechanical "picture language" that Coleridge all too successfully banished from Romantic poetics when he distinguished it from the Symbol capable of expressing transcendent realities (*Statesman's* 30).[7] Allegory "lived on in the quietest academic obscurity" until its twentieth-century rehabilitation eventually made it something quite thoroughly problematic (Piehler, "Allegories" 1). But allegory as ridiculed by Lessing was evidently nothing other than thematically significant description, part of a figurative network that becomes visible only in a larger poetic context. The figurative significance of individual descriptive passages, such as Homer's two scepters, does not emerge for Lessing or for any other reader until the reader becomes conscious of the interconnected network of which these elements are a part. In fact, it often seems easier and more plausible to dismiss such elements as an eight-hexameter scepter as merely "decorative" (or as "mere artistic devices" that cause us "to linger over a single object") than to look for their figurative function and psychological impact in some larger context.

Here, for instance, is a telling example involving the fiction of Achilles Tatius, a writer from the late second century who frequently engages in elaborate descriptions. Charles W. Hedrick explains:

> Frequently the narrator suspends the action to provide the reader lengthy decorative descriptions of various objects, locations, people, topics, and events. These lengthy descriptions play no immediately obvious role in furthering the story. For example, the narrator digresses to give a rather elaborate description of a large vessel used for mixing wine on the occasion of the festival of Dionysus. (180)

The description Hedrick alludes to is this, from Achilles Tatius's novel *Leucippe and Clitophon:*

> My father, wishing to celebrate it [the festival] with splendour, had set out all that was necessary for the dinner in a rich and costly fashion; but especially a precious cup to be used for libations to the god, one only second to the famous goblet of Glaucus of Chios. The material of it was wrought rock-crystal; vines crowned its rim, seeming to grow from the cup itself, their clusters drooped down in every direction: when the cup was empty, each grape seemed green and unripe, but when wine was poured into it, then little by little the clusters became red and dark, the green crop turning into the ripe fruit; Dionysus too was represented hard by the clusters, to be the husbandman of the vine and the vintner. As we drank deeper, I began to look more boldly and with less shame at my sweetheart. (qtd. in Hedrick 180)

Hedrick's view is that this elaborate description is "merely a meandering detail in the progress of the narrative," serving only to "inform the reader of the plush nature of the festival. There is no obvious connection to the love story" (181). Hedrick's allegiance to Lessing's heritage is clear. The narrator "suspends the action" to do something Hedrick, like Lessing, thinks he should not do.

Another reader, Shadi Bartsch, understands the passage quite differently. For Bartsch, the description of the bowl "serves as a metaphor and a parallel both for the moment in the narrative at which it is described *and for the outcome of the romance itself*" (Bartsch 146; my italics). The moment in the narrative is one of sexual arousal, and Bartsch finds it hard not to acknowledge a figurative connection between the growing sexual attraction between the lovers and the change in color from pale to deep red taking place in the bowl. It is in effect blushing on their behalf. But the figuration, she claims, goes much farther:

> More generally, the description of the [krater] and the transformation of the grapes from unripe to mature fruit foreshadow the entire progress of Clitophon and Leucippe's love affair and its final fulfillment at the end of the novel, when we find the protagonists finally [. . . in the narrator's words] "accomplishing the much-wished for marriage." (147)

Hedrick's response to Bartsch's reading is one of cool incredulity, and he is quick to admonish readers inclined to follow her example against what he views as an attempt "to read the author's mind" (181). Hedrick apparently feels it makes more sense to construe the novel as full of digressions and meandering details than to see it as a coherent unit, unless its coherence can be shown to be explicitly authorized by "clear guidance from the narrator" (181).

Henry James, well aware of this problem, dramatized it in "The Figure in the Carpet," whose narrator wants desperately to understand an inscrutable author: "For himself, beyond doubt, the thing we were so blank about was vividly there. It was something, I guessed, in the primal plan, something like a complex figure in a Persian carpet" (586). What is it that authorizes a description, no matter how many figures of speech it employs, to be read in its entirety not as a detachable fragment, but as integral to the "primal plan" of the work, like the figure in James's carpet? What, if anything, justifies understanding a "purple patch" such as Achilles Tatius's wine bowl (in this case quite literally purple) as a figure in the larger carpet of the novel rather than simply as a "meandering detail" meant only to enhance what twentieth-century theory might call the "reality effect"? The issue is one that has bothered several judicious readers of descriptive literature. Jean Hagstrum, for example, notes his own and Reuben Brower's sense of a need for a figurative function in descriptive detail:

> Pictorial imagery is most effective when it is in some way or other metaphorical rather than purely descriptive or purely imitative of visual reality. Professor Reuben A. Brower has said: "The failure of much eighteenth-century poetry [. . .] is not due to over-generality but to the lack of a metaphorical sense which connects and gives meaning to detail." The comment is shrewd, but it can be applied to *much* of the the poetry of any period. (*Sister* xx)

Indeed, it can be applied not just to the poetry but to all the literature of all periods. But Hagstrum and Brower are both hampered in their attempt to discuss the matter productively by an imprecision in their technical vocabulary. When they say "metaphorical," they probably mean something like "figurative." But is *metaphor* the term that best describes the figurative function of literary description?

It is instructive in this connection to examine the complex relationship between the classical rhetorical terms *metaphor* and *allegory* as they were understood in the first century, at about the time we find the first extant use of the term *ekphrasis* in Greek rhetoric, and not far from the time when Achilles Tatius wrote his novel. The problem that emerges from examining the relation between these two terms is the very same as that highlighted in the dispute between Hedrick and Bartsch: the nature of the relation between what a text explicitly states and what it might, indirectly and figuratively, mean to suggest. Quintilian, for example, is conscious of how complex figuration is patterned out of smaller components, and a theory of allegory derived in part from a consideration of his thinking on the topic is particularly helpful in providing a productive basis for understanding the figurative function of description in classical literature.

By Quintilian's time, *metaphor* and related terms had been classified into elaborate systems of tropes and figures, the various taxonomical principles of which Quintilian finds useless to the student of oratory. He writes wearily and prophetically that teachers of literature quarrel violently among themselves and with the philosophers about the correct classification. For his part, he rejects a narrow definition of trope as any expression necessarily involving a word-for-word substitution (301; 8.5.35–8.6.3). Instead he proposes a more semantically sensitive one: "By a *trope* is meant the artistic alteration of a word or phrase from its proper meaning to another" (301; 8.6.1). And metaphor is "the commonest and most beautiful of tropes" (303; 8.6.4). More than that, metaphor is essential to language, to the clear expression of meaning. Quintilian takes a step further Aristotle's sense that metaphor expands knowledge and understanding. For Aristotle, a good metaphor is a clear metaphor. Metaphor "most brings about learning; for when he [Homer, *Odyssey* 4.213] calls old age 'stubble,' he creates knowledge and understanding [. . .], since both old age and stubble are [. . .] things that have lost their bloom" (*Rhetoric* 244; 10.2; Kennedy trans.). Quintilian, in a passage that anticipates the nineteenth- and twentieth-century idea that metaphors are the growing-points of language itself, writes that metaphor

> adds to the copiousness of language by the interchange of words [. . .] and finally succeeds in accomplishing the supremely difficult task of providing a name for everything. A noun or a verb is transferred from the place to which it properly belongs to another where there is no literal term or the transferred is better than the literal. We do this either because it is necessary or to make our meaning clearer or [. . .] to produce a decorative effect. (303; 8.6.5–6)

Quintilian goes on to suggest that metaphor has an affective as well as a semiotic function: "For [. . .] metaphor is designed to move the feelings, give special distinction to things and place them vividly before the eye" (311; 8.6.19). These functions are indistinguishable from the functions of classical ecphrasis. But then, as if to undermine his contention that metaphor serves one's commitment to the classic ecphrastic goals of clarity and vividness, he links metaphor to obscurity—to allegories and riddles:

> While a temperate and timely use of metaphor is a real adornment to style, on the other hand, its frequent use serves merely to obscure our language and weary our audience, while if we introduce them in one continuous series, our language will become allegorical and enigmatic." (307–309; 8.6.14)

If we suppose that all the metaphors contributing to allegories and riddles are well formed and clear by Quintilian's standards, how can it be that too much accumulated clarity produces obscurity? Why should the extended form of a clear trope be an obscure figure called allegory?

Quintilian's terminology is imprecise in a way that bedevils ancient and much modern discussion of metaphor and allegory. The imprecision arises from a failure to distinguish clearly between the whole metaphor and the two parts of a metaphor, Aristotle's "this" and "that," the two parts involved in the substitution, comparison, or interchange that produces the whole metaphor. This problem, together with the problem of mistaking the metaphor, "the double unit including tenor and vehicle," for its meaning(s)

(I.A. Richards 132), motivated Richards to introduce his tenor-and-vehicle terminology:

> At present we have only some clumsy descriptive phrases [. . .] "The original idea" and "the borrowed one"; "what is really being said or thought of" and "what it is compared to"; "the underlying idea" and "the imagined nature"; "the principal subject" and "what it resembles" or, still more confusing, simply "the meaning" and "the metaphor" or "the idea" and "its image." (96)

The tenor is the principal, literal subject that the figurative vehicle refers to. In the metaphor "Achilles is a lion," Achilles is the tenor; the lion is the vehicle. For Richards, the challenge to the interpreter lies mainly in knowing enough about the literal meanings of tenor and vehicle—who is Achilles? what is a lion?—and in deciding exactly what the present interaction between them implies. To gain a purchase on that interaction is to construe some meaning of the metaphor, a meaning different from the possible meanings of its constituent parts.

Richard Moran writes that if the words of a metaphor undergo a "'meaning-shift' of some kind, it will have to involve a difference of meaning very different from that involved in ordinary ambiguity" (252). By ordinary ambiguity, Moran refers to the sort of misreading that is no longer interesting or relevant once the correct reading has been achieved. For example, if I say that "Heather" called, and you think I mean Heather A. when in fact I mean Heather B., once you find out which Heather I mean, all the other Heathers are no longer relevant to understanding the ambiguous message. Your understanding cancels out your misunderstanding. But "when an expression is interpreted metaphorically, the first interpretation (the literal one) is not cancelled or removed from consideration" (252). That is, the literal meaning of "lion" is not dispensable when we apply it to Achilles. "The literal meaning must be known to both the speaker and the audience for the metaphorical point of the epithet to be made. It has everything to do with clarifying the speaker's intentions" that he chose this particular word—lion—to refer to Achilles, who is not an animal, "and when we start to figure out the reason why the speaker is using this word with its literal meaning in this context, we have begun to interpret" the metaphor (252–253):

> Simply characterizing metaphor in terms of a change of meaning fails to capture the role of the original, literal meaning [. . .]. If we are to speak of a new meaning, this meaning will be something reachable only through comprehension of the previously established, literal meanings of the words that make it up. (253)

Literal meanings do not "just provide clues to help you get to the second one, like a ladder that is later kicked away," but somehow "remain 'active' in the new metaphorical interpretation" (253). It is this indispensability of the literal that sharply distinguishes metaphor, most allegory, and all thematically significant description from a code. For once we have deciphered a code, we are *only* interested in the meaning. The coded representation was a (possibly quite annoying) means to that end. We commonly betray our sense of a code's dispensability by speaking, with no regret, of having "broken" or "cracked" it.

We do not speak of breaking metaphors. Confronted with "Achilles is a lion" we ponder the relationship between our notion of Achilles and our notion of the lion; we keep on needing both Achilles and the lion. Significance flows back and forth between the two as we contemplate what relationship really is being proposed between Achilles and the animal. Moran points out that for recognizing such utterances

> as metaphorical (rather than ironic, say), [. . .] the principles the hearer employs to compute the speaker's meaning from the meaning of the sentence uttered, combined with the context of utterance [. . .] will appeal to features of resemblance, contrast, context, and emotional attitudes toward the subject that make the relation between literal and figurative meaning very much unlike the relation between a word and its substitution in some code. (262–263)

But even after the speaker's meaning is recovered, it does not follow that the meaning is restricted to the speaker's explicit intentions.

> The interpreter may need to presume various things about the beliefs of the speaker for the metaphor to succeed in picturing one thing in terms of another; but once that perspective has been adopted, the interpretation of the light it sheds on its subject may outrun anything the speaker is thought explicitly to have had in mind. And on the other hand, from the point of view of the speaker, the restriction to speaker-meaning seems inadequate, in that it construes metaphor as a kind of shorthand [. . .] for a given set of beliefs that she wishes to convey. What such a picture leaves out of consideration is the role of metaphor in thought, the fact that the composition of live metaphor is undertaken in the expectation that it will lead one's thoughts about the subject in a certain direction [. . .]. (264)

In fact, a creative speaker may well expect the metaphor to produce *new* thoughts about the subject rather than merely encapsulate the beliefs that *either* speaker or audience may already have about the subject (264).

Armed now with better tools for understanding metaphor, we may also begin to see more clearly why Quintilian wants to connect it to allegory.

He makes the connection more or less as an aside in a discussion of irony, when he claims: "Thus as continued metaphor develops into allegory, so a sustained series of tropes develops into this figure [irony])" (401; 9.2.46). The phrase *continua metaphora*, "continued metaphor," inaugurates a critical tradition that more or less equates allegory and metaphor and assumes that their effects differ only in the degree of extension suggested by the word *continua*. The phrase survives today not only as Quintilian's very definition of allegory but also as the most elegant formulation of what classical rhetoric has to say about the term. "The traditional rhetoric set forth by Cicero, Quintilian, and the Renaissance rhetoricians," writes Angus Fletcher, "asserts that allegory is a sequence of sub-metaphors which amount in the aggregate to one single, continued, 'extended' metaphor" (70). Allegory "does not use metaphor; it is one," claims Rosemond Tuve; it is "by definition a continued metaphor" (105–106). Moreover, discussions of metaphor often assimilate allegory to metaphor. Richards admits that he

> generalized, or stretched, the sense of the term metaphor—almost, you may think, to the breaking point. I used it to cover all cases where a word, in Johnson's phrase, "gives us two ideas for one," where we compound different uses of the word into one, and speak of something as if it were another. And I took it further still to include, as metaphoric, those processes in which we perceive or think of or feel about one thing in terms of another. (116)

Later on in the twentieth century, *allegory* would also stretch to the breaking point (Piehler, "Allegories" 2) until it meant exactly the same thing as Richards's overly extended *metaphor*.[8] Richards's generalization echoes one of Quintilian's, except that Quintilian (like his late-twentieth-century heirs) makes allegory rather than metaphor the central term. Again, Quintilian's topic is something else, euphemism this time instead of irony, when he remarks that "all saying one thing and wanting another thing to be understood is like allegory" (432; 9.2.92; my trans.)—*like* allegory, but exactly how?

As useful as such generalizations are in foregrounding similarities among various kinds of figurative language—and Quintilian's inter alia remarks about allegory nearly always point up one or another such similarity—generalization exacts heavy costs if it disables our perception of important differences in how figurative language is first recognized as such and then interpreted by readers. The finer structure and the interpretive strategies specific to all the subtypes one might imagine—irony, allusion, allegory, metaphor, metonymy, hyperbole, to name only a few terms that would be lumped together by either Quintilian's or Richards's generalization—get lost. In particular, metaphor and allegory announce themselves quite differently to readers and ask them to proceed quite differently if they are to arrive at an interpretation. The difference between allegory and metaphor that emerges from Quintilian's explicit account of allegory, from the examples themselves and from what he needs to do to interpret them, will be helpful in understanding thematically significant description.

The crucial difference between metaphor and allegory that emerges from Quintilian's examples of allegory—rather than from his attempt to define it—is that while both metaphor and allegory propose a significant relation (of likeness and/or disparity) between two terms, metaphor always specifies the two terms that are supposed to convey the figurative meaning of the metaphor—a tenor such as "Achilles" and a vehicle such as "lion." Allegory, on the other hand, specifies only the vehicle, usually in an extended imagistic or narrative form that provides enough structure for the knowledgeable to recover the missing tenor. The interpretation of metaphor is therefore potentially more straightforward; the challenge to the interpreter lies mainly in knowing enough about the literal meanings of tenor and vehicle—who is Achilles? what is a lion?—and in deciding exactly what relationship is being proposed in the immediate context. Allegory, even a brief allegory, elicits a more complex effort on the part of the reader. It is left to the reader to determine what the unnamed tenor of the text might be—and whether or not indeed there is one. Metaphors announce themselves more openly, by saying something so patently false ("Achilles is a lion") or so patently obvious ("Achilles is no pussycat") that the reader, having ruled out the possibility that the writer is writing nonsense or trivia, tries to figure out what relationship really is being proposed between Achilles and the animal. Whether or not the reader succeeds depends crucially on understanding the literal meanings of lion and pussycat and of the tenor, Achilles.

Unlike a metaphor, an allegory is not embedded in and dependent for its meaning upon the literal terms of the surrounding tenor (there is no tenor). Instead, allegory depends upon its own *tenorless* figurations and on larger-scale nonmetaphoric patterns established formally by (for example) puns, juxtaposition, repetition, contrast, analogy, and narrative extension—as well as an unusual amount of sophisticated "insider" knowledge on the reader's part—to provide all the structure for making this determination. The potential problems may be alleviated by providing an explicit "moral," as in the case of the Aesopian fable or medieval exemplum. But these are subgenres for wider, younger, or less sophisticated audiences. Allegory normally does not offer a built-in interpretation; it prefers to present itself to insiders who will approach it with the right knowledge and belief. "Impious intruders," as

Frank Kermode calls them, are bound to get it all wrong. Kermode explains that the

> history of the rules and theory of interpretation—of hermeneutics as it used to be, before philosophy appropriated it—is closely linked with that of Biblical exegesis; the exegetes drew up the rules or canons, refined them, distinguished between different kinds of hermeneutic activity, and expanded the whole subject to include such questions as what makes interpretation possible, how its process is affected by lapse of time between the writing and the interpreting, what may be controlled by prescriptive rules of conduct, and what must be left to the divinity genius of the interpreter. (vii)

Interpreters always belong to a cultural institution; they are the ones who know how to read. They have the duty and privilege of exhibiting the latent sense of the text, the spiritual sense, a sense that is always superior to the manifest and carnal reading available to anyone (2–3). "Carnal readings are much the same. Spiritual readings are all different" (9).

We are fortunate that such a distinguished institutional reader as Quintilian lets us read what he calls allegory over his shoulder, so to speak. We can watch him as he interprets text and context in such a way as to discover the missing term of the figure he assumes the text to be. Quintilian introduces his first example of allegory in a manner that seems to place it in perfect accord with the extended metaphor doctrine. Horace's *Ode* 1.14.1, says Quintilian, "is produced by a series of metaphors" (327; 8.6.44). He cites the opening lines:

> O ship, new waves will bear thee back to sea.
> What dost thou? Make the haven, come what may [. . .].
> (qtd. in Quintilian 327; 8.6.44)

Quintilian asserts that "Horace represents the state under the semblance of a ship" (327; 8.6.44). What is curious is that neither in the passage cited nor anywhere in the entire ode does Horace mention the state. Moreover, the *continuatis translationibus,* the "series of metaphors" that make up what is supposed to be the state under the semblance of a ship, are all "metaphors" with missing tenors. Only the vehicles—the waves, the sea, the port, and so forth—are present in the ode. None of these half-empty, tenorless metaphors could stand alone as metaphors of the state or anything else; for, taken separately, there is no way to know that any one of them *is* a metaphor. In fact the ode is so manifestly about a ship that, to understand the ode as being about anything other than a ship, readers need insider information of various kinds. They have to know about Roman politics. They have to be sufficiently aware of Horace's political context and poetical topoi to confidently guess at some point in reading the ode that Horace, the sophisticated political Horace he thinks he knows, could not possibly have written a manifestly unclever poem about a boat. And since the ode cannot possibly be about boats, all the boat rhetoric insists on being reread in some unified Horatian other-sense, an other-sense that is probably political. Thus the allegorical readers, the knowledgeable insiders, learn to read the ode as they go along. They progressively construct a well-coordinated set of missing tenors, using each completed half-metaphor as a clue for completing and possibly correcting the others. Finally, all the missing tenors come into view and cohere as an image of the imperiled state.

If the structure we have just discerned in Horace's ode is what Quintilian means by extended metaphor, we need to qualify the term. First, the metaphors are all obscure half-metaphors with missing tenors. Next, the extended or continued metaphor is unified by clarifying and elaborating the initial ship image while at the same time sustaining the "O navis" apostrophe with which Horace introduces the ship. But apostrophe is *not* metaphor.[9] Quintilian understands it as a diversionary turning away from the present audience: "Apostrophe [. . .] consists in the diversion of our address from the judge," as when one "turns to make some invocation such as 'For I appeal to you, hills and groves of Alba,' or to cry 'O Porcian and Sempronian laws'" (397; 9.2.38) to strengthen the emotional appeal of one's case. But apostrophe also applies "to utterances that divert the attention of the hearer from the question before them" (397; 9.2.39). It is this rhetorical tradition of diversionary forensic apostrophe that enables the ode to playfully announce itself to Quintilian as possibly a smoke screen hiding the real issue. The figure asks the sophisticated reader to look hard for what important matter the figure is diverting the reader from. Through the extended apostrophe—not an extended metaphor—the ship accumulates detail as the poet particularizes the danger it is in. This tightly integrated rhetorical extension—adding imagistic detail while sustaining the admonition—amounts to a cohesive set of clues enabling Quintilian and others who share his beliefs about the poet in his political context to read of "civil wars as tempests, and peace and good will as the haven" (327; 8.6.44).

Quintilian's next few examples are similar in that the figurative language he would have us understand as extended metaphor really contains only the vehicles of what the reader must construct as metaphors. But the most puzzling example with respect to the extended metaphor doctrine is Quintilian's example of allegory *sine translatione,* "without metaphor" at all (327; 8.6.46). The example helps us gain a purchase on just how much insider knowledge is implicitly involved in Quintilian's notion of allegory. Quintilian reads Virgil's

Eclogue 9 as an allegory because he believes the poem sustains what we would call an autobiographical allusion to the poet. Quintilian cites these lines:

> Yet surely I had heard that, from where the hills begin to rise, then sink their ridge in a gentle slope, down to the water and the old beeches with their now-shattered tops, your Menalcas had with his songs saved all. (*Eclogues* 9.7–10; qtd in Quintilian 326; 8.6.46)

Quintilian claims that all the words in this brief description are to be taken literally, except Menalcas, which he claims really refers to Virgil. Here we need to ask a question similar to the one I posed earlier in this chapter, a question central to making progress in understanding the figurative function of description: What, if anything, justifies interpreting this landscape as something other than an attempt to enhance what twentieth-century theory might call the "reality effect"? The answer, Quintilian suggests, is that this is an allegory, and like all great allegories, it succeeds by providing some reason for reading what might be quite satisfactory literal descriptions as part of an integrated figural pattern. Quintilian evidently believes that the shepherd saving the hills by his song is an allegory of Virgil saving his own farm from confiscation because of his celebrity status as an Augustan poet. And while modern readers might, while accepting Quintilian's allegorical reading, quarrel with his assessment of all the other terms—the hills, the beeches with their shattered tops, and so forth—as quite completely literal, the important point is that Quintilian does *not* consider them sufficiently removed in sense from the notion of "farm" to be metaphoric. For Quintilian, it is the cryptic political puzzle of how songs saved the farm that makes the poem an allegory. Supplying the missing tenor "Virgil" for the poetic vehicle "Menalcas" solves the puzzle and reveals the allegorical structure at a single stroke.

Coherence, Irrelevance, and the Reader's Expectations

We are now in a position to return with profit to the dispute between Hedrick and Bartsch on the right reading of the descriptive passages in Achilles Tatius's *Leucippe and Clitophon,* a novel that is structured on exactly the same principles as Horace's "ship of state" poem. We can now readily see that the basis for the disagreement has to do with the same sorts of problems encountered in any text whose literal descriptions we might be inclined to read allegorically. Like every allegorical element in the "ship of state," Achilles Tatius's description of the wine bowl that changes color is a tenorless vehicle. Because it is literally the sort of wine bowl a rich man might actually own, and because it is not explicitly metaphorical—that is, because it lacks a stated tenor—Hedrick proposes that any reading of it as figurative must be rejected as not authorized by a clear authorial intention. Since there is nothing disconcerting or out of place about such a naturalistic wine bowl, what need is there for a figurative reading of its decoration? But Bartsch appears to be implicitly arguing that the reading she proposes is indeed authorized, not by a specific tenor provided by the author but by what Henry James would call the "primal plan" of the novel. She assumes some guiding principle or "pretext" that is as clear to the knowledgeable insider as Horace's political preoccupations were to Quintilian, even if that guiding principle is opaque to Kermode's impious intruders. Bartsch in fact concludes that the descriptions in this novel and others like it are "no mere rhetorical showpieces but forge playful and intricate connections with the narrative and its events" (7). Such descriptions

> present themselves, for readers guided by the conventions of the epoch, as illuminators of the text; they promise insight into it; they call for acts of interpretation. As such they necessarily figure as crucial tools in the author's narrative strategy. (7)

The conventions she has in mind are the provocative uses of ecphrasis in the rhetoric of the period. Expecting to be provoked, and remembering just how the descriptions provoke or perplex, Bartsch finds "the figure in the carpet" that would be invisible to a reader who is committed to the notion that a description can only be locally relevant, if it is relevant at all. She argues that vivid presentations of the strange or irrelevant, coupled with the explanations that the characters or the narrator offer for these matters, form powerful hermeneutic clues by which the author engages and controls the reader's attention to the text. They are formal means by which the reader is stimulated to engage in more complex acts of interpretation. The most attentive and wholehearted readers

> are repeatedly lured into forming their own interpretations or into accepting the false ones. Often the author deliberately misleads by providing incorrect clues and including in the narrative events that seem to fulfill incorrect interpretations. Generally the truth is only apparent with hindsight or even with secondary hindsight; generally, too, it is the more sophisticated readers—those who look for clues and are confident in their ability to see where these point—who will be most deceived about the author's elaborately designed interweaving of foreshadowers, apparent fulfillments, and later events that prove to be the true fulfillments. In these works, the model readers are [. . .] those [. . .] who actualize the text in such a way as to secure their own deception. (172)

It should be mentioned that all this business is not quite as slippery as it sounds. The utterly conventional plot, by conforming to culturally enshrined models, constitutes a contract under which readers happily submit to much playful teasing, while authors rigorously uphold their end of the bargain. To a dead certainty, boy meets girl, boy loses girl, and boy gets girl in the end. The author's challenge is to make what is a dead certainty—the eventual marriage—come off as an unexpected wonder.

To readers who know how to read romance, Achilles Tatius offers the wine bowl gratis—with no hermeneutic deception at all—as a charmingly particular commentary on the assured outcome. He also integrates the wine bowl into a network of significant descriptions that includes the very setting in which Clitophon tells his long love story, a grove reminiscent of the *Phaedrus*. (Helen Morales, in her introduction to the novel, goes so far as to argue that the "novel dramatizes and explores the major concerns of *Phaedrus*—rhetoric, *eros,* and the form, unity and status of written communication" [xxi].) When the wine bowl appears in the novel's second chapter, it extends a pattern of erotic ecphrasis that the first chapter had established beyond all doubt in Clitophon's description of a flourishing garden where "leaf caressed leaf, beside frond embracing frond, beside fruit coiling around fruit, so intimate was this [. . .] intermingling of trees" (16); where a peacock courts his hen—"The bird's actions, you know, [. . .] are not without design. He is in love" (17); and where Clitophon is moved to describe a gardener who "revives the soul" of a lovelorn male palm tree by grafting a shoot from the female "into the heart of the male" who forthwith "recuperates, rejoicing in the embrace of its beloved" (17). Every such "irrelevance" that Clitophon lingers over in the opening chapter (while literally lingering in an evocative grove) thus in effect prefigures his erotic involvement with Leucippe and proves in the long run not to be irrelevant at all. So, too, the wine bowl, which Bartsch understands and interprets accordingly, while Hedrick remains an impious intruder into a genre that can loudly proclaim the course and outcome of its budding romance (in all senses of the word) in the ripening grapes of a blushing wine bowl.

It is ironic that the very structure Bartsch finds so compelling, the unexpected "irrelevance," was identified as such in 1912 by Samuel Lee Wolff, one of the genre's harshest critics. Irrelevancy, he writes,

> rests on a common basis with paradox. Both defeat expectation;—the one turning the expectant mind away [. . .]; the other by the surprising nature of its own content. In both its phases,—irrelevancy and paradox—this element of *the unexpected,* prominent in the form as in the matter of the Greek romances deserves attention. To turn aside to the irrelevant; to strain suspense by retarding the expected outcome; to introduce by the way—all unlooked for—as

many bizarre, ironical, paradoxical situations and dazzling phrases as possible; and finally to "spring" an issue which is itself a surprising combination of opposites—all these would seem to be consistent results of adopting the unexpected as the principle of the *genre*. (210–211; Wolff's italics)

While Bartsch attempts to understand how the unexpected functions hermeneutically for the reader, Wolff lays the unexpected open to view so that he can denounce it as conveying "a base view of life" that opposes his idea of the classical (235–236):

> So far from seeking to unify the divers phenomena of life under law, the Greek Romance prefers to keep them apart, in all their chance diversity, showiness, and separate sensuous appeal. Law, permanence, consistency, [. . .]—all this is too sober, too dull. Let us have what is truly interesting; let us have what moves and jingles and glitters. Let us have the passing show. (235)

Wolff hurls his final salvo toward the Renaissance, which felt at liberty "to choose according to its own unquiet taste," and so unfortunately placed these works within the "canons of classicism" (235–236). These works, as he so correctly points out, were "'made to order' for the entertainment of the Renaissance. [. . .]. Hardly any other kind of fiction, hardly any other view of life, could appeal more strongly" (235). Had Boccaccio, Sidney, Shakespeare, and Cervantes shared Wolff's taste for law and permanence and his aversion to the passing show, they could not have invented modern European drama and prose fiction. The "unquiet taste" of the later twentieth century makes it easier for critics such as Bartsch and Morales to discover much more than haphazardness in descriptive novels that so loudly proclaim the strange, attractive unexpectedness of life.[10]

The hermeneutic description that Bartsch finds in ancient novels is one of the ways in which description can be made programmatically figurative, and the compositional technique did not die out with the classical novel. Sometimes a descriptive passage in modern prose fiction or narrative poetry seems so strange or irrelevant for one reason or another that it puts readers on a high state of alert and intensifies interpretive activity. For example, the object or event described may be out of place and bizarre. Consider the vivid and strangely dissonant opening episode of *Madame Bovary*, where the young Charles (and not the heroine Emma) wears an outlandish hat to school and is cruelly humiliated in front of his class. By the end of the novel, the reader may understand that this little vignette of Charles at school is a miniature story of his life, as well as the narrator's way of introducing a thematic concern with spectacle: the public spectacle and humiliation of the heroine's career, and the venality and stupidity of her spectators. In another narrative situation, a description may involve something easily recognizable but now placed in a strange context: Byron has his hero Manfred offer a poetic description of the Roman Coliseum on the eve of his death. The topic is familiar enough, but why does Manfred offer such a discourse just then, as his life is about to end? The reader's initial effort to understand such passages often leads in turn to retrospective reinterpretations of what has happened before as well as to new expectations—which many be satisfied or not—and thus to further interpretations and reinterpretations that reach far beyond the passage in question. Local reading of a problematic passage thus creates a powerful incentive for a global reading that will resolve the problem. In this way, a strange description becomes a symbolic nexus for interpreting the narrative, and even for identifying its fundamental unity. Descriptive passages that seem to impede the local narrative but in fact create global coherence have figured prominently in the history of European poetry from antiquity to the present. One of them, Virgil's description of the harbor at Carthage in *Aeneid* 1 and its progeny, is the topic of the next chapter.

CHAPTER 3

A Sylvan Scene

> and, as the ranks ascend
> Shade above shade, a woody theatre
> Of stateliest view.
> —Milton, *Paradise Lost*

One way to gauge the vitality of the descriptive tradition that grew out of classical ecphrasis, and to suggest its impact on the poets of Romantic Britain, is to follow the trail of one historically significant example. For this purpose I have chosen the sublime mountain landscape that forms the Carthaginian harbor at *Aeneid* 157–72, where Aeneas and his crew find safe refuge after a ruinous storm. Virgil modeled his place description on Homer's lengthy discourse on the Ithacan harbor sacred to Phorcys at *Odyssey* 13 (Gordon Williams 637–46), one of the major Homeric descriptions that Lessing's *Laocoön* fails to mention. Because most elements of the passage are impossible to salvage as narrative, Lessing's theory would have to reject the description as "static," though it is anything but emotionally static in its context. It occurs at one of the great climactic moments of the poem, when Odysseus finally arrives home at Ithaca. But the hero, having slept through the voyage, is unaware that he has arrived and been left "on the sand, still overpowered by sleep" (13.119; Murray trans.) and that many travails still await him before he can reclaim his wife and his throne:

> There is in the land of Ithaca a certain harbour of Phorcys, the old man of the sea, and at its mouth two projecting headlands sheer to seaward, but sloping down on the side toward the harbour. These keep back the great waves raised by heavy winds without but within the benched ships lie unmoored when they have reached the point of anchorage. At the head of the harbour is a long-leafed olive tree, and near it a pleasant, shadowy cave sacred to the nymphs that are called Naiads. Therein are mixing bowls and jars of stone, and there too the

bees store honey. And in the cave are long looms of stone, at which the nymphs weave webs of purple dye, a wonder to behold; and therein are also ever-flowing springs. Two doors there are to the cave, one toward the North Wind, by which men go down, but that toward the South Wind is sacred, nor do men enter thereby; it is the way of the immortals. (13.96–112; Murray trans.)

These lines are no decorative irrelevance; they set a complex emotional tone combining warm welcome (the embracing headlands, the olive tree, the springs, and the honeybees) with ominous minor strains of danger (the heavy winds and, above all, the entrance used by the immortals) essential to the thematic development of the final books of the *Odyssey.* The landfall takes place at dawn on a spot near a gateway to the underworld, thus figuring the hero's homecoming as a rebirth.[1]

Virgil's Ecphrastic Triptych

Virgil demonstrably understood the figurative patterning at work in the Phorcys description and found his own way to deepen it even further into a false but attractive homecoming for Aeneas. Virgil's more problematic harbor energized a complex tradition that reaches not only back to Homer but also forward through Milton and Dryden to Wordsworth and indeed even to the present day. It is a formal set piece, a progymnasmatic ecphrasis carefully set in the poem right between two other figurative ecphrases of a great storm that Aeneas and his crew endure and a great Carthaginian temple that Aeneas visits. These three descriptions, the *Aeneid*'s first set of extended ecphrases, form an interdependent triptych that introduces and explores the idea, image, and place of Juno in the hero's physical and psychological progress.

The three ecphrases can be read with pleasure as detachable fragments in Hamon's sense, with one caveat: detach*able,* yes; but detach*ed,* no. The sequence of storm, harbor, and temple forms a counterpoint to Virgil's narrative, weaving relationships of comparison, contrast, and irony among themselves and to the main action. Occurring as it does at the beginning of the poem just on the heels of the epic argument, the ensemble illustrates Virgil's figurative embedding of description in particularly straightforward ways. No matter how much retrospective form we may discover later on, at this early point in the narrative the poet has to work particularly hard within the slim context of his opening if the descriptions are to fit seamlessly into the exposition, while at the same time arousing the kinds of questions and expectations that can later on be understood as commentary on complex future events. The poet has to count on his audience believing certain things about the nature of the world and about the history and politics of Rome, just as Horace relied on such beliefs when he composed his "ship of state" poem.

But the effect of these opening ecphrases is muddied when modern critics claim, as for example Michael C. J. Putnam does, that the ecphrasis of the temple murals is the "initial use of ekphrasis in the *Aeneid* [. . .] and serves to educate the reader in many of the imaginative patterns the poet will follow in subsequent descriptions" (23). Further confusing the issue, he also identifies the harbor as the poem's first ecphrasis (1). But he does observe in the course of a discussion of Dido's murals how

> we sense from the moment of the Trojans's landing on the Carthaginian shore, where threatening woods and black rocks [*sic*] form a backdrop (*scaena,* 164) against which evolving action will be performed, that tragedy, stemming from a chain of events riddled with instances of deception, will be a major concomitant of that action. (24–25)

D. Clay also notices the proleptic force of the harbor and makes the point more vigorously when he remarks (in an essay about the temple) that Aeneas's "first sight of this new land was theatrical" and that this *scaena* foreshadows the "Virgilian tragedy of Dido" (196). The proleptic force of the harbor is still more complex than these distinguished scholars suggest.

Putnam's wavering about the "first" major ecphrasis of the *Aeneid* is, I think, more than a careless or unimportant error. The error is symptomatic of how thoroughly ecphrasis, the ancient topos of vividness, has been redefined as a topos of stillness or stasis that modern critics associate primarily, or most compellingly, with visual artifacts they suppose to be more static than poetry and more instantaneously comprehended. Citing Murray Krieger with approval, Putnam writes that

> the ideal, but unrealizable goal of ekphrasis is to stop time, to place narrative momentum in a subservient position to the object under scrutiny, which we are meant to grasp in a flash of comprehension, just as we would react when first seeing a painting or a piece of sculpture in a museum. (2)

In addition to the wholly illusory assumption that sculpture and painting are "comprehended" at first sight, the view of ecphrasis that Putnam shares with Krieger and nearly every other critic since the middle of the twentieth century has another feature that requires careful qualification: the assumption that ecphrasis stops time. It is more accurate to say that ecphrasis stops the narrative in which it is embedded to embark on a contrasting discourse (which may be another, even *more* quickly paced narrative). Vividness is relative; ecphrasis is a figure that "speaks out" of its ground by contrasting with it in many possible ways. If we agree with the ancient rhetoricians—as we must, at least in reading Virgil's ecphrases—that battles and storms are typical subjects for ecphrasis, we have to concede that such vivid narratives as the storm of book 1 or the concise, impressionistic rendering of the fall of Troy in book 2 are ecphrases that are much more, not less, fast-paced than the surrounding material. Aeneas's ecphrastic banquet speech about the fall of Troy (temporally an early chapter in the *main* story) contrasts with particularly poignant vividness against the background of the slow and civilized gathering from which it emerges. Distinctions between "description" and "narrative" in the spirit of Lessing are inadequate to Virgil's interlaced story telling.

In this connection, it is instructive to review Putnam's main thesis. I align myself with him when he writes: "All of Virgil's notional ekphrases," descriptions of imaginary works of art, "are in consequential ways metaphors for the larger text which they embellish [. . .]; individually and as a group, they have much to teach the reader as a whole" (2). But I prefer to call descriptions that work like this "allegories" rather than "metaphors," since they do not have a stated tenor. Such descriptive allegories have an important figurative relation to the "larger text" that a careful reader like Putnam cannot ignore. In the *Aeneid*, it is not only the descriptions of imaginary works of art that have the properties Putnam attributes to works of art. Putnam implicitly acknowledges this fact in his brilliant chapter on Sylvia's deer; here his critical practice outstrips his own art description theory. It is ironic that animal ecphrasis, which has the explicit authority of Aphthonius as an ecphrastic category on a par with persons, places, and things—a prominence that none of the progymnasmatic authors give to works of art—is the atypical chapter. Nevertheless Putnam's acknowledgment of nonartifactual subject matter proves the rule about biased attention to artifacts, even among distinguished classicists.

Although storms and harbors are also well-attested ecphrastic subjects in the ancient progymnasmata, and although the particular storm of *Aeneid* 1 is cited as such in Lorich's redaction of Aphthonius (318), the storm and the harbor have not been considered integral with the ecphrastic program in *Aeneid* 1 that leads to the celebrated temple of Juno. When we so foreground the temple as ecphrasis (and give it this fancy Greek name), while denying a similar emphasis to the major ecphrases that precede it—the storm and the harbor—we obliterate part of the epic's structure and indeed fail to see how well Virgil prepares his audience for the temple, the later major ecphrases, and the concerns of the epic as a whole.

Indeed Putnam's thesis about the murals in the temple to Juno—that it educates the reader in the poem's imaginative patterns—is actually strengthened when we apply it not to the murals alone but to the opening triptych of storm, harbor, and temple. The temple is the third part of a coherent ecphrastic sequence that educates the reader in imaginative patterns of the sort that Putnam identifies. I would like to focus on the harbor and place it more securely into the figurative program it shares with the two ecphrases that frame it in book 1. In the subsequent sections of the chapter, I leave the immediate context of the *Aeneid* to discuss the remarkable afterlife of the harbor in much later English literature, primarily Milton's role in deepening the split perception of the harbor into a flexible model of how landscape description could figure moral artistry and creative perception.

Immediately after Neptune quells the storm, Aeneas and his crew find themselves, logically enough in terms of Neptune's intervention, in a safe haven:

> The wearied followers of Aeneas strive to run for the nearest shore and turn towards the coast of Libya. There in a deep inlet [*in secessu longo*] lies a spot, where an island forms a harbour with the barrier of its sides, on which every wave from the main coming [*ab alto*] is broken, then parts into receding ripples. On either side loom heavenward huge cliffs [*vastae rupes*] and twin peaks [*geminique minantur / in caelum scopuli*], beneath whose crest far and wide is the stillness of sheltered water [*aequora tuta silent*]; above, too, is a backdrop of shimmering woods [*silvis scaena coruscis*] with an overhanging grove [*nemus*], black [*atrum*] with gloomy [*horrenti*] shade. Under the brow of the fronting cliff is a cave of hanging rocks; within are fresh waters and seats in the living stone [*vivoque sedilia saxo*], a haunt of Nymphs. Here no fetters [*vincula*] imprison weary ships, no anchor holds them fast with hooked bite. Here, with seven ships mustered from all his fleet, Aeneas takes shelter; and disembarking with earnest longing for the land [*magno telluris amore*], the Trojans gain the welcome beach and stretch their brine-drenched limbs upon the shore. (1.157–73)

The first landfall is not only a dramatic turn in the narrative; it articulates, as Richard Jenkyns observes, one of the poem's thematic problems: "The desire to be firmly rooted on some particular portion of the earth" (60). Rome as a "city, a work of man" is one aspect of that "desire for a firm basis," but there is also in the *Aeneid* "a feeling for the ground, the very soil" (60). Aeneas and his men have been "all at sea," physically and emotionally; now they are on solid ground. Jenkyns notes that the very triteness of the English phrase *all at sea* "may suggest the deep, archetypal emotion to which Virgil appeals" (61).

Whether or not we respond emotionally to the scene in this way, we recognize the landscape as a generic opening description that introduces us to a new place and a new episode. As such, the device is as old as Homer. Shadi Bartsch shows, in *Decoding the Ancient Novel,* how Hellenistic novelists built on this ancient device and elaborated opening descriptions that are sufficiently strange or mysterious to function symbolically and hermeneutically in the narrative, far beyond their immediate context. We will find much the same reach in Virgil's harbor. As in the Greek novel (and in much later dramatic narrative as well), this opening description both sets the stage and presents puzzling or curious elements that play upon the reader's understanding of the whole plot and the reader's expectations about what is immediately to follow. After the storm, we certainly expect Aeneas's weary crew to be, as Jenkyns observes,

> full of gladness, and sure enough they possess the beach "magno telluris amore" (1.171). That is one of those simple Virgilian phrases that seem pregnant with a deeper significance. Its immediate sense is that the Trojans are overjoyed to be on dry land again, but beyond this we hear much more that larger theme: a man's "great love of the earth" is a fundamental part of his humanity, and goes beyond simple relief at escaping a watery grave. (62)

But why should such a simple phrase be pregnant with meaning here, and less so in an ordinary sea story?

The response of a sensitive reader depends on an often barely conscious apprehension of the poem's "motival" development, if motival is understood in a musical rather than literary sense. A literary motif is a "type of incident, device, reference, or formula" (Abrams, *Glossary* 121), but a musical motif or motive is more protean and dynamic. It can be a phrase as short as two pitches, or it can be long enough to contain several smaller motifs, as long as it is "sufficiently well-defined to retain its identity when elaborated or transformed and combined with other material." A musical motif "thus lends itself to serving as the basic element from which a complex texture or even a whole composition is created." Beethoven's Fifth, with its famous four-note opening motif, or his *Pastoral*, beginning with three motifs that together constitute a larger motif (or "theme"), are "paradigms of the technique" (Randel 513).

Nicholas Horsfall indirectly acknowledges such musically motival development in Virgil when he identifies ten thematic "strands" in the opening lines of the *Aeneid* (102–03), none of which appear to have sufficient structure to be called literary motifs, but whose motival potential (understood musically) drives the poem's retrospective form in much the same way that Beethoven's motifs drive the listener's sense of retrospective form. In a thesis that sounds remarkably like what Putnam will say several decades later about Virgil's ecphrases of works of art, Pöschl observes that the storm anticipates "the whole poem in thought as well as mood. It is the prelude of the work, announcing the basic motifs after the manner of an overture" (165). The description of the storm rhetorically expands and dramatizes the poem's central antagonist, wrathful Rome-opposing Juno, Aeneas's and Rome's enemy. This is the point that Pöschl develops so well in his classic essay on the first

296 lines of the *Aeneid* (164–82). It is remarkable that Pöschl mentions the harbor only in passing (as reminiscent of Phorcys) although the harbor falls within the first 296 lines and develops the same strands that Horsfall finds in the storm. The storm's introductory position, writes Pöschl,

> indicates that it is more than just another episode in the destiny of the homeless Trojans. The pulsating breath of tragedy and the atmosphere of wild pathos embody with the greatest compression the nature of the emotion which permeates the whole poem. It is, as it were, the "musical" motif that from the start marks the events with passionate grandeur and the demonic power of fate. (164)

Pöschl's musical analogy is no mere purple patch; it is apt and to the point. Many literary works use this organizing principle, usually without recourse to theorizing. Some writers, however, have been explicitly aware of the musical analogy. (Thomas Mann, for example, referred to his fiction-writing as "music-making" and enjoyed comparing his motival development with Wagner's.) The musically motival structure that Pöschl finds in the storm description of *Aeneid* 1 is actually felt throughout the epic at many scales, just like a musical motif that undergoes varying development. Virgil, like Beethoven, Flaubert, or Mann, is a motival composer. Like them, he relies on his work being reexperienced before the whole integrated configuration can be understood. The rhetorical descriptions, beginning with the fateful storm, are highly compressed, mid-range elements in the larger allegorical figure that is the whole work.

Pöschl's thesis about the storm (which he does not explictly call ecphrasis) is in the same spirit as those of Putnam, and R. D. Williams before him, concerning the murals that everyone calls ecphrasis.[2] This is no accident. All of these scholars have noticed some dimension of how, the closer we examine Virgil's descriptions, the more we find the developing figuration I have called "motival," and the more allegorical the descriptions therefore become as the retrospective form gradually emerges. W. R. Johnson describes the same phenomenon when he writes of what he calls Virgil's "polysemantic fictions" or "interdependent allegories":

> in the shifting patterns of polysematic [*sic*] fictions the separate themes illumine one another in new and different ways as now one and now another theme achieves a special prominence and as the various themes keep entering into new configurations with one another. (20)

When we examine all of Virgil's progymnasmatic descriptions—including descriptions of battles and storms, animals and people—as figurations on a par with descriptions of artifacts, we can even better discern the shifting patterns of Virgil's polysemantic fictions. Virgil the schoolboy, we can be sure, wrote independent exercises in description; in school he learned to write a good storm, a good harbor, a good temple. Virgil the mature poet weaves them together as interdependent parts of a larger work that is deeply committed to exposing the psychological and political operations of *furor.*

"Can such anger affect heavenly minds?" asks the poet with reference to Juno's fury (1.11; my trans.). Rage overwhelms warriors; it consumes Dido-in-love; it consumes Aeneas, "burning with anger and frightening in his obsession" (12.946–47; my trans.) at the problematic and much-discussed end of the epic, after the external threat from Juno has dissipated (Putnam 212–213). This large-scale pattern of escaping Juno as an external threat only to find Juno threatening from within, as uncontrollable emotional pressure, appears in miniature as the entire triptych's underlying irony. Aeneas's crew moves unwittingly from one mask of Juno, the storm, to two others, the harbor and the temple. At each stage, the dramatic irony increases as the reader's comprehension of Aeneas's ominous shipwreck increasingly outstrips his own until, in the temple, Aeneas responds with deep emotion but misconstrues the full significance of several scenes depicting the Trojan War, scenes that foreshadow the tragic future as much as they commemorate the past. In this way, Virgil sets the stage for the tragedy of Dido and for the uncontrollable sequelae that the Roman "insider" knows will occur outside the frame of the epic —the Carthaginian wars and the tragic destruction of Dido's nascent and promising civilization. Virgil's complex theory of Carthage's destruction, especially Aeneas's and Dido's unknowing complicity in its doom, serves as a cautionary adumbration of the potentially self-destructive challenge that unconsciousness and uncontrollable anger will set for the still-to-be established Roman empire.

The need to begin the great project of building Rome already resonates in the harbor description in the brief phrase "magno telluris amore" (1.171), "with great love of the earth." The whole description functions as a medium-scale motif condensing how the idea of founding Rome will be analyzed in the quite particular context of the excursion into and finally out of Carthage. The three-word motif enfolds the largest theme, desire for Rome, and it interlaces other structures large and small. Its nouns "love" and "earth" immediately become problematic, for at the most literal narrative level Carthage is a problematic site of both love and city-founding. There in Carthage each concept splits, into right earth/wrong earth, right love/wrong love. Such an analysis of basic thematic terms (i.e., differentiation and splitting apart) is presented emotively and imagistically through the mixed tones of the diction describing the harbor. The landscape supports all sides, so to speak, of the argument about love and earth and what they have to do with each other. I want to illustrate how the landscape works motivally, how a few small textual motifs mesh in a landscape description (a medium motif) that articulates themes that operate at a larger scale in the Carthage episode as well as at the largest scale of the epic as a whole.

The Shimmering Sylvan Scene: *Silvis Scaena Coruscis*

Virgil depicts a winding shore with sensuously welcoming set-back bays, "sinus [. . .] reductos" (1.161). The word *sinus* not only refers literally to gulfs and bays but, in this context, evokes *sinus* as the cleft in the chest to which children and others are drawn as a gesture of affection or protection, or held dear in the psychologically innermost sense: *in sinu* corresponds to English "in my heart," the deepest seat of affection. Virgil's coastal scene is anthropomorphic and female-gendered: Virgil again evokes a protective bosom when he writes that the island makes a port "obiectu laterum" (1.160), literally by throwing out its flanks or chest. The men reciprocate the gesture, embracing the beach with open arms, just as Aeneas will soon embrace the gracious queen who falls in love with him and so keeps him happily there. Dido, like the harbor, will need no chain and anchor to tie down Aeneas and his fleet. On the contrary, it will take extraordinary efforts by the gods to pry Aeneas away. The safe seas are "being quiet": "aequora tuta silent" (1.164). The sea's behavior is, as Jenkyns puts it, "like the watchful silence of a living thing" (64). The crags are "vastae" (1.162) vast and awe-inspiring; but the interior, domesticated by helpful Nymphs, flows with sweet waters.

Yet Virgil's cliffs are distinctly troubling: "minantur"; they "loom" or "threaten" (1.162). Jenkyns notes that the same root is picked up by "imminet" three lines later at 1.165, communicating a kind of awesome suspense (63–64). Although Jenkyns even observes that we can compare the cliffs to Dido's looming city walls: "minaeque murorum ingentes" (4.88–89), his too-local reading is not explicit about what this iterative looming implies about the larger epic structure: the imminent, destabilizing threat from Dido's love and the long shadow her failed love will cast over relations between Rome and Carthage.

Moreover, the second line of the description tells the contemporary Augustan reader something disturbing and unknown to Aeneas's lost crew, that they are approaching Libya, the site of Carthage, a protectorate of Juno's (Tanit's) and home to Rome's historic foe:

> The Romans' fear of Juno is reflected in the many reported propitiatory offerings to her, which succeeded (according to Ennius) only during the Second Punic War in winning the goddess over to the Roman side. (Perkell 34)

To a Roman, or to a modern insider familiar with Roman political history, Juno/Tanit's Libya (modern Tunisia) would be about as secure a place to wash ashore as, say, late-twentieth-century Libya might have been for an American crew. The dissonance between what the reader knows as a spectator and what Aeneas knows is also thematic, both in this description and in the epic as a whole. Aeneas is often lost and uncomprehending, as he was in the opening storm; he misreads signs and portents, as soon he will misread the murals in Dido's temple to Juno; he ends up in the wrong places, makes false starts; has an affair that is disastrous to his lover and to his own future city; and, most notoriously for critics who want to see the *Aeneid* as imperial propaganda, when Aeneas returns from an underworld vision of Rome's future, he emerges unawares through the ivory gate, the gate of false dreams, and remains unconscious of the potentially troubling implications for the dream of Rome's future. But already in Carthage, the narrator offers a number of clues to the reader that do not make any impression at all on Aeneas, for whom the place is an unproblematic refuge and not anything like a harbor or shelter for false dreams.

Constructing a dissonance between what the audience knows and what a character knows is an ancient principle of construction so closely associated with drama that we now call it dramatic irony. Although, as Frances Muecke explains, the term was first defined by Bishop Thirlwell in 1833 with illustrative examples from Sophocles (134), drama has for centuries been associated with the powerful effect of double perception that ensues when the audience has access to information that a character or set of characters does not have. Before Oedipus even sets out to find the culprit, *we* already know who it is. It is precisely this dramatic irony of unshared perception, learned from the Greek tragedians, that Virgil adapts to his epic when he embeds crucial privileged information in a rhetorical description, beyond earshot, so to speak, of his characters.[3]

The sharp dramatic irony of landfall in Libya, complicated by the mixed safe-and-menacing tone of the descriptive diction, is further augmented by a striking figure at 1.164–65 that has been noticed (if not fully discussed) by many readers. Here the technical rhetoric of the actual theater describes the mountain landscape: "Above, too, is a backdrop [*scaena*] of shimmering woods, with an overhanging grove, black with gloomy shade" (1.164–65; Fairclough trans.).[4] Consider two more translations:

(1) Fitzgerald: "Over these, / Against a forest backdrop shimmering, / A dark and shaggy grove casts a deep shade."
(2) Mandelbaum: "The backdrop—glistening / forests and, beetling from above, a black / grove, thick with bristling shadows."

The translations foreground a problem: What is the relationship between the shimmering or glistening forest and the black grove, so different is "black" from "shimmering"? Fitzgerald sees the black grove against the backdrop; the other translators see the black grove above the forest backdrop. To begin to understand the figure, we need to know that for Virgil the word "scaena," translated by all as "backdrop" and from which we get the many meanings of English *scene,* is a technical theatrical term from the Greek (*skene,* "tent" or "hut"). In this passage, "scaena" literally means a decorated piece of stage architecture, "scenery." Virgil takes a technical Greek term referring to the stage building in a theater and applies it, evidently for the first time, to an actual landscape.

"A sylvan scene" (a loose translation of *silvis scaena coruscis* much favored, as I will discuss below, by English poets) is now such a hackneyed phrase that, as with so much else that is original in Virgil, it takes some effort of the imagination to hear the freshness of Virgil's metaphor. How Virgil came to this figure can only be fully appreciated by examining the way in which theaters were constructed in Virgil's day. The most comprehensive study on this subject is that of Margarete Bieber, who provides descriptions of the theaters of the Augustan period, including in particular Pompey's theater, one with which Virgil and his audience would have been well acquainted. From Bieber we learn that the "stage house, orchestra, and auditorium were intimately connected with each other with the help of side buildings (*versurae*) which took the place of the paraskenia of the Greek theater" (181). These "versurae" projected forward from the "scaena" toward the audience on each side. On the basis of this and a wide variety of other evidence gathered by Bieber, we can say with some confidence that the stage building at the front of a Roman theater in the time of Augustus was constructed in a broad U shape. The *scaenae frons* (the wall of the stage-building that faced the audience) formed the bottom of the U, and the two identical "versurae" made up the legs. The spectator in a Roman theater such as that built by Pompey would thus have looked into a space that had two tall projecting structures on each side, the "versurae," and an equally tall "scaena" at the rear. The stage platform itself (the *pulpitum*) filled the space in the center of this U.[5] The harbor at Carthage as Virgil describes it has exactly this form, with the "twin crags" forming the legs of the U-shaped bay. It must have occurred to Virgil that these *scopuli* were rather like gigantic versions of the "versurae" of the theaters he and his audience knew, and thus it would make poetic sense to call the plane at the back of this embracing space a "scaena."

It would have been normal for the scaenae frons to be adorned with paintings appropriate to the performance, and in the right circumstances these decorated backdrops might very well have "shimmered" in the light.

The backdrops were made of wood, which was both visually and acoustically functional. Vetruvius Pollio, in about 15 b.c., described the architecture and acoustics of the Roman theater. He was well aware, as Bieber explains, that the acoustics were "improved by the fact that wood continued to be used for the floor of the stage, also for doors, barriers, and painted panels set into the stone 'scaenae frons'" (187).

And in particular, evidence suggests that "the theater of Pompey originally had a straight scaenae frons [. . .] with rectangular sinkings, probably for the insertion of paintings" (182). It seems almost certain that some plays would have called for paintings that represented forests. In any case, Virgil's intention here is apparent: the harbor of Carthage, with its embracing promontories, encloses a theatrical space at the rear of which is a backdrop of woodlands analogous to the painted stage decorations familiar to Augustan audiences.

The metaphorical theater, the home of the nymphs, is also furnished with seating, "sedilia." *Sedilia* literally denotes something physical to sit on—"seating"—and theater seating in particular: "Under the brow of the cliff face is a cave with hanging crags; within are sweet waters and seating of living rock [*vivoque sedilia saxo*], the home of the Nymphs" (my trans.). Like the sea that is not merely quiet but "being quiet," the nymphs are potential spectators. Indeed, in *Aeneid* 4 they will provide the howling chorus for the ill-fated tryst of Dido and Aeneas when the poem's next great storm drives them into a cave for shelter: "And the Nymphs howled on the mountain-top" (4.168; my trans.). Virgil's verb *ululaurunt* denotes the vocalization of wolves or ghosts; here the Nymphs reveal the demonic aspect of the uncanny landscape surrounding their theatrical home in the cave. The domestic seating is strangely animated. Gordon Williams points out that the expression *vivo saxo,* "living rock,"[6] which sounds (along with the bold "scaena" metaphor) like modern English usage, seems to have been invented by Virgil and is also used at *Aeneid* 3.688 (642).[7] As Jenkyns further explains, the phrase

> appealed to Ovid, and we find it also in Tacitus. In some of these later instances it appears to mean little or no more than [. . .] unquarried rock, still fixed in its original position. But in at least one place Ovid suggests that rock is "alive" in a stronger sense, likening it to organic nature: "saxo quod adhuc vivum radice tenetur" (rock which is still held living by the root).[8] [. . .]. Virgil has made the rock within the cave instinct in some mysterious way with life. (63)

The life of the stone is in uncanny counterpoint to the artifice of the theater.

Stage scenery suggests illusion—of love? of founding a city?—as well as the tragedy of Dido, which is about to unfold. Moreover, other figurative extensions of "scaena" that are attested in writers earlier than Virgil also inform and strengthen the metaphor. "Scaena" can also mean the stage, the stage performance itself, or any "sphere in which actions, etc. are on public display" (*OLD*). Carthage will indeed be a tragic "scaena" on, in, and in front of which Dido is presented as a noble fugitive queen who is already accomplishing everything for the remnant of her people that shipwrecked Aeneas desires for his own, and who tragically devolves into a public spectacle of humiliation and madness. The enormity of the "scene" is Virgil's way of dramatizing the calamitous enmity of Carthage and Rome as, at bottom, irrational *furor,* and of bringing the spectator-reader into some empathic relationship to Rome's utterly devastated foe : "And the black woodland [*nemus atrum*] looms with shuddering shade [*horrenti* [. . .] *umbra*]."

A sense of awe and dread is expressed by the black and shuddering woodland: *horrenti* means "bristling" and in this sense suggests conifer leaves. It also means "shuddering" with religious awe or dread. *Nemus* is a wood, often a sacred wood, and it is moreover *atrum,* a heavily freighted word for "black." Before offering some 11 meanings, the *OLD* admonishes: "N.B. The word is used emotively, especially by poets; and meanings such as 'dark,' 'funereal,' 'ill-omened,' ' terrible' merge into one another in many instances." This is one such instance. The primordially ill-omened wood is a fearsome darkness, a terrifying numen.[9] Virgil's woody theater is as dark as the harbor is safe. The dissonance between black wood and sweet waters figure the ambivalence of the sweet but fatal attraction that will unfold in the Carthaginian tragedy. The shimmering forest is a painted theatrical backdrop, but the dark woods are actual.

The evidence of the ill-omened wood would alone be enough to require revising Jenkyns's surprising conclusions that "there is very little in the passage to suggest disagreeable emotion" and that "if the scene is in some degree symbolic of future events, the symbolism is of a rather muddy kind" (64–65). Jenkyns can arrive at this lopsided solution only by simplifying the complex emotion denoted by *horror* in the metaphor "horrenti umbra," "shuddering shade," by not pursuing the fully tragic implications of the patently theatrical "scaena," and by ignoring the black woods—his own translation elides "atrum" entirely; Jenkyns's "nemus" is a mere " woodland" with no modifying adjective at all (60). The full significance of Virgil's ambivalent diction, intensified by the physical split between the shimmering painted forest and the actual black grove, can only be comprehended when it becomes clear in book 4 that Dido is, as Muecke has shown, a generically tragic heroine who would be recognized as such by Aristotle. The problematic theatrical landscape is vividly there, but only as part of the larger epic pattern.

Indeed the theatrical motif soon recurs, en route from the harbor to the temple. Just before Aeneas arrives at Juno's temple during his incognito tour of Carthage, he stops to admire the actual civic theater under construction: "Here others placed the deep foundations of a theater, and quarried huge columns to adorn the future stage" (1.427–29; my trans.). The massive pillars out of which are formed the theater's columns precisely echo the twin peaks that form the metaphoric wings in the harbor theater. Aeneas's stop at the theater that is so reminiscent of the harbor, yet one step better developed into architecture, immediately precedes the celebrated ecphrasis of the temple to Juno, which is still more completely finished and in fact decorated with murals.

I cannot of course do justice here to Putnam's brilliant reading of Dido's murals, where he shows how carefully Aeneas's interpretive response to the battle scenes depicted on them is linked to both Dido's and Aeneas's fates (23–54). I want rather to step back from the details of the feature Putnam rightly identifies as the overarching imaginative pattern of this ecphrasis so as to reveal just how much the storm and the harbor participate in the same pattern: split perception between the reader and the viewer(s) inside the text. When Aeneas tours the temple and examines the murals, he is, writes Putnam, "both viewer and object of view" (53). Putnam asks:

> Why does Virgil place Aeneas in this privileged role as contemplative and critic, especially at the challenging moment when the poet is experimenting for the first time with ekphrasis and with the tension in narrative techniques its embedding in epic requires? Why at this particular instant is he both a passive figure, pondering his own active past frozen in art, and yet dynamic, beholding his own passivity but responding as well? (54)

We might ask the same question, and with more justification, during the storm when Aeneas is given his first speech of the epic in the midst of what is actually the first ecphrasis. At this rhetorically challenging moment (for the poet and for Aeneas) the hero first presents himself in his own words as a vulnerable and passive figure, pondering his past (just as he will later on at the temple) and wishing he had died in Troy. The speech presents the first of many disjunctions between Aeneas's psychic interior and the resolute, dynamic persona he presents in his actions and in his speeches to his men. It is the first intimation of how difficult it is for him to understand and assimilate his fate, as well as the first intimation of how effortlessly the Juno-engendered violence he must counter in the outer world is interiorized as destructive emotion, suicidal despair in this case. The brutally energetic ecphrasis slows down, is punctuated by a moment of brutal self-reflection, and resumes again with even more violence.

The *Aeneid*'s motival development, so evident in the ecphrastic triptych of book 1, operates at textual scales from the word or phrase to the descriptions and speeches and further out to the episode and book and so forth, and can only be synoptically comprehended upon rereading. We cannot fully hear the small motifs as a motival condensation of theme until we have heard the whole poem through, any more than we can fully hear the first four notes of Beethoven's Fifth until the whole symphony has taught us to hear this simple motif reflected and developed in the larger musical elements that ultimately constitute the whole. Repeated exposure to the whole is what makes the four notes become pregnant with meaning. Because Virgil's "interdependent allegories" (as W. R. Johnson calls them) are so motival, we can get a fair idea of the technique by examining the global reach of a few of the small but interrelated motifs in just one description. Each description is in turn a tenorless vehicle connected motivally to the others and to the work as a whole. Interdependent meanings form retrospectively, but only inasmuch as readers have access to the cultural models and historical realities that orient Virgil's descriptive practice.

The Idea of Natural Scenery

We have seen that Virgil's theatrical metaphor is the first attested Latin application of the term to what we—registering our linguistic debt to Virgil—now call natural scenery. Virgil's "scenic" harbor exists in a world already nostalgic for the more primitive and numinous homeopathy of his Homeric model, where Odysseus awakens under an olive tree to the protective custody of wise Athena. Aeneas's "great love of earth," however, is never so reciprocated. His protectress Venus entangles him in a disaster for himself and his people, and he never does get all the way home. Virgil's "scaena" metaphor founds an entire discourse of "scenic" and picturesque landscape description in which civilized human subjects find themselves nostalgic spectators of an objectified world that they cannot fully inhabit.

Two strongly contrasting late-seventeenth-century British responses to Virgil's "sylvan scene," in Dryden's *Aeneis* and in Milton's *Paradise Lost,* show what was at stake in the representation of landscape in the century to follow and in Wordsworth's transformation of place description into the poem of the mind. They will also help us to explore a set of questions taken up with particular urgency by Wordsworth. What is the point of accurately depicting a "scene" from the natural world? What makes reproducing the appearances of things relevant—aesthetically, intellectually, or in any other way—to human concerns? But before we can appreciate what later poets have done with Virgil's "scaena," we need to defamiliarize the familiar English words *scene* and *scenery,* which come into English through French as theatrical terms, but were applied only recently in English to nature. Not until 1660 do we have a phrase like "a scene of . . . lovely trees." The *OED* cites *scenery* in Cowper's 1784 *Task* as the first usage meaning "the general appearance of a place and its natural features, regarded from the picturesque point of view." William Gilpin, however—a major creator of the picturesque point of view that Cowper embraces—edges out Cowper by at least two years, in *Observations of the River Wye* (1782), when he evaluates the pictorial composition of the living landscape as follows: "From Wallingford to Oxford, the road scarce affords one good view, except at Shillingford; where the bridge, the river, and its woody banks exhibit some scenery" (3).

Milton's "sylvan scene" at *Paradise Lost* 4.140–42 and Dryden's "Sylvan Scene" in his 1697 translation of the harbor at Carthage authorize many an eighteenth-century sylvan scene, such as Pope's 1704 "See what delights in sylvan scenes appear!" ("Summer" 59). The opening lines of "Summer" remember the harbor in another way: "Verdant alders form'd a quiv'ring Shade" (4). Although Pope's diction clearly alludes to Virgil's harbor, already in Pope the epic and theatrical resonance is nearly gone; Pope writes pastoral. This is not the case for Dryden and Milton, who recognized and transformed Virgil's natural theater, each in his own way, into different kinds of epic theater.

Dryden wrote an English translation of the *Aeneid* that remains much admired, and as such it documents a stable British idea of Virgil. Moreover, Virgil is a canonical, almost sacralized, European author. When anyone bothers to translate such authors at all, it is out of a desire to reveal their greatness "as it really is" to a new audience. Such a desire places the translator under enormous (though not necessarily conscious) pressure to adapt his text to the highest possible contemporary canons of taste. The translation has to speak for itself in answer to the question: Why read Virgil? Or Homer? Or Sophocles? Dryden's translation of Virgil's landscape reliably documents a neoclassic strain in British aesthetics, greatly at odds with Milton's nearly contemporary poetics.

Dryden nicely renders the theatrical quality of the sylvan scene, but in contrast to Virgil, the theater is diminutive and almost scaled down to an indoor space:

> Betwixt two rows of Rocks a Sylvan Scene
> Appears above, and Groves for ever green:
> A Grott is form'd beneath, with Mossy Seats,
> To rest the *Nereids,* and exclude the Heats. (1.233–36)

Dryden understands that Virgil's "sedilia" are physical seats, but Dryden's Nereids are merely polite ladies seated in the protective shade waiting for the show to begin on a well-bounded stage "betwixt two rows of rocks." The crisp, rhythmic alliteration of *t*'s and *r*'s renders the texture of the rocks, contrasts them with the flowing "Sylvan Scene / Appears above," and sets the rocks off visually from the untroubled "Groves for ever green." Dryden's rocks no more loom or threaten than does a heavily carved rococo picture-frame. The theater is polished and civilized, as is the total effect of Dryden's elegant presentation of the whole landscape. Dryden achieves that effect at the expense of the awe-inspiring force that Virgil inextricably weaves into his Carthaginian harbor. Dryden attenuates the cliffs, collapsing Virgil's many words for rocks and rock-formation—*rupes, scopuli, saxo, antrum*—into "rocks," mentioned just once and only to frame the scene. He transforms Virgil's black and shuddering woods into a woodland "forever green," and mutates the shade into sun-protection for Nereids who have none of the numinous quality of Virgil's nymphs. Dryden, like Jenkyns three centuries later, does not want to shade too much darkness into Virgil's description of the harbor, as if granting the description its full rhetorical force would interfere too much with the undeniable picturesqueness of the harbor and the undeniably warm reception actually accorded to Aeneas and his crew by the doomed queen who rules there. Dryden's choices (and Jenkyns's) are good examples of that strain in British taste for the beautiful as smooth, with all the rough edges and dark tones polished away or carefully contained: Burke's idea of the beautiful in his *Philosophical Inquiry into the Origin of our Ideas of the Sublime and Beautiful.*

Dryden's transformation of Virgil is tone deaf to the sublime aspects of the place, but it would be mistaken to read Dryden's taste back into Virgil, as Wordsworth clearly recognized. Bruce E. Graver explains:

> Dryden's Virgil had long been one of the poet's bugbears: "In his translation from Vergil," wrote Wordsworth to Sir Walter Scott in 1805, "whenever Vergil can be fairly said to have had his eye upon his object, Dryden always spoils the passage." (Introduction 157)

When Wordsworth tried his hand at translating the harbor scene into heroic couplets, he restored the original vastness and picked up the menacing overtones that Dryden had "spoiled." In Wordsworth's version, the woods "gloomily impend," the rock are "vast," the twin cliffs are "heaven-threatening." "Wild crags and lowering rocks" form the cave of the nymphs ("Translation" 219–224). Wordsworth found in Milton a far more sensitive interpreter of Virgil than Dryden. The poet of *Paradise Lost* deepened the psychological foundation of this description in a way that was directly and massively influential on Romantic descriptive practice.

In 1674, some two decades before Dryden's *Aeneis,* Milton had taken the expression "sylvan scene" from Virgil's harbor and applied it to Eden (Gordon Williams 642); but the aesthetic contrast with Dryden's untroubled and diminutive theater could not be sharper. While Dryden attenuates the dramatic irony of the Trojans' "safe" arrival in Libya by homogenizing the tone of the descriptive diction, Milton intensifies the powerful effect of double perception and adapts Virgil's theater to a purpose as deeply figurative as in Virgil's original. While Virgil's theater is the setting for the tragedy of Dido, Milton's "sylvan scene" is at once the setting for the Fall of man and a seminal image for the purely mental theater of fallen and unfallen perception. Milton's dramatic irony sets the narrator's illumined Eden against Satan's fallen consciousness of the place.

Milton found in Virgil's harbor-theater a rhetorical model for the arrival at Eden of its most intrusive actor, the personage who inaugurates the drama of the Fall.[10] Satan, "disfigured, more than could befall / Spirit of happy sort" (4.127–28) takes the role of Virgil's weary crew, and the border of "delicious Paradise" echoes the sublime coast of Libya:

> So on he fares, and to the border comes
> Of Eden, where delicious Paradise,
> Now nearer, crowns with her enclosure green,
> As with a rural mound, the champaign head
> Of a steep wilderness whose hairy[11] sides
> With thicket overgrown, grotesque and wild.
> Access denied; and overhead up-grew
> Insuperable highth of loftiest shade,
> Cedar, and pine, and fir, and branching palm,
> A sylvan scene, and, as the ranks ascend
> Shade above shade, a woody theatre
> Of stateliest view. (4.131–42)

Access denied: but access to "delicious Paradise" is more experiential than physical. Satan does of course get in: " in contempt, / At one slight bound," Satan "high overleaped all bound / Of hill or highest wall, and sheer within / Lights on his feet" (4.180–83). Satan, having trespassed and alighted on the Tree of Life, "yet not true life / Thereby regained, but sat devising death / To them who lived" (4.196–98). Predatory Satan uses the Tree only "For prospect" (4.200). Milton exploits the technique learned from Virgil's harbor, where at landfall a tension is established between the crew's simple joy and the more nuanced narrative description. Milton even more severely differentiates Satan's "prospect" from an illumined vision of the place.[12] Satan's prospect from the tree is "To all delight of human sense exposed," but the exposure does not register: "the Fiend / Saw undelighted all delight" (4.285–286).

Satan's predatory prospect of innermost Eden from the Tree of Life contrasts with Adam's magisterial prospect of the world outside, from over the top of Satan's steep and perplexing wilderness:

> Yet higher than their tops
> The verdurous wall of Paradise up-sprung;
> Which to our general Sire gave prospect large
> Into his nether empire neighbouring round. (4.142–45)

But Satan's dominion (enormous though it will be) cannot be "heav'n on earth" (4.208). The phrase "Heaven on Earth" both echoes and mocks Satan's own bold psychological declaration: "The mind is its own place, and in itself / Can make a Heaven of Hell, a Hell of Heaven" (1.254–55), for *his* mind can only "make" hell, as he realizes on his journey to Eden:

> Me miserable! which way shall I fly
> Infinite wrauth and infinite despair?
> Which way I fly is Hell; myself am Hell. (4.73–75)

The same theme of fallen and illumined perception is recapitulated at Adam and Eve's expulsion from Eden, when Michael consoles them with the possibility of redeeming paradise by recreating it within:

> Only add
> Deeds to thy knowledge answerable; add faith;
> Add virtue, patience, temperance; add love,
> By name to come called Charity, the soul
> Of all the rest: then wilt thou not be loth
> To leave this Paradise, but shalt possess
> A Paradise within thee, happier far. (12.581–87)

Milton's description of Eden as relative to the perceiver presents the poem's concern with conscious human choice in a persuasively vivid way, as the freedom to "make" the world beautiful or otherwise by moral choice.[13] Moral artistry makes and loses paradise and can make it all over again. Such artistry is utterly beyond the competence of Satan. The narrator's illumined Eden is precisely what Satan's barren consciousness cannot "conceive" and bring into being; the garden is a state of mind and spirit. Rhetorically it is a classical locus amoenus, but a nonnaturalistic one. Its very artificiality reinforces the idea that it is consciously made, and it is instructive to examine just a few of the ways that Milton's vision respects, transforms, and renews such an ancient and well-rehearsed descriptive topos. Libanius's "six charms" are as systematically described as ever before in a classical ecphrasis such as Tiberianus's "amnis ibat." The onrushing imagery engages the aural, visual, olfactory, tactile, and kinesthetic imagination for over 200 energetic lines (4.131–355), and sometimes all at once in a single sentence:

> The birds their choir apply; airs, vernal airs,
> Breathing the smell of field and grove, attune
> The trembling leaves, while universal Pan,
> Knit with the Graces and the Hours in dance,
> Led on the eternal Spring. (4.264–68)

The sentence, for all its unrelenting sensuous detail and pagan color is not, in Marmontel's expression, "décrire pour décrire" ("describing for the sake of describing") ("Descriptif" 442); its exuberant energy figures unfallen life, and Satan's response to all this figures the barrenness of fallen consciousness. Consider, for example, the breeze wafting from the garden as Satan approaches it:

> so lovely seemed
> That lantskip. And of pure now purer air
> Meets his approach, and to the heart inspires
> Vernal delight and joy, able to drive
> All sadness but despair. (4.152–56)

Satan, "Infinite wrauth and infinite despair" (4.74), is impervious to the breeze because he bears into Eden his private hell, "A mind not to be changed by place or time" (1.253). "Native perfumes" and "balmy spoils" (4.158–59) cannot permeate the mental barrier.

Wherever Satan is, the local geography has a Satanic aspect that contrasts with its illumined aspect. Edenic space is relative, not absolute. To get to the garden proper, Satan has to climb through "steep wilderness" (4.135) and "thicket overgrown, grotesque and wild" (4.136). The stalking fiend

> further way found none; so thick entwined,
> As one continued brake, the undergrowth
> Of shrubs and tangling bushes had perplexed
> All path of Man or Beast that passed that way. (4.174–77)

Demaray points out that the "tangled wood through which Satan wanders, though apparently of a high spiritual order in nature, is comparable to the spiritually inferior but equally tangl'd Wood [181] in which Comus dwells" (77), but Demaray does not explore this apparent paradox. On the one hand, nature, including its thickets, must be unfallen; on the other, Satan clearly lives in a "steep wilderness," and this utterly traditional metaphor of spiritual distress gives the montane thicket its negative tone. But it is crucial to recognize that for Milton, a wilderness, like any other place, has its fallen and illumined aspect. Milton redeems the very term *wilderness* by making it a metaphor for an illumined vision of Eden:

> A wilderness of sweets; for Nature here
> Wantoned as in her prime, and played at will
> Her virgin fancies, pouring forth more sweet,
> Wild above rule or art, enormous bliss. (5.294–97)

Eden is the oxymoronic wild garden. The same wild, steep mountain that perplexes Satan and gives Adam an imperial prospect beneficently dominates the garden proper as the source of rivers and springs that water the plantation. According to the narrator's illumined poetic vision,

> Southward through Eden went a river large,
> Nor changed his course, but through the shaggy hill
> Passed underneath ingulfed; for God had thrown
> That mountain, as his garden-mould, high raised
> Upon the rapid current, which, through veins
> Of porous earth with kindly thirst updrawn,
> Rose a fresh fountain, and with many a rill
> Watered the garden. (4.223–30)

The word *steep* is picked up again to describe the mountain, this time in its illumined aspect. "Down the steep glade" (4.231) the waters flowed, dividing into steams and brooks that

> Ran nectar, visiting each plant, and fed
> Flowers worthy of Paradise, which not nice Art
> In beds and curious knots, but Nature boon
> Poured forth profuse on hill, and dale, and plain. (4.240–43)

The description of the flowers—how they are and are *not* arranged—proclaims an aesthetic ideal that aligns the distinction between illumined and fallen consciousness with a distinction between two kinds of artistry. It has often been observed that when Milton rejects the Continental aesthetic of "beds and curious knots" he is Romantic *avant la lettre* in opposing neoclassical rules. The "artless" beauty of Milton's Eden looks much further back, however, to *classical* Latin descriptions of the Golden Age. As C. S. Lewis notes, Eden's flowers, poured forth by nature and "not nice art," echoes Seneca's description of the Golden Age at *Epistles* 90.43: "meadows beautiful without the use of art" (139). The aesthetic ideal is harmonious, generous, and free. Eden in its wild splendor broke with Continental landscaping practice and "became almost a sacred text" for British gardeners, giving them authority for "serpentine lines, natural treatment of water, rural mounds, wooded theatres" (Hunt and Willis 79). At the same time, Milton's Eden and the British gardening it inspired have been felt as fully sharing the "poetic" or idealizing aspirations of seventeenth-century landscape painters (Hunt and Willis 79).

Indeed the poem's concern with art and aesthetics goes well beyond the low valuation of the "curious knots" of geometrical garden beds. It can be felt in certain technical borrowings used metaphorically. We have already seen how Milton emulates Virgil in borrowing *scene* from the theater and applying it to nature when such usage was still fresh in English. Milton borrows other terms from the arts and applies them to nature, two of which, *landscape* and *grotesque,* I would like to discuss in some detail. Like *scene,* they are now commonplace and easy to miss as the technical borrowings they were in Milton's day. Moreover, Milton's usages have implications for the transformation in British taste that (however we explain it) we broadly understand as the eighteenth-century picturesque and its Romantic sequelae.

The mount, says Milton's narrator, is "grotesque and wild" (4.136). *Grotesque* meant "romantic, picturesquely irregular." Milton's text marks a place where two words that come into English from French and Italian art rhetoric during the seventeenth century, *grotesque* and *picturesque,* coincide in meaning and are moreover barely distinguishable from *romantic* as applied to landscape. *Grotesque* has entirely negative aesthetic connotations in modern English, but the Italian etymology of the word *grotesque* documents a positive aesthetic valuation of the rough, the broken, and the irregular. Before Milton applied *grotesque* to landscape, the word had come into English in 1561 with the meaning "a kind of decorative painting or sculpture, consisting of representations of portions of human and animal forms, fantastically combined and interwoven with foliage and flowers." According to the etymological discussion in the *OED,* the adjective appears in both of Florio's dictionaries: "A kinde of rugged vnpolished painters worke, anticke worke" (Florio 1598); "anticke or landskip worke of Painters" (Florio 1611). The *OED* notes that Florio in both his dictionaries also "has *crotesca* as an *Italian* word, explained as 'antique, fretted, or carued worke.'" The *OED* discloses a further dimension of the word that has to do with describing paintings found on the walls of ancient ruins:

> The etymological sense of *grottesca* would be "painting appropriate to grottos." The special sense is commonly explained by the statement that *grotte,* "grottoes" [*sic*], was the popular name in Rome for the chambers of ancient buildings which had been revealed by excavations, and which contained those mural paintings that were the typical examples of "grotesque."

When Milton picks out this strange foreign term, he evokes a formal aesthetic principle—the free and playful combination of forms—that harmonizes Eden as both natural and man-made: Eden, the natural locus amoenus *grotto* covered with moss and ivy, merges with an Eden reminiscent of the purely artifactual Roman excavations that astonished Renaissance Italy. Thus Eden becomes a potent figure for the naturally harmonious spiritual state about to be lost through human choice.

Milton's tone is wistful: "so lovely seemed / That lantskip" (4.152–53). Milton's "lantskip" (landscape), like "grotesque" and like "sylvan scene," was then metaphoric. *Landscape* came into English early in the seventeenth century, as a "technical term for painters" meaning "A picture representing natural inland scenery." Eden seemed like a picture. Milton might have had in mind "any number of Italian and Flemish paintings" (Hunt and Willis 79). In Paradise

> fruit, burnished with golden rind,
> Hung amiable—Hesperian fables true,
> If true, here only—and of delicious taste. (4.249–51)

Milton's liberal and innocent wilderness—like a fable, like a landscape, only *true*—functions in his poem as an emblem of *human* moral and imaginative freedom to make hell heaven and heaven hell. Goethe once praised Claude as having "the highest truth but no trace of actuality" (qtd. in Howard clxvii). British landscape gardeners understood that the elements of Claude's landscapes *are* actual—naturalistic enough to step out of a picture into the world. They labored to make such compositions actual on British soil.

What is Milton up to, using rhetorical tactics that suggest artistry when describing unfallen nature? The point of using so many aesthetic terms is not merely to show that Eden is pretty as a picture, artificial, or illusory in either a negative or absolute sense (that would be blasphemous). Milton foregrounds Eden's constructedness —the fact that it is made—in ways that both recapitulate the ancient idea of the divine artificer and deepen Virgil's theme of theatrical reality and illusion. Milton's Eden is made in the first place by a divine artificer, and then made over again, and variously, according to the moral artistry of the perceiving mind. Eden to the narrator's illumined vision is

> A Heaven on Earth: for blissful Paradise
> Of God the garden was, by him in the east
> Of Eden planted. (4.208–10)

Romantic poets understood Milton's place description neither as simply a program for making pictures or gardens nor as a fanciful depiction of an unreal world beyond human experience, but as an aesthetic manifesto asserting the power of imagination to see the world truly. For Blake, the union of the true world with illumined vision is particularly intense and polemically set forth. In a 23 August 1799 letter to a potential client who had just rejected a few of his watercolors, Blake wrote:

> To Me This World is all One continued Vision of Fancy or Imagination, & I feel Flatterd when I am told So. What is it sets Homer, Virgil & Milton in so high a rank of Art? Why is the Bible more Entertaining & Instructive than any other book? Is it not because they are addressed to the Imagination, which is Spiritual Sensation, and but mediately to the Understanding or Reason? Such is True Painting, and such was alone valued by the Greeks & the best modern Artists. ("Two Letters" 89)

Wordsworth, too, aspired to something like Blake's True Painting and made this aspiration the center of the aesthetic and spiritual program he set forth in his self-consciously Miltonic "Prospectus" at the end of the Preface to the 1814 *Excursion:*[14]

> Paradise, and groves
> Elysian, Fortunate Fields—like those of old
> Sought in the Atlantic Main, why should they be
> A history only of departed things,
> Or a mere fiction of what never was? (xii)

Such is Wordsworth's response to Milton's Eden, the true fable of the Hesperides. That the world is continuously offering itself to the imagination is a Miltonic theme that all British Romantics confronted and explored in one way or another. For Blake, Wordsworth, and Coleridge, the deliteralization of landscape into double perception, illumined and fallen, exalted

Milton as nature poet above any poet who wrote about natural places as if they were external scenic "givens."

Recall how on the top of Mt. Snowdon just before dawn, with the full moon illuminating the "ethereal vault," (1850 *Prelude* 14.50), Wordsworth saw "the emblem of a mind," (14.70)

> the type
> Of a majestic intellect, its acts
> And its possessions, what it has and craves,
> What in itself it is, and would become. (14.66–69)

Wordsworth's "emblem of a mind" bears comparison with Petrarch's epiphany after hiking up Mont Ventoux with his brother in the fourteenth century. After admiring the view, Petrarch opens Augustine's *Confessions* and

> happens to hit on the admonition against going off to admire the high mountains and all the other wonders of the earth while neglecting [. . .] one's own self. Shocked by the realization that he is still admiring earthly things, he recalls Seneca's adage that "nichil preter animum esse mirabile" [there is nothing admirable that surpasses the mind] and resolves to turn his eyes inward towards the soul. (Piehler, "Allegory" 99)

Petrarch, as Piehler further explains, went up the mountain as a medieval "participant in the allegorical consciousness of his age" for whom the landmarks and errors of the physical ascent corresponded to his inner struggles. After reaching the top, however, he turned his back on the prospect and descended with a consciousness that made a "sharp distinction between physical and internal environments" (99). All the medieval allegorical machinery—the otherworldly dreamscape of dark woods, steep mountains, and spiritual visitations—was dead for Petrarch as a mode of representing the inner life. Like Petrarch, and unlike the medieval visionary, Wordsworth climbed an actual mountain in the waking world. But Wordsworth found in the prospect a fit emblem of mind, and he turned away neither from the emblem nor from the mind. They illuminated each other.

Wordsworth transformed the "scenic" consciousness that dawned on Petrarch into a view of nature not only as a quite wonderful spectacle out there in the world but also as a reflection of an equally wonderful internal universe. This transformation would not have been possible, however, had Wordsworth not been able to call upon a tradition of landscape depiction in the visual arts. Late in the seventeenth century John Ray wrote that "the Mountains are pleasant Objects to behold," as witness the fact that "the very Images of them, their Draughts and Landskips, are so much esteem'd" (qtd. in Nicolson 261). Ray's observation was prescient. It suggested how Britain's rapidly changing visual culture was affecting the perception of natural scenery. This change accelerated during the eighteenth century when landscape prints became cheaper and more widely available to the middle class. Terms such as *scene, scenery, landscape,* and *grotesque,* borrowed from the arts and applied to living nature, gave Britain a new vocabulary for describing and evaluating nature and the human relation to it.

Romantic assimilation of this new vocabulary was not without its problems. In *Biographia Literaria,* for example, Coleridge praises Dryden's and Milton's usage of *scene* and criticizes Wordsworth for using *scene* to characterize a landscape in "There was a Boy" without (in Coleridge's view) "keeping the original" theatrical signification "full in the mind." Coleridge finds Wordsworth's usage obscure and confusing and objects "to any extension of its meaning because the word is already more equivocal than might be wished"; that is, the word can mean both stage scenery and the "characters and actions presented on the stage" (2:103). As we have seen, this equivocation was already present in Latin "scaena." The phrase that offended Coleridge reappeared in the 1805 *Prelude* and remained unchanged in the 1850 *Prelude:*

> Then sometimes, in that silence while he hung
> Listening, a gentle shock of mild surprise
> Has carried far into his heart the voice
> Of mountain torrents; *or the visible scene*
> Would enter unawares into his mind,
> With all its solemn imagery, its rocks,
> Its woods, and that uncertain heaven, received
> Into the bosom of the steady lake. (1805, 5.406–13; my italics).

Coleridge seems to have missed the point of Wordsworth's metaphor. Wordsworth's "scene" is a creative visionary remembrance or internalization of natural form. The theatrical term suggests the enhanced replaying of past perception initiated by a certain emotion, "a gentle shock of mild surprise." Wordsworth's "scene" is as much a creative transformation of Virgil's harbor with its sublime heavenward cliffs, living rocks, and silent watery bosom as it is of Milton, from whom Wordsworth learned the visionary potential of *scene.*

This and other aesthetic metaphors in Milton's national epic developed the tension between artifice and living nature that Milton read in Virgil's harbor-theater. This metaphoric development meshed historically with seventeenth- and eighteenth-century changes in the visual culture and religious outlook of the British so that eventually, under the nationalistic pressure of the Napoleonic Wars, Britons found themselves the increasingly self-conscious spectators, creators, and connoisseurs of a national sylvan scene that could rival Continental landscape, whether natural or pictorial. The eighteenth-century quest for a taxonomy of landscape forms that would be adequate to such a rationalized aesthetic program is the topic of the next chapter.

CHAPTER 4

The Universe Dead or Alive: Gilpin, Wordsworth, and the Picturesque

> Springs crystal-clear and streams not spoiled by man's work [. . .] and meadows beautiful without the use of art.
>
> —Seneca, *Epistle 90*

Milton's *Paradise Lost* opened a new and decisively important theme in the modern history of ecphrastic place description: the interplay between nature and the human mind that is central to much Romantic poetry. Even in a straightforward guide to lake scenery, Wordsworth pauses for an impassioned excursus on the traveler's mind: "After all, it is upon the *mind* which a traveller brings along with him that his acquisitions, whether of pleasure or profit, must principally depend.—May I be allowed a few words on this subject?" ("Description" 65). The gesture is so characteristic of Wordsworth, Byron, and the whole Romantic movement, and indeed so central to any coherent reading of the history of figurative place description, that it is worthwhile to explore how certain trends in eighteenth-century natural philosophy, visual culture, and aesthetic theory intersected with Wordsworth's experience of the natural world to shape some of the key concepts in his descriptive rhetoric.

It will be important to explore the development of an aesthetic category peculiar to Wordsworth's time, the "picturesque." Although this concept arose primarily in the context of expanding middle-class tourism during the late eighteenth century, it had profound consequences for the locodescriptive poetry of English Romanticism and for the development of the tradition of classical ecphrasis. The entire project of picturesque travel was founded on the possibility of visiting nearby and partially familiar locations, but looking on these everyday scenes as if they were exotic, unfamiliar, and worthy of representation in art. How much Wordsworth's poetic project owes to the impulse that animated the picturesque tourist can be readily seen in a passage from the 1805 *Prelude,* where Wordsworth declares, "In life's everyday appearances / I seemed [. . .] to have sight / Of a new world" (12.369–71). The poet foregrounds his sense of wonder, a commonplace in the rhetoric of vividness that surrounds ancient discussions of ecphrasis. He also describes himself in terms that would be entirely familiar to the devotees of the picturesque, though in Wordsworth's hands the concept is transformed into something far more complex and far better suited to a locodescriptive poetry committed to an exploration of the interplay between nature and the human mind. It is essential to this inquiry, then, to examine in some detail the origins and development of the picturesque as an aesthetic category and to explain how Wordsworth incorporated it into his own work, even as he reacted vigorously against it.

Aesthetic Categories in the Eighteenth Century

A central current of eighteenth-century aesthetics divides aesthetic experience into two basic contrasting categories. The terms and definitions for these experiential categories vary, and the objective and/or subjective sources of the experience vary as well. Lessing's opposition of verbal and visual art is typical. In British aesthetics, however, an important third category partakes of or mediates between the two. Although this middle third term is missing in Lessing's aesthetic theory and its postmodern progeny, it is of vital importance in the development of Romantic poetics.

Addison established the pattern in *Spectator* 412 (23 June 1712) when he spoke in terms of the Great, the Uncommon, and the Beautiful. The Great has to do with

> Stupendous works of Nature. Our imagination loves to be filled with an Object, or to graspe at any thing that is too big for its Capacity. We are flung into a pleasing Astonishment at such unbounded Views, and feel a delightful Stillness and Amazement in the Soul at the Apprehension of them. (540)

Beauty, on the other hand, "diffuses a secret Satisfaction and Complacency [. . .] strikes the Mind with an inward Joy, and spreads a Chearfulness and Delight through all its Faculties" (542). The hallmark of the middling Uncommon is variety and surprise, but well-modulated variety and surprise. Addison's Uncommon makes the mind "a little agitated and relieved" (542). For Addison, the imagination finds its greatest pleasure when the three principles merge, when " there be a Beauty or Uncommonness joined with [. . .] Grandeur, as in a [. . .] spacious Landskip cut into Rivers, Woods, Rocks, and Meadows" (541). Addison's theoretical structure bears a family resemblance to later accounts of the sublime and the beautiful, though not to the aesthetic dualisms popular in the late twentieth century. His high valuation of a middling category or mixture as "the greatest pleasure" looks forward to the later craze for the picturesque and to the British effort to define and dignify *picturesque* as an aesthetic category on a par with *beautiful* and *sublime*. For the purposes of this inquiry it is necessary to discuss just one such effort, that of William Gilpin, and the response of just one poet, Wordsworth, whose aesthetic program takes a sharp turn away from the fashions and doctrines that had accumulated around Gilpin's popular enterprise by the end of the eighteenth century.[1] Wordsworth learned about the picturesque primarily from Gilpin, who was unquestionably the foremost exponent of picturesque tourism. Martin Price has shown that although Wordsworth also later read some other theoreticians of the picturesque such as Uvedale Price and Richard Payne Knight, these were of less consequence in the development of his thinking ("Picturesque" 389). At the critical moment when Wordsworth was interested in such matters, it was Gilpin whom he read, and it was Gilpin against whom he reacted.

Gilpin's attempt to establish the picturesque as an aesthetic category is best understood as emotionally informed by Addison's great middling "pleasures of the imagination" and as rationally motivated by Burke's science of taste in terms of polar opposites, the sublime and the beautiful. Burke describes the emotions pertaining to each, the objects that excite these emotions, and he presents a physiological theory of how those objects excite their corresponding emotions. Sublime emotion has to do with self-preservation and entails an awareness of great danger averted (47; 1.18).

> And indeed the ideas of pain, and above all of death, are so very affecting, that whilst we remain in the presence of whatever is supposed to have the power of inflicting either, it is impossible to be completely free of terror. (59; 2.5)

In this sense, the sublime is for Burke "founded on pain" (113; 3.27). Beauty, on the other hand, is "that quality or qualities in bodies by which they cause love, or some passion similar to it." Burke hastens to add that he confines his definition "to the merely sensible qualities of things" (83; 3.1). In this sense, the beautiful is founded on pleasure. Burke's dualism of the sublime and the beautiful coordinates, literally and systematically, with the properties of objects. "For sublime objects are vast in their dimensions," explains Burke, while

> beautiful ones [are] comparatively small; beauty should be smooth, and polished; the great, rugged and negligent; beauty should shun the right line, yet deviate from it insensibly; the great in many cases loves the right line, and when it deviates, it often makes a strong deviation; beauty should not be obscure; the great ought to be dark and gloomy; beauty should be light and delicate; the

great ought to be solid, and even massive. They are indeed ideas of a very different nature, one being founded on pain, the other on pleasure. (113; 3.27)

Gilpin is concerned with the gray area that Burke himself realizes he leaves open between these two poles. Burke insists that although the distinct causes of the sublime and the beautiful (pain and pleasure respectively) "keep up an eternal distinction between them" that must never "be forgotten by any whose business it is to affect the passions," we must nevertheless expect to find the qualities of both

> united in the same object. We must expect also to find combinations of the same kind in the works of art. But when we consider the power of an object upon our passions, we must know that when any thing is intended to affect the mind by the force of some predominant property, the affection produced is like to be the more uniform and perfect, if all the other properties or qualities of the object be of the same nature, and tending to the same design as the principle. (114; 3.27)

For Burke, the senses of the sublime and the beautiful are as distinct and stable as the sensory perceptions of black and white:

> Black and white may soften, may blend, but they are not therefore the same. Nor when they are so softened and blended with each other, or with different colors, is the power of black as black, or of white as white, so strong as when each stands uniform and distinguished. (114; 3.27)

To appreciate Gilpin, we will need to remember Burke's shades of gray and not expect much in the way of precision from Gilpin's picturesque. Gilpin locates the picturesque as the area between the poles of the sublime and the beautiful. Near one pole is the picturesquely sublime, rough, shaggy, and big, but without formless terrors and infinitudes, while near the other pole is the picturesquely beautiful, smooth and well formed but without an overly elegant finish.

While Gilpin accepts Burke's premises and tries to define, describe, and promote Burke's gray area as the picturesque, Wordsworth rejects the black and white analogy as an altogether misleading account of the mind's colloquy with nature. Wordsworth, himself a travel writer, became a vocal critic not only of the vogue for picturesque sightseeing but of the entire enterprise of labeling nature with literal and stable emotive designators such as "sublime," "beautiful," or "picturesque." For Wordsworth, as for Milton, perception itself is a kind of creative artistry that often reveals nature as an emblem of mind. Wordsworth, manifestly a nature poet, takes Milton one psychological step further when he elevates the idea of relative perception to an aesthetic program for nature poetry that makes "the Mind of Man"—not external, objective nature—"My haunt, and the main region of my Song" ("Prospectus" xii). Wordsworth moreover disavows the eighteenth-century impulse to systematize emotion and nature. "It is not the Author's intention formally to announce a system," as he writes in the Preface to the 1814 *Excursion,*

> it was more animating to him to proceed in a different course; and if he shall succeed in conveying to the mind clear thoughts, lively images, and strong feelings, the Reader will have no difficulty in extracting the system for himself. (x)

The emphasis on clarity and vividness in these lines says much about their participation in the tradition of classical ecphrasis. Wordsworth is obviously far more interested in these qualities than he is in systematic philosophy. For us it will be essential to show how this ecphrastic turn of mind fits together with Wordsworth's attitude toward the picturesque. It will soon become clear just how deeply Wordsworth's antipathy toward the picturesque is implicated in his most serious aesthetic and philosophical commitments.

The Picturesque Tourist

The Reverend William Gilpin, a "reluctant theorist," wanted to be known by his religious works; but

> he had created a fashion for which the public had developed an insatiable hunger; and as he was, in the words of the *Monthly Review,* "the venerable founder and master of the Picturesque School," his hundreds of tourist pupils would not easily let him return to his primary vocation. (Andrews 56–57)

Unlike Wordsworth, Gilpin had an explicit system for encountering the natural world. The epigraph for his *Two Essays* (1804) encapsulates the didactic spirit and intention: "Non minus otii quam negotii rationem exstare oportet." ["There ought to be no less a system for leisure than there is for conducting business."] The aim of his discourse on the picturesque was to provide a system for engaging nature in a particular way: touring in quest of the visual aesthetics of nature and documenting the results in sketches made according to Gilpin's program. It was a disciplined program for amateur, middle-class connoisseurship that developed out of a relatively new kind of middle-class leisure activity, scenic travel in Britain.

Intrepid aristocrats such as the first Duchess of Northumberland (b. 1716) had paved the way for Gilpin with systems of their own.

The Duchess structured her 1760 country house visits with 150 preplanned queries on anything that might conceivably be of interest, from the emotions evoked by the landscape to the particulars of household butter consumption. Here are just a few of the questions she wrote up in her travel journals:

> Is the place chearful melancholy romantic wild or dreary. . . . what is the situation of the House good or bad sheltered or exposed. . . . Who was the architect. . . . Is the furniture rich plain neat mean Elegant Expensive. . . . Is there a menagerie. . .What curious fowls does it contain. . . . How much meat wine malt liquor coals charcoal corn butter do they usually consume [. . .]. (qtd. in Percy and Jackson-Stops 150)

What most merits attention in the Duchess' system is the broad virtuoso curiosity that places descriptions of coal consumption, menageries, site planning, and romantic landscape all on one copious agenda. The inclusive descriptive program of her travel journal is similar to the one in Thomson's *The Seasons* (1727–1730), a work, which "initiated a literary fashion for poems describing the working conditions and settings of agricultural life, the pictorial elements of landscape, anecdotal details of rustic existence, and man's relation to nature" (Webb and Weller 286).

The British reinvented tourism for the middle class and made Britain itself a tourist destination, eventually even for the aristocrats of Europe, by methods similar to those by which the civilized pleasure trip was invented and promoted in antiquity: safer transportation, geographical and descriptive literature, and appeals to the cultural resonances of history, myth, and poetry. The last half of the eighteenth century saw a vastly expanded turnpike system, smoother roads, lighter carriages with steel springs, stronger horses, new large-scaled maps with both roads and points of interest marked, and several innovations in book production including aquatint for mass-produced illustrated books (Piggott 123–125). Early illustrated books about landscapes and ruins, such as Allan Ramsay's *Tea-Table Miscellany* of the 1720s, could by late century function both as advertisements for visiting the now-accessible sites and as a library of classicist model drawings for the amateur artist-tourist who might want to document his tour.

The Duchess' queries capture something of the exotic feeling and expectation that eighteenth-century British tourists had for exploring their own isle, either for the first time or in a new light. Her queries are not the sort one asks of familiar neighbors but the sort one asks when carefully documenting the strange ways of a strange land explored for the first time. The Duchess took on the role of an anthropologist from Northumberland, striking out on new roads into the wilds of Scotland, during the same year (1760) that

James Macpherson published his *Fragments of Ancient Poetry, Collected in the Highlands of Scotland, and Translated from the Galic or Erse Language.* Macpherson was also touring just then in quest of material for the two forged Scottish epics, *Fingal* (1762) and *Temora* (1763) that would fascinate all of Europe. From the 1760s onward, Macpherson's fictive world of Ossian evoked a heroic past that rivaled European fantasies of Homeric antiquity. The distant Celtic past invented by Macpherson for Britons' right in England's backyard eventually became in turn an exotic destination for Europeans. In 1819, the dramatic date of *Eugenie Grandet,* Balzac could quickly sketch the stereotypical aristocrat Annette simply by placing her on tour in Scotland. An actual aristocrat, the Duchess of Northumberland, was touring Scotland in quest of absolutely everything just when the confluence of better transportation, print technology, and a range of descriptive and evocative literature was beginning to enable what would later become a national craze for making, documenting, and publishing tours with an aim more specialized than we find in either Thomson's, Macpherson's, or the Duchess' broader agenda. That special aim was to find and capture the picturesque.

Although the British became even more passionately attracted to British travel as nationalism flourished under the geopolitical pressures of the French Revolution and the Napoleonic Wars, Stukely rightly points out that as early as 1725 a tour of the Lakes might substitute for a Grand Tour of Italy; significantly, his description reprises the central metaphor of Milton's Edenic "woody theater" (*Paradise Lost* 4.141) and Virgil's "scaena":

> When one stands at the end of these lakes, the prospect is exceedingly delightful; the mountains on each side rising to a great height, one behind the other the whole length and broke off into short ones, like scenes at a playhouse: nor need a painter go to Italy for variety and grandeur of prospects. (Stukely, qtd. in Piggott, 122)

In "Description of the Scenery of the Lakes," Wordsworth cites the authority of West's mid-eighteenth-century *Guide,* in which it is argued that the scenery of "our northern mountains" provides "in miniature" a perfectly adequate idea of the Alps and the Appenines, "not inferior in beauty [. . .] but in height and extent only" (West qtd. in "Description" 75). When the Napoleonic Wars made the Grand Tour impossible or undesirably dangerous, the wealthy patriot who otherwise might have taken the tour was as prepared as were the middle class to delight in British travel and Edenic British scenes. Gilpin's contribution was to show just how to do it.

Gilpin's 1768 *Essay upon Prints* gives his first definition of picturesque as "that peculiar kind of beauty, which is agreeable in a picture" (x).[2]

His more theoretical *Three Essays* and *Two Essays* attempt to answer the question of what it is in objects that makes them picturesque, and what are the principles of picturesque composition, but his theoretical writing never strays too far from the practical problem of how and why to document a tour. He began publishing his enormously popular aquatint-illustrated tours in 1782, all of them bearing titles of the form *Observations* [upon some part of Great Britain] *Relative Chiefly to Picturesque Beauty.* The picturesque tourist as embodied in his tour books is a resourceful, low-budget, do-it-yourself version of the Grand Tourist who traveled through France and the Alps into Italy and Rome, the main cultural destination. The wealthiest might take along an artist to document the trip and might have a portrait done in Rome. Lord Byron, for example, commissioned in 1817 a portrait bust from life by Thorvaldsen, one of the most distinguished classicist sculptors working in Rome at the time. The Grand Tourist might bring back original Italian art but more often souvenir prints, especially prints of the great ruins. Gilpin scales the pattern down to a petite tour for Everyman. Stay in Britain. Be your own artist. Not only be your own artist, but create your own sights if what you actually see is wanting in picturesque beauty. (It usually will be.) Make the requisite portrait a self-portrait. Just sketch yourself into the landscape; Gilpin often did. But just what is the picturesque tourist looking for?

Gilpin's "On Picturesque Beauty," the first of the *Three Essays,* opens by stating the problem as follows:

> Disputes about beauty might perhaps be involved in less confusion, if a distinction were established, which certainly exists, between such objects as are *beautiful,* and such as are *picturesque*—between those, which please the eye in their natural state; and those, which please from some quality, capable of being illustrated by painting. (3; Gilpin's italics)[3]

After paying lip service to the idea that beauty is also partly in the eye of the beholder, he forgets about this notion and sets himself the question: "*What is that quality in objects, which particularly marks them as picturesque?*" (4). Framing the question in this way shows that Gilpin accepts Burke's premise that aesthetic qualities are (one way or another) stable properties of objects. Objects with certain formal qualities elicit certain responses, and Gilpin wants to isolate the picturesque quality so that he can amplify it in a picture. In this connection, Gilpin is troubled by Burke's high valuation of smoothness. "Mr. Burke," writes Gilpin, "considers *smoothness* as one of most essential" properties of beautiful objects, "indeed the most considerable" (5). Gilpin quotes Burke:

> For take any beautiful object, and give it a broken, and rugged surface, and however well-formed it may be in other respects, it pleases no longer. Whereas,

let it want ever so many of the other constituents, if it want not this, it becomes more pleasing, than almost all the others without it. (Burke qtd. in *Three Essays* 5)

Gilpin takes exception: "How far Mr. Burke may be right in making smoothness the *most considerable* source of beauty, I rather doubt" (5). In fact, Gilpin's own eye simply does not share Burke's perception that smoothness is the most considerable source of beauty. Gilpin attempts to replace, or somehow supplement, Burke's "objective" taste for smoothness with his own taste for roughness, by sharpening a distinction (already suggested by Burke in his discussion of the sublime) between the aesthetic response to a natural object and the aesthetic response to a picture of the same:

> in *picturesque representation* it seems somewhat odd, yet perhaps we shall find it equally true, that [. . .] the ideas of *neat* and *smooth,* instead of being picturesque, in reality strip the object, in which they reside, of all pretensions to *picturesque beauty.*—Nay, farther, we do not scruple to assert, that *roughness* forms the most essential point of difference between the *beautiful,* and the *picturesque;* as it seems to be that particular quality, which makes objects chiefly pleasing in painting. (6)

Thus the picturesque has more to do with rough and shaggy things than with smooth and finely finished things.[4] He observes, however, that "it is not so obvious, why the quality of *roughness* should make an essential difference between objects of *beauty,* and objects suited to *artificial representation*" (26).

Gilpin's discovery in nature of scenes suitable for artificial representation links his idea of the picturesque to modern notions of ecphrasis as literary depictions of works of art. While Gilpin does not engage in the description of art objects, his quest for the picturesque involves searching nature for the protoartificial, then realizing that potential for artifice by making a sketch that corrects nature's defects. Just as in twentieth-century art ecphrasis, the representation (whether as process or product) may be more interesting than what is represented. Gilpin was by no means alone among eighteenth-century aestheticians in looking at nature in this way. No less a figure than Kant himself resorted to a very similar double-think when he tried to explain the beauty of natural landscape:

> Self-subsisting natural beauty reveals to us a technic of nature which shows it in the light of a system ordered in accordance with [. . .] a finality relative to the employment of judgement in respect of phenomena which have thus to be assigned, not merely to nature regarded as aimless mechanism, but also to nature regarded after the analogy of art. (92)

Natural beauty exists in that moment of double perception in which nature, a process without purpose, seems to be arranged according to the purposes of art.

The author of the third *Critique* seems entirely comfortable with such moments of double perception, but the author of "On Picturesque Beauty" is not. Gilpin in fact rejects every definitive statement he makes about the protoartificial quality to be found in nature: "The picturesque eye abhors art," preferring nature; but no, Gilpin likes art too (26–28). Picturesque beauty is "the happy union of simplicity and variety"; but no, simplicity and variety are sources of the beautiful too (28–29). Painting is "*strictly imitative,*" and rough objects have strong features that present most easily to the eye; no, Gilpin has to admit that smooth objects are as easily imitated (29). Each of his rejected solutions reveals another aspect of the underlying paradox in defining picturesque as suited to artificial representation (in pictures) while at the same time maintaining that the picturesque entails a response to nature, not art. Unable to find his way out of this quandary, he throws up his hands "puzzled, bewildered, but not informed, all is uncertainty; a strife of words" (33). Caught for the time being in this almost postmodern aporia, he moves on to the second *Essay,* "On Picturesque Travel," in which an answer of sorts emerges implicitly from Gilpin's portrait of the traveler as sketch artist.

"On Picturesque Travel" attempts a theory of his popular tour book practice. The "general intention of picturesque travel," he says, is "searching after effects" (41). The implication is clear, after the first essay, that the traveler is searching for those hard-to-define impressions that can be converted into a picturesque representation. Gilpin, aware of this narrow purpose, disclaims

> competition with any of the more useful ends of travelling. But as many travel without any end at all [. . .] we offer one end, which may possibly engage some vacant minds; and may indeed afford a rational amusement to such as travel for more important purposes. (41)

The traveler, writes Gilpin, seeks "beauty of every kind," (42) especially "picturesque" beauty, which brings him right back to the "strife of words" he abandoned in the first essay.

Gilpin tries once again to capture just what picturesque beauty is when he observes that not only landscape can be the object of picturesque attention but also beautiful artifacts "far too neat and elegant for the use of the pencil" (*Three Essays* 45; by "pencil" Gilpin means watercolor brush). Gilpin only parenthetically mentions the pencil; but what it does best is essential to Gilpin's aesthetic: "Nothing is wanting, [in these artifacts] but what his imagination can supply—a change from smooth to rough" (45). The change that makes the artifact more picturesque is the transformation effected by the fluid autographic gesture of the pencil. Like Lessing, who wants subject and medium to correspond, Gilpin wants to bring his subject and his medium into picturesque accord.

Gilpin's self-conscious concern with how to transform the subject matter into a picture that evokes the desired aesthetic emotion reflects his understanding of an important distinction Burke makes between the aesthetic response to subject matter and the aesthetic response to a picture of it. "It is one thing to make an idea clear," writes Burke,

> and another to make it *affecting* to the imagination. If I make a drawing of a palace, or a temple or a landscape, I present a very clear idea of those objects; but then (allowing for the effect of imitation which is something) my picture can at most affect only as the palace, temple, or a landscape would have affected in the reality. (55; 2.4)

Burke distinguishes the sublime as particularly problematic for pictorial representation:

> I have been at a loss, in all the pictures I have seen of hell, whether the painter did not intend something ludicrous. Several painters have handled a subject of this kind, with a view of assembling as many horrid phantoms as their imagination could suggest; but all the designs I have chanced to meet of the temptations of Saint Anthony, were rather a sort of odd wild grotesques [. . .]. (58–59; 2.4)[5]

Disjunctions like this between phenomena and the responses that are supposed to be elicited by their depictions or descriptions create a space for irony in Romantic and later literature. In *Pride and Prejudice,* Elizabeth Bennet rebuffs an outdoor party of three (including Darcy) by saying: "No, no; stay where you are. You are charmingly grouped . . . The picturesque would be spoilt by adding a fourth" (qtd. in *OED,* "Picturesque" 5). In 1796 Austen can count on her audience to get the joke, for a clump of three trees must not be squared off by a fourth. Such compositional rules were well known. The detached urbanity of Blake's "Memorable Fancy" parodies Gilpin, when the narrator introduces himself and his copious tour notes from Hell:[6]

> As I was walking among the fires of hell, de-
> -lighted with the enjoyments of Genius; which to An-
> -gels look like torment and insanity. I collected some
> of their Proverbs: thinking that as the sayings used
> in a nation, mark its character, so the Proverbs of

> Hell, shew the nature of Infernal wisdom better
> than any description of buildings or garments.
> (*Marriage of Heaven and Hell,* copy C, plate 6.15–21)

Coleridge, on the other hand, tends to take it all more seriously. Just how hard it is to keep Gilpin's (or Addison's or Burke's) aesthetic categories seriously aligned with emotions can be illustrated by a story told by Coleridge. The poet comes upon a cataract with a party of travelers. The cataract, writes Coleridge, was "of great height, breadth, and impetuosity, the summit of which appeared to blend with the sky and clouds, while the lower part was hidden by rocks and trees" (367). When Coleridge observed that "it was, in the strictest sense of the word, a sublime object, a lady present assented with warmth to the remark, adding—'Yes! And it is not only sublime, but beautiful and absolutely pretty'" ("Essays" 367). Or picturesquely sublime, as Gilpin might say. Coleridge mocks the unlearned lady's response, supposing her a little ridiculous in her warm and theoretically confused outburst. But Coleridge does not report the sublime cataract as a vivid, sublime *experience* over which his rational powers have scant control. Rather he locates the sublime in the visual characteristics of the cataract and gives a coolly detached description that is "picturesque" in the formal sense, that is, suitable for a picture. Coleridge frames and delimits the scene, describing it in visual terms that mark its top and bottom as if it were a picture. Having read his Burke and Kant, he sees a cataract and calls it "in the strictest sense"—he has thought it through—"sublime." The term in no way accords with his emotional response, actual or imagined.[7] His rational functions have identified and controlled the impression made by the cataract. He can see and name, but not feel the emotion he names, just as in "Dejection": "And still I gaze—and with how blank an eye / [. . .] / I *see,* not *feel*" (30–38). The more effusive lady feels the cataract, and her emotional pressure to find words for what she cannot express spills out naively in a confused and spontaneous concatenation of terms. She really wants to produce an ecphrasis, to make her reader share her intensity of feeling, though she is not quite up to it. Her warm delight owes as much to Gilpin as does Coleridge's tendency to describe the scene without extravagant emotional participation. The lady cheerfully domesticates the wild cataract into absolute prettiness, Coleridge into a textbook instance of sublime appearance. Neither Coleridge nor the lady is quite awed by the cataract.

Coleridge's lady and Blake's traveler might be compared with Hannah More, who wrote as follows in a letter of September 1789 to Horace Walpole:

> I have been an arrant stroller—amusing myself by sailing down the beautiful River Wye, looking at abbeys and castles, with Mr Gilpin in my hand to

teach me to criticize, and talk of foregrounds, and distances, and perspectives, and prominences, with all the cant of connoisseurship, and then, to *subdue* my imagination, which had been not a little disordered with this enchanting scenery, I have been living in sober magnificence with the Plantagenet Dowager Duchess at Stoke, where a little more discretion, and a little less fancy was proper and decorous; and then I have had Mrs Montagu at my cottage, and then I have had Mrs Garrick, and then I have had Mr Wilberforce. (September 1789, More qtd. in Walpole, *Horace Walpole's Correspondence* 31:320–321)[8]

More's witty letter does not take Gilpin any more seriously than the enchanting scenery or her only slightly disordered imagination, or the many visitors who figure more specifically than the Wye tour. But all the same, she is eager to demonstrate her fashionable acquaintance with "all the cant of connoisseurship" as she is to document her fashionable social life. Mrs. More, with her round of not-too-passionate amusements, might have stepped out of an Austen novel.

The picturesque eye is never too carried away by extremes. Gilpin writes that the picturesque eye is not so fond of the fantastic and curious as of nature in her "*most usual* forms" (*Three Essays* 43). Gilpin does, however, openly concede that nature can inspire the traveller with "religious awe" (47), but the manner in which he acknowledges Burke's sublime is almost comedically telling: "We derive our chief pleasure [. . .] when some grand scene, tho perhaps of incorrect composition, rising before the eye, strikes us beyond the power of thought—when the *vox faucibus haeret*" (49), when the voice is stuck in the throat, "and every mental operation is suspended," and we "rather feel, than survey" (50) the place. Consider first how closely Gilpin has paraphrased Burke on the astonishment evoked by the natural sublime. Burke explains astonishment (already a key term, as we have seen, in Addison's 1712 *Spectator* 412) as follows:

> The passion caused by the great and sublime in *nature*,[9] when those causes operate most powerfully, is Astonishment; and astonishment is that state of the soul, in which all its motions are suspended, with some degree of horror. In this case the mind is so entirely filled with its object, that it cannot entertain any other, nor by consequence reason on that object which employs it. (53; 2.1)

Gilpin, however, even when speaking of suspended mental operations, cannot help thinking about rearranging the furniture; he duly notes the potentially "incorrect composition" of what supposedly lies "beyond the power of thought." But Gilpin's main point here is that the picturesque traveler should not, in any case, be looking for Burke's Astonishment. Normally the traveler happily settles for more modest amusement. "Yet even this may be of some use," Gilpin remarks, "in an age teeming with licentious pleasure; and may in this light at least be considered as having a moral tendency" (*Three Essays* 47).

Gilpin outlines the sources of this harmless amusement in what amounts to the case for picturesque travel. First, the pleasure of the pursuit itself is a pleasure akin to hunting:

> And shall we suppose it a greater pleasure to the sportsman to pursue a trivial animal, than it is to the man of taste to pursue the beauties of nature? To follow her through all her recesses? To obtain a sudden glance, as she flits past him in some airy shape? To trace her through the mazes of the cover? To wind after her along the vale? (48)

The traveler finds his quarry, the picturesque scene, sometimes whole but more often in parts that need reconfiguring: "We examine what would amend the composition: how little is wanting to reduce it to the rules of our art" (49).[10] In *Observations,* Gilpin notes what a poor composer nature is: "Either the foreground, or the background, is disproportioned: or some awkward line runs through the piece: or a tree is ill-placed: or a bank is formal: or something, or other is not exactly what it should be" (18). But, as he explains in *Three Essays,* pleasure attends the traveler's enlarged mental stock of the new bits and pieces that enhance his understanding of the familiar. "We get it [the familiar] more by heart" (50). And sketches, " a few scratches [. . .] legible at least to ourselves" (51) are the traveler's memorials. "There may be more pleasure in recollecting, and recording, from a few transient lines, the scenes we have admired, than in the present enjoyment of them" (51). Besides, the memories enjoyed in the comfort of home are "unallayed with that fatigue, which is often a considerable abatement to the pleasures of traversing the wild, and savage parts of nature" (52).

Gilpin, spiritual godfather to all tourists who love their snapshots and videos more than their vacations, unabashedly encourages tourists to make up the memories as they go along, for the truly imaginative traveler can create and represent "*scenes of fancy*" inspired by bits and pieces of scenery (*Three Essays* 52). Gilpin (in sharp contrast to Wordsworth and Coleridge) uses the words *fancy* and *imagination* indistinguishably to refer to the image-forming capacity of the mind: "The imagination can plant hills; can form rivers, and lakes in vallies; can build castles, and abbeys; and if it find no other amusement, can dilate itself in vast ideas of space" (56). And the traveler can simply enjoy the dreamscapes, "the very visions of fancy itself" (54) that are beyond his powers of representation:

> Often, when slumber has half-closed the eye, and shut out all the objects of sense, especially after the enjoyment of some splendid scene; the imagination, active, and alert, collects its scattered ideas, transposes, combines, and shifts them into a thousand forms, producing such exquisite scenes, such sublime arrangements, such glow, and harmony of colouring, such brilliant lights, such depth, and clearness of shadow, as equally foil description, and every attempt of artificial colouring. (54)

It is easy to see why Gilpin's pictures only loosely interpret what he sees. Picturesque tourism was neither photojournalism nor literal topographical documentation. Rather, its procedures gave amateurs open to a new and wholesome experience—those "vacant minds" Gilpin addresses—a framework for arousing and organizing a sensuous aesthetic response to the landscape. Gilpin's aesthetic manifesto anchors his readers in compositional rules familiar to them through classicist landscape prints, while his high valuation of the spontaneous brush stroke and rough, unfinished textures anticipates the formal preferences of Romantic and modern art. It attempts a kind of forced merger between place description, the favored form of classical ecphrasis, and art description, the sole form of ecphrasis recognized by twentieth-century theory, though in the medium of painting rather than in words. It would take a master of words to exploit the impulse toward the picturesque and transform it into an ecphrastic practice that would change the poetic landscape forever.

"The Cold Rules of Painting": Wordsworth

Wordsworth began arguing against the picturesque, both as an aesthetic category and as a cultural process, early in his career. One line of criticism takes on the picturesque in practice. He deplores some unintended consequences of what the picturesque aesthetic is producing on the actual land. Wordsworth himself, an enthusiastic promoter of British tourism, praises the indigenous cottage as a natural outgrowth in "Description of the Scenery of the Lakes." The cottages, he writes, have been inhabited by many generations and have "received without incongruity additions and accommodations adapted to the needs of each successive occupant." These accretions over time make the buildings seem to be "productions of nature" that may "rather be said to have grown than to have been erected [. . .] to have risen, by an instinct of their own, out of the native rock" (39).

Wordsworth notes how the very popularity of the region attracted settlers who wanted to establish residences from which to see and be seen. He finds the region disfigured by buildings constructed with the express purpose of being "looked at and commented upon" and placed upon "the summits of naked hills" to have the best and most unobstructed views (47–48). Wordsworth witnesses how industrialization has so destroyed the economic base of traditional cottage artisans that opportunities for disfiguring the landscape are widespread: since the proprietors and farmers can no longer maintain their small farms, they are obliged to sell them to the rich, who "erect new mansions out of the ruins of the ancient cottages" (61).[11] It might be argued that Gilpin himself anticipates Wordsworth's critique of the picturesque traveler as despoiler of landscape when he writes that he is

> disgusted [. . .] with houses, and towns, the haunts of men, which have much oftener a bad effect in landscape than a good one. He is frequently disgusted also when art aims more at beauty, than she ought. How flat, and insipid is often the garden scene; how puerile and absurd! The banks of the river how smooth, and parallel? The lawn, and its boundaries, how unlike nature! (*Three Essays* 57)

But Gilpin's objections are to "the haunts of men," and they rest on purely visual and formal grounds. He objects to the flat, the straight, and the smooth. Wordsworth's position is more nuanced in that he does not find all human habitation unaesthetic. He objects primarily to homes whose economic purpose is inappropriate to their setting in the natural landscape.

The picturesque traveler in Wordsworth's writing, at worst a wealthy despoiler of the landscape and the rural economy, at best an idler in quest of mere formalist delight in the visual surface of things, entirely misses nature as understood by Wordsworth. Picturesque touring is for Gilpin an innocent pleasure, but his idea of the picturesque quest as chase, as an impatient quest for what looks like a representation—a familiar picture or rhetorical description—is for Wordsworth an important part of what is wrong with the picturesque aesthetic. The impatient eye, and travel as a kind of organized visual impatience, undermines the proper imaginative rapport with nature, a reciprocal and patiently developed communication with the land. For Wordsworth, picturesque attention, rationalization, and rearrangement preclude rapport and communication.

In a note to *Descriptive Sketches* (1793), Wordsworth objects to applying the term *picturesque* to scenery that has the power to communicate the strong emotion that inheres in nature, whence it flows into the properly vacated human mind. He objects to the term precisely because it evokes "the cold rules of painting":

> I had once given to these sketches the title of Picturesque; but the Alps are insulted in applying to them that term. Whoever, in attempting to describe their sublime features, should confine himself to the cold rules of painting would give his reader but a very imperfect idea of those emotions which they have the irresistible power of communicating to the most impassive imaginations. (72)[12]

Wordsworth's objection to cold rules should not be construed as a rejection of all painting. "Cold rules" are programs and schemata, such as Gilpin's, that have grown too rigid to accommodate nature's power. Recall that Gilpin defines *picturesque* as beauty that is "agreeable in a picture" and systematically looks for the protoartificial. Wordsworth objects to Gilpin's notion that nature is the not-quite-good-enough raw material for a picture, that it needs to be visually rearranged by "the cold rules of painting" before it evokes the right emotion. It is not that Wordsworth hypocritically claims that his own poetry somehow offers unmediated nature; he never makes such claims for his own work. Rather, procedures such as Gilpin's add, in his view, so much noise that the signal is drowned out. In what follows, I will argue that Wordsworth wants to dampen the cognitive noise so that he can pick up a clearer signal.

At the heart of Wordsworth's response to the picturesque and to his own re-creation of the landscape poem is a remark he makes in the Preface to *Lyrical Ballads*. He distinguishes *Lyrical Ballads* "from the popular Poetry of the day" in that the "feeling therein developed gives importance to the action and situation, and not the action and situation to the feeling" (283). For Wordsworth, aesthetic categories such as the sublime, the beautiful, and the picturesque, including whatever feelings are supposedly associated with them—awe and exaltation with the sublime, love and gentleness with the beautiful, or the pleasant, middling excitements between the two that are associated with the picturesque—are not determined by the surface structure of objects but by the mind's engagement with the sense and feeling that inheres in natural objects. Wordsworth's ideas are far more radical than the commonplace notion that beauty is in the eye of the beholder. Moreover, Wordsworth insists that the same landscape can at different times elicit various responses, just as a living person can. For example, an object's "obtrusive qualities," writes Wordsworth in "The Sublime and the Beautiful," can "imperiously" preclude "the perception of beauty which that object if contemplated under another relation would have been capable of imparting" (264). In another jibe at the scenic traveler, he writes that

> the true province of the philosopher is not to grope about in the external world and, when he has perceived or detected in an object such or such a quality or power, to set himself the task of persuading the world such is a sublime or beautiful object, but to look into his own mind and determine the law by which [. . .] the same object has power to affect him in various manners at various times. (271)

Just what governs the mind's dynamic colloquy with nature is thematic in Wordsworth's poetry and literary theory.

The historical context of Wordsworth's ideas about mind and nature is the topic of H. W. Piper's *The Active Universe*. Though Piper's book has been available for decades, it has been unjustly disregarded by subsequent scholars. This is not only a grave injustice to a careful and original contribution to Romantic studies, it is an injustice to literary history itself. Because my own position develops some of his more provocative suggestions, which may not be well known, I would like to recapitulate the salient points here.

Wordsworth's ideas about the mind's relationship to nature came about, according to Piper,

> from deliberate thought about the Imagination [. . .] . But this deliberate thought did not occur in an historical vacuum. Contemporary philosophical speculation—particularly speculation concerning emergent scientific ideas—influenced both Coleridge and Wordsworth. (1)

Wordsworth's associates in revolutionary France placed him in a current of late eighteenth-century thought that

> swept away the Newtonian mechanical "universe of death" [1805 *Prelude* 13.141] and brought a new conception of life, development and purpose in the natural world. In the eighteenth century the poets had seen the universe as the beautiful handiwork of God; the Romantics were able to see it as full of human significances and full of a life which answered to man's.(1)

Piper points out—and this is crucial to my discussion of Wordsworth—that although Wordsworth and Coleridge both distinguish between *fancy* and *imagination*, two terms that were often used interchangeably, Wordsworth's distinction is not the same as Coleridge's. Piper's concern is "with the Wordsworthian notion of the Imagination as the power to communicate with the life in natural objects" and he shows that this particular notion "was an integral part of a comprehensive philosophical view, the theory of an 'active universe'" (2).[13]

Key Wordsworthian abstractions such as *nature, life, sense, form,* and *power* (often capitalized quasi-personifications in Wordsworth's poetry) are associated with the living qualities of matter (Piper 73–74). The same terms were also favored by the later philosophes who argued that all matter was "living, organic and animal, that all natural objects had their own life and sensibility, and that the whole organization of the natural world was capable of intelligent purpose" (25). Wordsworth uses the word *form,* for example, as Robinet uses the term, to denote an organized body of sentient matter and not simply a visible shape or other surface structure (73).[14] A *form* in Wordsworth's rhetoric is "animal" and alive.

Wordsworth found in this line of natural philosophy the beginnings of a scientific theory that could explain his ecstatic experiences. The rhetoric of the philosophes enters Wordsworth's poetry as a way of accounting for his ecstatic experiences in a 1794 revision of "An Evening Walk." In "lines that might epitomize the whole new creed as it has developed in France" (Piper 72), it is easy to hear young Wordsworth finding his distinctive voice:

> A heart that vibrates evermore, awake
> To feeling for all forms that Life can take,
> That wider still its sympathy extends,
> And sees not any line where being ends;
> Sees sense, through Nature's rudest forms betrayed,
> Tremble obscure in fountain, rock, and shade;
> And while a secret power those forms endears
> Their social accents never vainly hears. (125–132)

The "forms" of these rocks and springs are clearly animate, as evidenced by their "social accent." What is distinctive about Wordsworth's use of French thought is that Wordsworth posits imagination as the "full response to, and implication with, the living qualities of natural objects" (Piper 2). Wordsworth's "imaginative animism," the belief that the universe is a living unity, knowable through the imagination, is more than the *animus mundi* of the Stoics and the Platonists. What is new is the belief that humanly significant communication is possible between human beings and the other forms of nature (3–5). "In short, the crucial point in the history of English Romanticism came when the concept of the 'active universe' met the developing theory of the Imagination" (2). When we read in the 1805 *Prelude* that imagination is "the prime and vital principle" (13.194), we need to hear "vital" as literally pertaining to life, not as a hyperbole for something (merely) very important.

Wordsworth became quite aware during the 1790s that his developing theory of imagination explained only moments of ecstasy. These ecstatic experiences "had not yet been tested by any attempt to explain the miseries of the world, and to those that mourn they had nothing to say" (Piper 75). Wordsworth's own disillusionment with political Godwinism motivated an ongoing concern with despair that he would eventually explore in detail in the 1814 *Excursion*. Wordsworth had tried to analyze despair in "The Baker's Cart," one of the fragments from which he developed the story of Margaret for *Excursion* 1. This fragment recounts a visit to a ruined cottage whose occupant's melancholy mood was as marked by rebellion against nature as the ecstatic mood "had been by sympathy with nature. In short, the two states were those which he [Wordsworth] would later have described as the imaginative and the fanciful" (Piper 75–76). This fragment, as Carl Woodring explains, "introduced Wordsworth's distinctive melding of self into others and of the objective into self, as when he quotes the simple words of the impoverished, incipiently mad mother" who comments, concerning a baker's cart (189): "That waggon does not care for us" (Baker's Cart" 16). The mother's mind, made "sick and extravagant" by poverty, rebelliously seeks emblems of its own despair, and misreads the forms:

> —by strong access
> Of momentary pangs driv'n to that state
> In which all past experience melts away
> And the rebellious heart to its own will
> Fashions the laws of nature. ("Baker's Cart" 21–25)

In Wordsworth then, we have not one but two kinds of "half created" nature that are reminiscent of the double perception that Milton dramatizes in Eden; the sick and extravagant creation (fallen in Milton's terms) becomes for Wordsworth the delusional work of Fancy, pathologically fashioning the laws of nature; Wordsworth's unfallen (or redeemed) nature is the true cognitive work of imagination allied with love:

> This love more intellectual cannot be
> Without imagination, which in truth
> Is but another name for absolute strength
> And clearest insight, amplitude of mind
> And reason in her most exalted mood. (1805 *Prelude* 13.166–70)

Imagination thus understood as under threat from excessive fancy is at the core of Wordsworth's cognitive-perceptual psychology. A struggle to redeem or protect imagination from excessive fancy can be discerned in his most serious poetry.¹⁵

Three Short Antipicturesque Poems

"As Bréhier said of Plotinus, all of Wordsworth seems to exist in each unit of his work," observes McFarland, and "sometimes briefer and less complex statements reveal the structure of an attitude more unequivocally than do more ambitious works" (152). Indeed, Wordsworth himself saw his entire oeuvre as one gothic cathedral. In the spirit of McFarland's shrewd observation, I would like to examine three short poems that sharply set Wordsworth's notions of nature, imagination, and fancy against the fashions and doctrines that had clustered around the picturesque by the late eighteenth century. These poems are helpful by way of preface to *Excursion* 1, "The Wanderer," a more complex and nuanced poem that will be the topic of the next chapter.

In "To M. H." (for his fianceé, Mary Hutchinson), we find the Wordsworthian ideal, the antitype of "Incipient Madness." The landscape, the cottage, the woman, and the poet-cottager are so mutually incorporated that the living "spot" (15) survives as an "image" (22) in the cottager's immortal soul. The spot to be inscribed in the cottager's thoughts is also inscribed with the beloved's name. In this way, the inscription (which is the poem itself, as well as the formally inscriptive title "To M. H.") substantiates the reciprocal, life-sustaining bond among the cottager, M. H., and the spot. The poem sets what the spot is against what it is not and never will be, an inert point of interest for the picturesque tourist-voyeur:

> The spot was made by Nature for herself;
> The travelers know it not, and 'twill remain
> Unknown to them; but it is beautiful. (15–17)

Someone who is part of nature can partake of the spot by unobtrusively *planting* a cottage and by gently incorporating the spot into his very body:

> And if a man should plant his cottage near,
> Should sleep beneath the shelter of its trees,
> And blend its waters with his daily meal,
> He would so love it, that in his death hour
> It's image would survive among his thoughts:
> And therefore, my sweet Mary, this still Nook,
> With all its beeches, we have named for You! (18–24)

"To M. H." studiously avoids framing or describing this spot as if it were a picture, because picturesque attitudes, the "cold rules of painting," are hostile to the right kind of care and attention. What can merely be seen in the Nook is throughout the poem subsumed to what can be felt and lived there. The trace of this loving incorporation survives. "To M. H.," composed between 20 and 28 December, 1799 (Hayden, Notes 525) rehearses the idea of the mutually reinforcing life of cottager, cottage, trees, and spring that would later be dramatized as Margaret's flourishing in "The Wanderer." The "M. H." spot emblematizes how the "human" and the "natural" mesh in ways precluded by the aesthetics of picturesque travel. "The travelers know it not, and 'twil remain / Unknown to them" (16–17).

Pictures and painting are not the most common topics in Wordsworth's poetry, but when the rhetoric of pictures and painting does occur, it often figures a contrast between actuality and illusion, insufficiency, or immaturity, as in "Tintern Abbey": "I cannot paint / What then I was" (76–77).

> For I have learned
> To look on nature, not as in the hour
> Of thoughtless youth; but hearing oftentimes
> The still, sad music of humanity. (88–91)[16]

The more mature way of "looking" is, significantly, figured by music instead of visual art.

The need to supplant an inadequate or immature outlook by something with a stronger social accent becomes urgent in "Elegaic Stanzas Suggested by a Picture of Peele Castle, in a Storm, Painted by Sir George Beaumont."[17] Unlike "Tintern Abbey," however, "Elegaic Stanzas" presents three distinct visions of the same literal subject, one memory and two paintings; the same castle is twice "contemplated under another relation" (264), as Wordsworth suggests in "The Sublime and the Beautiful." A "sublime" Beaumont imperiously precludes a "beautiful" pictorial fancy as well as a faded memory of life and peace.

The first three stanzas of "Elegaic Stanzas" present the castle of memory. It takes the form of an apostrophe to a living, socially significant castle, a neighbor: "I was thy neighbour once, thou rugged pile!" (1). The castle-neighbor is instinct with life: "Thy Form was sleeping on a glassy sea" (4). "Whene'er I looked, thy Image still was there; / It trembled, but it never passed away" (7–8). Since the poem is an elegy, these last lines invite comparison with the brother who was lost at sea. Two lines conclude the memory in a way that suggests that the unpaintable picture to follow, if it could exist at all, would substantiate a fanciful illusion: "I could have fancied that the mighty

Deep / Was even the gentlest of all gentle things" (11–12). The key term introducing the picture stanzas is *fancied*; the poet's transformation of his memory becomes for a few stanzas the work of Fancy. Like all explicit constructions of Fancy in Wordsworth, its attractiveness is somehow morbid and does not in fact console him. The overt artifice of the picture contrasts with the imaginatively perceived Form, the life that has in fact passed away. The poet takes pains to distinguish the remembered Form from the fancied picture—they occupy separate stanzas—precisely because the fancied and unpaintable picture figures the now unrealizable life of his brother.

The picture-making fantasy yearns to rearrange things as they are into an artificial Gilpinesque scene of fancy that adds, transplants, and changes the background:

> Ah! Then, if mine had been the painter's hand,
> To express what then I saw; and add the gleam,
> The light that never was, on sea or land,
> The consecration, and the Poet's dream;
>
> I would have planted thee, thou hoary Pile
> Amid a world how different from this! (13–18)

The poet exposes this ironically picturesque seascape as "the fond illusion of my heart" (29). "A Power is gone, which nothing can restore / A deep distress hath humanized my soul" (35–36). The loss of his brother trumps Nature, Forms, and Power.

If the elegy's unpaintable painting is a "beautiful" or "beautifully picturesque" emblem of both the lost brother and the poet's inaccessible dream of joy in nature, the contrasting painting, the actual Beaumont that is referenced in the title, is the "sublime" or "sublimely picturesque" emblem of both the overwhelming grief and the stoical resolve that supplants both the lost Power and the fanciful dream.[18] A "sublime" picture, in collusion with the poet's grief, "imperiously" precludes the "perception of beauty which that object if contemplated under another relation would have been capable of imparting" ("Sublime and Beautiful" 264).[19] The poet's grief so empowers the obtrusive qualities of the seascape that he can only experience it as in Beaumont's picture: "This sea in anger, and that dismal shore" (44) with "this huge Castle, standing [. . .] sublime" (49) in "lightning, the fierce wind, and the trampling waves" (52). Grief in collusion with the "sublime" aspect of the picture turns the poet's faded and now unfeeling memory of Peele Castle into a Fancy he would like to paint and thereby fix somehow. Such a project is, in Wordsworth's view, futile and demoralizing.

The fact that Wordsworth, who is generally suspicious of picturing, deploys pictures as contrasting emblems *both* of former joy and present grief invites us to ask whether either picture can express the true imaginative vision. Woodring is correct in noticing how strangely little there is of the "ut pictura poesis" doctrine in a poem so manifestly concerned with pictures (87). The explanation is that the poem opposes any equation of picture and poem. Instead it sets both its pictures against the verbally realized memory of the first three stanzas, before the poet tries to fix the Form in a mere picture. Only the castle of memory is alive, just as only the brother of memory is alive. Although full communication with life is emotively inaccessible to the poet, he creates some distance from grief by objectifying and thereby containing it in Beaumont's picture, from which the poet may be able to detach himself just as he was able to detach himself from the picturesque fancy.

The Beaumont painting, as read by the aggrieved poet, may be understood as not so much an epiphany of the true state of things as a product of the distempered mind, for yet another reason. Wordsworth's antithetical pictures, as emblems of sharply contrasting emotions, are thoroughly in keeping with the generic conventions of elegy. A sharp contrast between complete joy "then" and complete grief "now" is among the genre's most ancient and consistent topics (Race 92). By developing this generic topic as antithetical works of art, with each picture firmly associated with a canonical aesthetic category, Wordsworth's poem invites us to read the pictures through the lens of his own critique of the sublime and the beautiful as stable, objective aesthetic categories. In Wordsworth's own terms, we must question the truth and permanence of either picture. The lost imaginative rapport is figured by the inaccessible life of the poem's opening "Form [. . .] sleeping on a glassy sea" (4), before the distempered picturing begins.

Wordsworth most clearly links morbid melancholy with the picturesque in "Lines left upon a Seat in a Yew-tree, which stands near the lake of Esthwaite, on a desolate part of the shore, commanding a beautiful prospect." This nature inscription rehearses a didactic situation that will be more fully developed later on in the quasi-dramatic "Wanderer." As in "The Wanderer," we have a traveler halted at a bench for instruction that goes against the grain of picturesque aesthetics as well as the entire rhetorical tradition of the locus amoenus:

> Nay, Traveller! rest. This lonely Yew-tree stands
> Far from all human dwelling: what if here
> No sparkling rivulet spread the verdant herb?
> What if the bee not loves these barren boughs? (1–4)

In other words, what if Gilpin would find the scene totally devoid of "effects" amenable to picturesque composition? And what if the place is not a locus amoenus of the "amnis ibat" type, with sparkling rivulets and verdure? The inscription includes a cautionary tale about an aggrieved and fanciful man who used to sit daydreaming on the bench, "Fixing his downcast eye" on the "barren rocks, with fern and heath / And juniper sprinkled o'er" (28–32; 19). He would look up at the prospect; but, as with the *Excursion*'s tragic heroine, Margaret, his grief precludes the perception of beauty; like her, his fancy isolates him from both humanity and nature.

In "Yew-tree," alienation fed by visionary fancy contrasts with the imaginatively fed incorporation of the couple into the land that we found in "To M. H." Instead, we have a lost man who

> would sigh,
> Inly disturbed, to think that others felt
> What he must never feel: and so, lost Man!
> On visionary views would fancy feed,
> Till his eye streamed with tears. (42–46)

The yew-tree inscription itself, as well as the "beautiful" but (significantly) undescribed prospect that can be seen from its perspective, is so easy to miss on the unattractive and desolate shore. The obscure inscription and the unseen beauty together figure the life, "the one soft impulse" (7), the power that is absent from both the picturesque surface and the melancholy mind. Wordsworth would have the traveler simply stop and become quiet as the "lost Man" (44) could not:

> Yet, if the wind breathe soft, the curling waves,
> That break upon the shore, shall lull thy mind
> By one soft impulse saved from vacancy. (5–7)

Wordsworth's phrase "saved from vacancy" is somewhat obscure now, in a way that it would not have been when it was written, because both "saved" and "vacancy" are used in senses now rare. A definition of *save* from Dr. Johnson's *Dictionary* suits Wordsworth's context better than any other: "To take or embrace opportunely, so as not to lose." The "one soft impulse" is what the inscription urges the resting traveler to embrace and preserve "from vacancy" should it opportunely happen to be found there.

Wordsworth's "vacancy" is a certain open state of mind that both echoes and deepens Gilpin's "vacant" when Gilpin writes, for example, that picturesque travel can harmlessly "engage some vacant minds" (*Three Essays* 41).

Gilpin's *vacant*, like Wordsworth's *vacancy*, has no negative connotations; Gilpin is not imagining dull or stupid people. He imagines minds that are free from pressing concerns, available for some elective activity, and open to influence. Reverend Gilpin wants to provide a harmless amusement to these vacant minds, lest they make bad choices "in an age teeming with licentious pleasure" (41). As a minister, Gilpin surely has in mind such usages as the following: "How much more ought Christians to bee vacant to God alone on the Lord's day" or "vacant and liable to crimes"; or, as Dr. Johnson wrote, "when the heart is vacant to every fresh form of delight" or "vacant to every object and sensible of every impulse." Wordsworth's "vacancy" resonates with the perceptual, religious, and moral connotations of these seventeenth- and eighteenth-century usages that were still close to those of the Latin cognate. Lucretius, for example, in an apostrophe to the reader in the proem to *On the Nature of Things*, uses "vacuas" in the same spirit that Wordsworth uses "vacancy." Before revealing the true design of the universe, Lucretius asks for "open ears" ("vacuas auris") and a quiet unprejudiced mind (6; 1.50–53; my trans.). In "Yew-tree," vacancy is a state of accessibility to the positive and negative spiritual influence of the spot, whether the "one soft impulse" of illumined vision or the picturesque and melancholy temptations the prospect offers to the fanciful, distempered eye.

"Yew-tree" fuses melancholic and picturesque fancies and combats them both by appealing to "the holy forms / Of young imagination," the living organs of true perception and cognition:

> If Thou be one whose heart the holy forms
> Of young imagination have kept pure,
> Stranger! Henceforth be warned; and know that pride,
> Howe'er disguised in its own majesty,
> Is littleness; that he who feels contempt
> For any living thing, hath faculties
> Which he has never used; that thought with him
> Is in its infancy. (48–55)

We should not be surprised that for Wordsworth, pride is the food of fancy and the enemy of imagination as an organ of true perception and communication. Milton's proud Satan is the immediate literary model for the lost man's fallen consciousness and desolate world. The late eighteenth-century philosophes countered human pride from another direction that also persuaded Wordsworth. In their quest for an evolutionary theory that would counter Newton's "universe of death," they insisted that all matter is animal, sentient, and purposive. As Diderot puts it in *Rêve d'Alembert*, "From the elephant to the flea, from the flea to the living, sensitive molecule there is not a point in all nature which does not suffer and rejoice" (qtd. in Piper 24).

Wordsworth has no confidence at all that "cold rules" of the sort Gilpin advocates can prepare or "vacate" the mind, as "Yew-tree" urges, so that the imagination sees into the life of such forms as molecules and fleas or "desolate" landscapes, but he is not satisfied with merely dismissing what does not work. In *The Excursion* Wordsworth sets himself the more ambitious task of trying to dramatize in a travel story just what does nurture and educate the imagination. Wordsworth transfigures Gilpin's impatient picturesque traveler, all too prone to distempering fancies, into a halted wanderer with an imaginative response to the living Forms postulated by the philosophers. The old Wanderer has long since been such a patient traveler; and the young Poet, along with the reader, is supposed to learn how to become one.

CHAPTER 5

The Visionary Eye: Wordsworth's Antipicturesque *Excursion*

> An author's paramount charge is the cure of souls, to the subjection, and if need be to the exclusion, of the picturesque.
> —Henry James, Miss Prescott's "Azarian"

Wordsworth's 1814 *Excursion,* firmly embedded in the classical tradition of place ecphrasis that informed Milton's Eden, self-consciously explores the Greco-Roman rhetorical theory of image and emotion that underpins that tradition. But Wordsworth surely contributed as much to the tradition as he takes from it. The very word *loco-descriptive* (now usually written without the hyphen) was coined by Wordsworth in his Preface to the 1815 *Poems* (374), after he had utterly assimilated and transformed the species of classical ecphrasis to which he gave this now-standard English name. *The Excursion* melds the allusive blank-verse nature poem as developed by the eighteenth-century Miltonists, the graveyard meditation as practiced by Young and Gray, the descriptive-didactic georgics of Thomson, the British pastoral in modern dress that Ambrose Philips tried to make respectable, and the picturesque travel essay as popularized by Gilpin. While Wordsworth retained many of the salient features of all these genres, he firmly relocated the center of discourse away from the place being described to the human minds perceiving and participating in the place, as inhabitants or visitors.[1] My aim in this chapter is to clarify how vivid descriptions produce the psychological complexity often felt in "The Wanderer," the first book of *The Excursion,* and to offer a more satisfactory account of what still remains its central interpretive problem: the Wanderer's lesson, the poet's reception of it, and the calm shared response to Margaret's story that poet and Wanderer achieve at the end. A fresh reading of *Excursion* 1 may in turn make the rest of *The Excursion,* a poem much admired by Lamb, Keats, Shelley, and the Victorians, more accessible to a twenty-first-century audience.

From travel writers like Gilpin, Wordsworth takes as a framing rubric the excursion or pleasure trip to a place of interest. The word *excursion,* which had for more than a century meant a round-trip journey from home or any other specific place, had by the time Wordsworth chose his title only as recently as 1779 acquired its specialized and entirely benign meaning of "pleasure travel." The root metaphor is *running out,* and most of the early English usages of the word have some connotation of speed or aggression, as in the very old and still current usage *military excursion.* In any case, speed made the picturesque tourist possible: faster vehicles, faster horses, better highways, maps, tour books, and other efficiencies made travel sufficiently pleasant and methodical for the first time for many (Piggott 122–124). One way to gain some purchase on what is happening in this poem is to imagine Wordsworth transfiguring Gilpin's impatiently selective picturesque tourists by slowing them down until they develop responses to places that are *at the same time* expressive emblems of the human mind participating in them. Locodescription functions as dual figuration: mind figures place, and place figures mind, interactively.

Wordsworth's method is excursive in an even more complicated way. The adjective *excursive,* very common throughout the eighteenth century, would later in the century lose its sense of departure and return and mean "capable of, or addicted to, varied flights; having a wide range of pursuits or interests" or "apt to diverge from a definite course; prone to stray; erratic; digressive," as first attested by James Thomson in 1744 with the phrase "your Eye excursive roams" (*Spring* 956). *The Excursion* roams and stops, both as a literal five-day trip and as rhetoric. Bruce Graver aptly points out that the "title itself is derived from the Latin term for rhetorical digression, *excursio,* a fact strangely absent from critical discussion of a poem that celebrates 'the mind's excursive power'" ("Oratorical" 95).

Wordsworth elevates excursiveness in and out of places and genres into a unifying principle of composition that might be called excursive frustration. The poem arouses, frustrates, suspends, and tries to resolve a wide range of generic locodescriptive expectations from pastoral, georgic, travel writing, and so forth, into a new unity. Witness how Annabel Patterson discusses the poem as georgic, Geoffrey Durant as elegy, Charles Lamb as descriptive and didactic; William Hazlitt "as a philosophical pastoral poem—as a scholastic romance" (326); and all of them are right. Woodring is perhaps more right than others when he calls *The Excursion* (as well as Byron's *Don Juan*) "a modern reconstitution of the epic" (194), the genre that enfolds so many others. Wordsworth's assimilation of genres into an epic of the mind, a "somewhat allegorical objectification of an interior struggle" (Woodring 185), is characteristic of Romantic art and gives expression to Romantic ideas of mind and nature as too lush and complex to be adequately expressed or represented through conventional forms.

Woodring's observation that the poem is "somewhat allegorical" reflects a perception that the work is structured by a related set of tenorless vehicles, the vivid place descriptions that dictate the poem's slow pace. It is structured like Horace's "ship of state," but instead of a ship we have locations, and instead of the state we have the human heart. This allegorical quality will not go away, even if one agrees with Alan Liu (as I do not) that "*there is no self or mind. Therefore, there is no Imagination.* What there 'is' is history" (39; Liu's italics). The need for allegorical interpretation remains, and even the need for mind or self remains. In Liu's reading, as in any reading that appeals to "ideology" or "false consciousness" as the key to interpretation, the tenorless vehicles figure forth acts of the mind, the poet's complex feats of self-delusion. Although there is general agreement that self-delusion is indeed thematic in Romantic poetry, there is heated disagreement over the nature of the reality against which self-delusion asserts itself. *The Excursion*'s bold experiment is to open up and enact this very problem, with human characters speaking in a landscape of fluctuating human significance.

The Poem as Therapeutic Psychodrama

The Excursion's psychodramatic structure recurs to that of medieval allegory, wherein "extensive dialogue between hero and spiritual guide" explicates the "visionary mysteries" (Piehler, "Allegory" 100). *The Excursion*'s visionary mysteries, boldly outlined in the "Prospectus," concern the holiness of the things of this world:

> —Beauty—a living Presence of the earth,
> Surpassing the most fair ideal Forms
> Which craft of delicate Spirits hath composed
> From earth's materials—waits upon my steps;
> Pitches her tents before me as I move,
> An hourly neighbour. (xii)

The hero is a young poet, and the spiritual guide is a visionary Wanderer under whose tutelage the poet achieves the desired apocalypse of consciousness as "A simple produce of the common day" ("Prospectus" xii).[2] The poem is as classical as it is Romantic. It resonates with the many classical genres that informed Wordsworth's imaginative assimilation of eighteenth century and earlier descriptive practice going all the way back to Virgil. But it also recapitulates literary history in characteristic Romantic fashion, as intimate participation in natural processes.[3] This mixture of the classic and Romantic suits, as we shall see, Wordsworth's epic plan to disclose and teach everything he knows, but by a very indirect method. He brings topics from many genres into conversation and juxtaposition, and thus experimentally transforms them, to see if new contexts can spark and awaken knowledge in the characters and in the reader. Hazlitt could see that even if such a grandiose plan fell short, the lapse was a magnificent one; he suggests that the poem, "this most original and powerful performance," is a monumental ruin "like one of those stupendous but half-finished structures, which have been suffered to molder into decay, because the cost and labor attending them exceeded their use or beauty" (325). Hazlitt's judgment gives some indication of how its excursive structure has made the poem's reception problematic from the beginning.

Charles Lamb, another positive reviewer who worried about the poem's reception, focused on its depiction of rapturous emotion: "A writer, who would be popular, must timidly coast the shore of prescribed sentiment and sympathy," writes Lamb:

> If he has had the good fortune to be bred in the midst of the most magnificent objects of creation, he must not have given away his heart to them; or if he have, he must conceal his love, or not carry his expressions of it beyond that point of rapture, which the occasional tourist thinks it not overstepping decorum to betray, or the limit which that gentlemanly spy upon Nature, the picturesque traveller, has vouchsafed to countenance. He must do this, or be content to be thought an Enthusiast. ("Wordsworth's 'Excursion'" 110)

Lamb correctly understood that Wordsworth's experiential grounding in an active and expressive universe was on a collision course not merely with the manners expected of polite tourists but, more seriously, with institutionalized religion. The problem of how to square the epiphanies of his youth with his Christianity dogged Wordsworth, too, and motivated some of the most ill-advised changes he made to *The Excursion* later on.

This problem was among several factors that contributed to the decline in the poem's popularity. After discovering the magnificent *Prelude,* the twentieth century all but turned its back on *The Excursion,* although Charles Lamb's review had distinguished it as "without competition among our didactive and descriptive verse" (106), Keats had welcomed it as one of "three things to rejoice at in this Age" (qtd. in Woodring 181); and, as Stephen Gill documents in *Wordsworth and the Victorians, The Excursion* finally secured Wordsworth's fame among such scientists, philosophers, writers, and critics as Charles Darwin, John Stuart Mill, George Eliot, and Leslie Stephen. Jonathan Wordsworth rightly reminds us that the 1814 *Excursion* was for the most part favorably reviewed and that even the usual crowd of negative reviewers often "showed a grumpy awareness of the poem's stature" (Introduction 2), as did Merivale when he admitted that the poem has "innate qualities of genius" which not even Wordsworth has the "power wholly to conceal" (128). Still, Francis Jeffrey's fatal curse in the *Edinburgh Review*, "This will never do" (1), has become, as Kenneth Johnston puts it, "posterity's favorite excuse for not reading the poem" (*Wordsworth and "The Recluse"* 334). Jeffrey's review not only foreshadowed typical twentieth-century views of *The Excursion*, it also inaugurated many later, more comprehensive "narratives of Wordsworth's poetic decline" (Hickey 1). "The case of Mr. Wordsworth [. . .] is now manifestly hopeless" writes Jeffrey, "altogether incurable, and beyond the power of criticism" (2).

Not that Jeffrey had ever been a great admirer of an earlier, more healthy Wordsworth. He panned the 1807 *Poems* in the *Edinburgh Review:* "trash"; "traits of delicate feeling and original fancy [. . .] obscured in the mass of childishness and insipidity"; an "open violation of the established laws of poetry" (231). He quotes the "Intimations" ode at length for particularly dishonorable mention as "the most illegible and unintelligible part of the publication" (227). The problem Jeffrey has with *The Excursion* is the problem he has with most of what Wordsworth wrote. *The Excursion* is, so to speak, Wordsworth in spades: "Rapturous mysticism which eludes all comprehension" (10). "Mr. Wordsworth delineates only feelings—and all his adventures are of the heart" (19), continues Jeffrey—a fair enough paraphrase of Wordsworth's self-professed aim as expressed in the Preface to *Lyrical Ballads,* where "the feeling developed therein developed gives importance to the action and situation, and not the action and situation to the feeling" (283). The "Prospectus" published in the Preface to the 1814 *Excursion* even more decisively reminds Wordsworth's readers of his poetic enterprise: "Of the individual Mind that keeps her own / Inviolate retirement [. . .] / I sing:—'fit audience let me find though few'!" (xi). This poet's topic, as Jeffrey well knows, is "the Mind of Man / My haunt, and the main region of my Song" ("Prospectus" xii). "And if," continues Wordsworth,

> I [. . .] with the thing
> Contemplated, describe the Mind and Man
> Contemplating; and who, and what he was,
> The transitory Being that beheld
> This Vision, [. . .]
> Be not this labor useless. (xiii–xiv)

Because the frequently anthologized "Prospectus" is so well known apart from its original context in the Preface to *The Excursion,* it is instructive to remember that Wordsworth published it there as the aesthetic manifesto by which he sought the poem to be judged. Notwithstanding Jeffrey's almost perfect blindness to Wordsworth's enterprise, Gill in 1998 summed up Jeffrey's critical acumen as

> a consistent and not undiscriminating probing of all the most difficult aspects of Wordsworth's poetic project—his metaphysics, his choice of "low and rustic life" for subject-matter, his egotism, his diction, his attitude to learning, civilization, refinement, to "society" in short. (18)

Gill's choice of "difficult aspects" shows how seamlessly the conservative Jeffrey and his "established laws" could be appropriated by radical twentieth-century desacralizers of Wordsworth as Victorian culture hero. What was difficult for an eighteenth-century mind became difficult again in the twentieth, after being less problematic in the nineteenth. Fortunately for Wordsworth, he found "fit audience" for the *Excursion* in contemporaries more sympathetic than the cynical and witty Francis Jeffrey, whose genius for invective is what I think compels us all to keep quoting him.

Hazlitt, whose taste was another of the great contemporary things Keats rejoiced in, carefully registered how Wordsworth had internalized place description. His review praised what Jeffrey condemned:

> It is less a poem on the country, than on the love of the country. It is not so much a description of natural objects, as of the feelings associated with them [. . .]. [Wordsworth] does not present the reader with a lively succession of images or incidents, but paints the outgoings of his own heart. (326)

After Lamb had received a copy of *The Excursion* from Wordsworth, he wrote back on 9 August 1814 that reading it had been "A day in heaven [. . .]. My having known the story of Margaret [. . .] did not make her reappearance less fresh" (*Letters* 95). Lamb's review in October 1814 was just as enthusiastic: "the stream, the torrent and the stirring leaf—seem not merely to suggest associations of deity, but to be a kind of speaking communication with it" (102). Lamb understands that Wordsworth has described the active universe of eighteenth-century theory: "In his poetry nothing in nature is dead. Motion is synonymous with life" (103).

Lamb's review instances how the Wanderer describes his participation in the life of Margaret's forsaken spring:

>   Beside yon Spring I stood,
> And eyed its waters till we seemed to feel
> One sadness, they and I. For them a bond
> Of brotherhood is broken: time has been

> When, every day, the touch of human hand
> Dislodged the natural sleep that binds them up
> In mortal stillness; and they minister'd
> To human comfort. (27)[4]

Lamb had heard a version of this description at Nether Stowey during the summer of 1797, some 17 years before its publication as the first book of *The Excursion*.[5] The frequently revised material that Lamb heard and that eventually found its way into "The Wanderer" is seminal to Wordsworth's poetic enterprise, and this helps account for how often the poet rethought and reworked it. By March 1798, not long after Lamb's visit, Coleridge and Wordsworth understood the ruined cottage material as the seed from which Wordsworth could grow a great philosophical poem called *The Recluse*. On 6 March 1798, Wordsworth wrote to James Tobin that *The Recluse* was to contain "most of the knowledge of which I am possessed. My object is to give pictures of Nature, Man, and Society. Indeed I know not any thing which will not come within the scope of my plan" (*Letters* 1:212). *The Recluse* was never completed.[6] But in 1814 Wordsworth published *The Excursion, Being a Portion of The Recluse, a Poem*. In the Preface he explains that it is the second part of a three-part project. The first two parts

> have the same kind of relation to each other as [. . .] the Anti-chapel [*sic*] has to the body of a gothic Church. [. . .] His minor pieces, which have long been before the public, when they shall be properly arranged, will be found by the attentive Reader to have such connection with the main Work as may [. . .] be likened to the little Cells, Oratories, and sepulchral Recesses, ordinarily included in those Edifices. (1814, viii–ix)

The first part, the antechapel, would be the much-revised 1850 *Prelude;* but we have an initial sketch of such a poet's biography in the Wanderer's biography in *Excursion* 1.

The Excursion differs considerably from most of Wordsworth's other poetry. From one perspective the core of *The Excursion* is stories, the story of Margaret being only the first of some 22 elegiac tales told during a five-day excursion in the country. From another perspective, the core of *The Excursion* is not so much the stories as the drama of storytelling as active communication between storyteller and audience. In the 1814 Preface, Wordsworth explains how his procedure in *The Excursion* differs from other parts of the planned *Recluse* in that it does not "consist chiefly of meditations in the Author's own Person"; rather, "the intervention of Characters speaking is employed, and something of a dramatic form adopted" (x). Wordsworth immediately adds a comment that is crucial for our interpretation of any didactic message we wish to take away from the drama:

> It is not the Author's intention formally to announce a system: it was more animating to him to proceed in a different course; and if he shall succeed in conveying to the mind clear thoughts, lively images, and strong feelings, the Reader will have no difficulty in extracting the system for himself. (x)

Wordsworth had more explicitly expounded the same educational philosophy, that the readers's task is to extract knowledge on their own, in the 1809 "Reply to Mathetes":[7]

> There is a life and spirit in knowledge which we extract from truths scattered for the benefit of all, and which the mind, by its own activity, has appropriated to itself—a life and a spirit, which is seldom found in knowledge communicated by formal and direct precepts, even when they are exalted and endeared by reverence and love for the Teacher. (108)

Wordsworth, in replying to "Mathetes," trusts that the assistance the pupil requests will come less from the advice he gives in his letter than it "will in course of time flow naturally from my labours, in a manner that will best serve him" (108).

On 22 May 1815, Wordsworth wrote to Coleridge in a similar vein, telling his friend that he intended *The Excursion* "to put the commonplace truths, of human affections especially, in an interesting point of view; and rather to remind men of their knowledge, as it lurks inoperative and unvalued in their own minds" (*Letters* 3:238). Indeed, the rationale for dialogue in *The Excursion* is to dramatize the possibilities and limitations of indirectly and informally awakening latent knowledge; that is, the possibility of anamnesis or "reminding" through poetic labor. Wordsworth confided his psychotherapeutic aspirations to John Wilson in a letter of 7 June 1802: "A great Poet ought [. . .] to a certain degree to rectify men's feelings, to give them new compositions of feeling, to render their feelings more sane pure and permanent, in short, more consonant to nature, that is, to eternal nature, and the great moving spirit of things" (*Letters* 1: 355).

For the most part, the "stories" the characters tell each other are vivid descriptions that figure mental activity, whence the frustration of critics like Jeffrey who complain about the "profuse and irrepressible wordiness" (1) of descriptions that figure forth adventures of the heart. To borrow Kermode's metaphor, Jeffrey is an "impious intruder" into a matter he does not understand, a psychodrama set in the Wordsworthian "haunt," the shared human mind of the depicted characters and the participating reader. The voices of one Wordsworthian mind reminds itself of its knowledge, with main characters such as the Wanderer (and later the Pastor) as types of the authoritative visionary reminder and with the young narrating poet (and later the despondent Solitary) as types of the "remindee" who extracts or fails to extract the life and spirit of their own inoperable and unvalued knowledge.

"The Wanderer" is a tale within a tale with two interacting narrators. Wanderer and poet relate sequences of descriptive vignettes that set the conventions of picturesque locodescription and picturesque touring against the visionary nature poem as recreated by Wordsworth. In its persistent concern with what needs to be said about a place, and to what end, it coasts away from Charles Lamb's "shore of prescribed sentiment and sympathy" toward a world Wordsworth describes in the 1805 *Prelude:*

> in life's everyday appearances
> I seemed [. . .] to have sight
> Of a new world, a world, too, that was fit
> To be transmitted and made visible
> To other eyes [. . .]. (12.369–73)

The outermost frame, the young poet's tale, dramatizes just such a transmission of a new world seen in life's everyday appearances.

The young poet recounts his progress, under the tutelage of a retired itinerant pedlar whose history he expounds, from agitated discomfort in the face of natural processes—death, decay, and punishingly hot weather—to "a state of wisdom that enables him to see into the moving form of things and to accept as an end in itself the deep tranquility at the heart of change" (Rudy 156). The pedlar-Wanderer, by transforming the young poet through telling the tale of Margaret and her ruined cottage, models the process of poetry achieving its aim in the mind of an ideally receptive audience. The main action of the framing narrative is simply this: the aspiring poet meets the Wanderer and hears a story.

For the reader, the tale of Margaret told to the responding young man unfolds as if in real time. We witness a characteristically Wordsworthian depiction of rural life as it is being composed by a Wanderer in communion with a familiar landscape seen through the medium of his memories. Memory also dominates the young poet's framing narrative, for no sooner does he see the Wanderer than he gives a long account of what he personally remembers about him and what he has learned about the old man's more distant past—his family, his youth, and his formative experiences.

The first part of the young poet's frame tale describes his approach to the cottage and then digresses into a biographical sketch of the Wanderer's developing mind. Although the long account of the Wanderer's education is considered by many to be a digression that spoils a more strongly desired emphasis on Margaret's story, Hayden is certainly right to point out, as several others have noted, that separating the two robs "the poem as a whole of its psychological complexity" (Notes, *Selected Poems* 551). He also observes that the Wanderer's role as an educator who credibly instills "natural wisdom" disappears entirely when the two pieces are severed, with the unacceptable result that the pedlar's tranquil reaction to Margaret's sufferings is simply puzzling and unmotivated (Notes 551). My aim is to build on and amplify observations such as Hayden's by clarifying how the cumulative pattern of descriptive figuration brings into focus what the Wanderer has to teach the poet, and how the poet learns the lesson.

First Excursion: The Life of the Wanderer

I would like to begin approaching this problem by looking at the pedlar's biography within the context of the whole, but from a slightly different angle: as one of *The Excursion*'s significant antipicturesque excursions, an excursion into memory. The imaginative arts of memory are, of course, such a common theme in Wordsworth that whenever a character begins remembering, and keeps remembering little vignettes for hundreds of lines, we have good reason to suspect that the figurative energies of these recollections have something to do with when they begin, how they end, and what comes afterward. Here, the recollections begin after describing in an emotionally engaging way a definite topographical spot to which the narrator returns his attention after the recollection. He makes an excursion in the oldest departure-and-return sense of the word. But he apprehends this place differently through the medium of memory, thereby destabilizing and complicating the significance of a place (like Milton's Eden) whose basic character varies with the perceptual artistry of those who experience and describe it. While this excursive structure dramatizes Wordsworth's visionary memory, the particulars of the recollected history provide a model of the growth of the ideal poet and the ideal reader as seen through the reverent eyes of a young man who presents himself as knowing something about literature. His portrait of the pedlar provides a context both for interpreting his tale and—since the portrait is drawn by this particularly open and receptive young man—for evaluating how the story of Margaret could have the effect that it evidently does have on the young man. For it will turn out that the Wanderer's successive vignettes of Margaret's decay have points of contact with the poet's vignettes of the Wanderer's growth that help ground the shared compassion the two men find.

The Excursion begins at high noon on a hot summer day: "Southward, the landscape indistinctly glared / Through a pale steam" (3), observes the young man. Then, contemplating what lies in the opposite direction from this discomfiting and uncertain landscape, he describes a distant contrasting landscape, the Downs. The prospect, dappled with atmospheric effects that nicely situate it between bright beauty and the ascending and brooding sublime, is as picturesque as Gilpin might have desired and quite as static as a picture. As if sketched in by an artist, the spotty shadows lay "determined," "unmoved," and with sunshine "interposed" (3). The young poet introduces a further level of picturesque indirection by fancying that the set piece is seen by someone else at ease there "who on the soft cool moss / Extends his careless limbs along the front / Of some huge cave" that casts "an ample shade, / Where the wren warbles," looking out to a distant "scene" (3–4).

The imagined locus amoenus is Virgilian, with a man watching at graceful ease, "viridi proiectus in antro," "stretched out in a green cave" (*Eclogues* 1.75; my trans.). Wordsworth discusses this very passage in "Essay Supplementary": "In the first Eclogue of Virgil, the shepherd, thinking of the time when he is to take leave of his farm, thus addresses his goats:—'Non ego vos posthac viridi projectus in antro / Dumosa pendere procul de rupe videbo'" (377) ["Stretched out in a green cave, I shall no longer watch you *hanging* from a bushy cliff".] What interests Wordsworth is Virgil's imaginative *pendere,* "hanging," because it shows us how the speaker's "mind, in its activity, for its own gratification contemplates [the goats] as hanging" when of course they are not literally (377–378). The metaphoric *pendere* is crucial, for, according to Wordsworth, Virgil's imagination is here

> employed upon images in a conjunction by which they modify each other [. . .]. The apparently perilous situation of the goat, hanging upon the shaggy precipice, is contrasted with that of the shepherd contemplating it from the seclusion of the cavern in which he lies stretched at ease and in security. Take these images separately, and how unaffecting the picture compared with that produced by their being thus connected with, and opposed to, each other! (379–380)

Wordsworth applies this lesson learned from Virgil when he establishes a valedictory antithesis of his own in "The Wanderer."

Like Virgil's shepherd taking leave of his farm, Wordsworth takes leave of imitating Virgil, and with comparable subtlety. Wordsworth doubly frames the poetic reminiscence of Virgil's tender lines within a distancing gaze-within-a-gaze, then has his poet-narrator awaken into a more perilous landscape. As soon as the young poet constructs the rhetorical landscape, he realizes he is not there; he is someplace else experiencing something else.

Wordsworth makes this point dramatically by abruptly breaking off the reverie: the young man all at once abandons his visually stimulated fancy to describe how his body is experiencing the present landscape. He abandons his gaze-within-a-gaze, no longer looking into the distance while entertaining a fantasy about someone else out there doing the same thing, and replaces the visual and doubly distant rhetorical landscape with the tactile and immediate. The only visual descriptor in the passage, the phrase "bare wide" (4), serves to mark the landscape's lack of visual interest. How the ground looks, whether brown or green or dappled, is subjugated to how it feels, both physically and emotionally. The turf is "slippery." It "baffled" his "languid" steps (4). The emotional body is puzzled, depressed, and weak in the face of what feels like a major assault by insects. The "host" of insects is both enemy army and miniature heavenly host, nature ironically sacralized and in a pestering mood (4).

The young man finds his refuge, "a Grove, / The wished-for Port to which my steps were bound" (4). The word "port" suggests a harbor, shelter, or haven as well as an opening or gateway into a different—and, we expect, refreshingly shady—physical and emotional place. But, again, the young man's and our expectations are frustrated. The desired tree-shade is "gloom / Spread by a brotherhood of lofty elms" (4). The personified elms seem intent on perpetuating the young man's discomfort; the price of their shade is a more somber mood that is only deepened further by the personified walls that the young man finds "amid the gloom" (4): "a roofless Hut; four naked walls / That stared upon each other!" (4). Rooflessness exposes the lack of refuge here, and "hut" is among the starkest habitational terms, the word "cottage" stripped down. The young man's ambivalent port, like Virgil's Carthaginian harbor, has a double character as both shady refuge and enclosing tomb. The staring naked structure, a specter of what will be disclosed about the linked destruction of an abandoned woman's psyche and her world, is a ghost of the past animated as narrative foreshadowing.

Given the mood the place evokes, it is not surprising that the young man looks around away from the hut. And, in any case, he has come to see the old man, not the old hut; but the lack of continued interest in the ruin is also an emphatic antipicturesque gesture. Nothing, of course, is more canonically picturesque than ruins in a landscape. For a Gilpin-trained tourist, the site would stimulate picturesque rearrangement into a suitable sketch. Instead, the young man focuses on an old man sleeping on a bench, and the feelings evoked by the old man (not the ruin) begin to transform both the site and the young man's emotional state. The old man's comfort contrasts with the young man's discomfort. Unlike the young man, he simply fits in; and the young man is happy to have found "Him whom I sought; a Man of reverend age [...] upon the Cottage bench, / Recumbent in the shade, as if asleep" (4–5). The description actualizes the pastoral Virgilian fantasy "viridi proiectus in antro," "stretched out in a green cave" (*Eclogues* 1.75) of *The Excursion*'s opening lines. The word "recumbent" intensifies the allusion to Virgil by echoing the first line of the same *Eclogue,* "patulae recubans sub tegmine fagi," "lying down under the shelter of a spreading beech," placing what was the poet's distant literary fantasy in the actual here and now: graceful ease becomes "A simple produce of the common day" ("Prospectus" xii). Just as Wordsworth has quietly domesticated Virgil, the old man has quietly domesticated the place and made himself vulnerable to it by making a habitational refuge of what is now the "cottage" bench.[8] Wordsworth dramatizes the old man's meditative repose, his being at ease as if asleep, by leaving him alone on the bench for a few hundred lines while the young man turns introspectively to his own memories of his friend. This turn away from the outwardly visual description toward recollection—a turn even from a full visualization of the sought-after friend—is another antipicturesque move. Memory takes the young man away for a while from his discomfort, and away from the easy diversion of a picturesque scene. Memory creates the proper medium through which the reader and the young man later "see" the old man and the landscape and properly hear his tale.

At this point, poet and Wanderer are both halted travelers. The reader is halted too. The excursion into the old man's history frustrates the reader's expectation of a charming tale about an ominously fascinating place. It repeats on a larger scale the excursive frustration established at the beginning when the Virgilian refuge was presented as if a mirage, only to be displaced by the actual gloom and fatigue. Wordsworth insists on stopping on the spot, on dramatically extending the reader's stoppage into a real-time parallel of the young man's patient hesitation and the old man's meditation.

Wordsworth's travelers, invariably slow-moving pedestrians frequently stopping for rest and contemplation, need to be imagined against the new late eighteenth-century fashion for the speedier "excursion," the pleasure-trip that gives the poem its title. At this point, Wordsworth stops the implied reader, Lamb's "gentlemanly spy upon nature," and transforms Gilpin's impatiently selective quester for the picturesque into a halted wanderer without a paint brush or a travel journal. The reader will need a moment of patience to settle receptively into the spot and become open to what it has to say. The Wanderer has long since been such a traveler; and the poet, along with the reader, is supposed to learn how to become one. The method is excursive, but when the poet and the reader return to this spot, the prospect will be different. This moment of patience is informed by the poet's biographical sketch, presented as descriptive vignettes of successive stages of life.

The young man's account of the pedlar's development provides a model of how the ideal poet prepares the mind to receive what nature communicates, a model of the ideal poet's effect on his audience, and a richly textured context for evaluating and interpreting the old man's melancholy tale. Having found the old man, the sought-after port, the parched young man's first refreshment is not water but a memory of something waterlike. He remembers as a boy asking his friend for "Old songs—the product of his native hills" (6). The phrase establishes the organic link between nature, folk tradition, and the old man's art. The young man likens the songs to water, himself to a parched meadow, the old man to a farmer skilled at irrigation. An elaborate agricultural metaphor sets abstract economic rhetoric—"skillful distribution," "industrious" (6)—against the flowing water to point up the careful combination of the deliberate and the spontaneous that forms the old man's "pure discourse" (7). Purity and refreshment is assured by the old man's care of and control over the Wordsworthian spontaneous overflow.

The biographical sketch develops the antithetical pattern of this initial agricultural metaphor. The pedlar's early education moved productively, and with a certain tension, between reading and nature. He tended cattle on the hills in the summer, went to school in the winter. In response to nature, the young pedlar cultivated an "active power to fasten images / Upon his brain" (10). His brooding internalized what he remembered seeing, giving "pictured lines" the "the liveliness of dreams" (10–11), a process well attested by ancient rhetoricians. "The Wanderer possesses exactly the imaginative capability that Quintilian believed necessary for eloquent speech," writes Graver. Quintilian's *visiones* are the Wanderer's lively dreams" ("Oratorical" 98). In a passage that was so much a favorite of Wordsworth's that he mounted part of it, "pectus est enim quod disertos facit et vis mentis" (translation italicized below), as epigraph to the 1802 and 1805 versions of *Lyrical Ballads,* Quintilian explicitly links *phantasiai* to the untutored speaker:

> We must therefore form in our minds those images [*visiones*] [. . .] called *phantasiai,* and keep before our eyes and take to our hearts everything that we shall be speaking about—persons and questions, hopes and fears. *It is the heart and the power of the mind that makes us eloquent.* This is why even the unskilled, so long as they are stirred by some emotion, are not short of words. (379–381; 10.7.15)

Wordsworth also quoted from this passage in the letter to Fox that accompanied a complimentary copy of the second edition of *Lyrical Ballads*

(*Letters* 1:315), explaining that the two poems "The Brothers" and "Michael" had "emboldened" him to call himself a poet (313). They

> were written with a view to shew that men who do not wear fine cloaths can feel deeply. [. . .]. The poems are faithful copies from nature; and I hope [. . .] that they may excite profitable sympathies in many kind and good hearts, and may in some degree enlarge our feeling of reverence for our species. (315)

The pedlar, too, makes "faithful copies from nature" with the goal of helping the poet to enlarge his "feeling of reverence" for Margaret and the others of our species.

The pedlar's imaginative participation in nature and in the folk arts closest to nature gave him, on the one hand, "small need of books" (11). But a few lines later the other side of the educational pattern appears again, and with considerable emphasis: "But eagerly he read, and read again, / Whate'er the Minister's old Shelf supplied" (12). The importance of these lines and those that follow is considerable, especially for readers inclined to suppose that Wordsworth always preferred to read the book of nature rather than the books made by people. One reason for this misapprehension is that modern readers generally pay little or no attention to *The Excursion*, one of the most influential works published in the poet's lifetime. The impression left by the works widely read today is that the injunction in "The Tables Turned" to "close up these barren leaves" (30) of man-made books and study instead "the lore which Nature brings" (25) was Wordsworth's last and best word on the subject. But it was not. One must keep in mind that "The Tables Turned" was written in early 1798 while the poet was engaged in a strenuous course of self-imposed reading (Butler and Green 8–10).

The pedlar, we learn, is not only literate; he is in many respects learned. He reads Milton with pleasure and insight, and in *Excursion* 4 he discourses widely on ancient Greek and Middle Eastern mythology (171–180). In the same conversation he reminds the despondent Solitary that "treasure lies" within the "silent chambers" of books. "These hoards of truth you can unlock at will" (166). Indeed, the Wanderer's erudition is such that Jeffrey complained about it in his negative review, arguing that it rendered the character of the pedlar ridiculous and unbelievable. Later on in *Excursion* 9 the Wanderer corrects the too-picturesque biography offered by the young poet in *Excursion* 1 by confessing that, as a child, he had to struggle through poverty and ignorance like "a Bird that breaks / Through a strong net, and mounts upon the wind, / Though with her plumes impaired" (395).

Nature is simply not enough for the rural populace: they need universal education in literacy as well. Children should not, the Wanderer argues,

> be forced
> To drudge through weary life without the aid
> Of intellectual implements and tools;
> [. . .]
> A servile Band among the lordly free! (401)

Wordsworth obviously went out of his way to make sure that his natural man should also be a bookish man. This characterization shows unmistakably that Wordsworth valued the written word just as highly as the observation of nature. The Wanderer is equally open to both.

As a youth he was often drawn to dark and serious matters: "The life and death of Martyrs, who sustained, / With will inflexible, those fearful pangs / [. . .] / Of Persecution" (12). Illustrated fairy tales, just the sort of literature Wordsworth and Coleridge actually did endorse for educating a child's imagination, had an uncanny appeal: "Romance of Giants, chronicle of Fiends, / Profuse in garniture of wooden cuts / Strange and uncouth" (12). Active remembering, "the active power to fasten images," first introduced to describe the pedlar's deepening mental impressions of nature, now extends to the verbal and visual impressions in books. The boy's imagination animated the ghostly figures with "dire faces" and "ghostly shanks" in a ruined book that is "straggling," "torn and incomplete" (12), as if both book and figures were the ruined bodies of the persecuted martyrs who fascinate the boy, just as later Margaret will fascinate him. The passage begins to forge the link we will find between ruined person and ruined artifact, Margaret and cottage, that was foreshadowed near the beginning of the poem by the naked staring walls. It reestablishes the somber mood of that first encounter with the roofless hut; but here, strangely, the topic is the young pedlar's reading.

The idea of reading as an imaginative process that animates both text and reader is further reinforced by a complicated allusion to Milton, one of Wordsworth's poet-heroes. The mention of an incomplete volume that "left half-told the preternatural tale" (12) alludes, as Hayden points out (550), to the half-told story in Milton's ode to Goddess Melancholy, "Il Penseroso":

> But, O sad Virgin, that thy power
> Might raise Musaeus from his bower
> Or bid the soul of Orpheus sing
> Such notes as warbled to the string,
> Drew Iron tears down Pluto's cheek,
> And made Hell grant what Love did seek.

> Or call up him that left half told
> The story of Cambuscan bold. (103–110)

The allusion to Chaucer's incomplete "Squire's Tale" clinches the broad thematic connection between Milton's poem and Wordsworth's. In each poem both poetry and melancholy have a redemptive function that entails revivifying and extending the work of the dead by imaginatively subjugating the visual to the visionary. Both poems figure deliverance as relief found in an unseen place away from the aggressive sun: "in close covert by som Brook, / Where no profaner eye may look, / Hide me from Day's garish eie" (139–41). Both poems treat the secluded contemplative poet as the object and agent of resurrection, whether figured by Musaeus, Orpheus, Chaucer, or by his anonymous descendants, Wordsworth's retired Scottish pedlar and young Englishman. Milton dismisses "deluding joyes, / The brood of folly" (1–2), "fancies fond" possessing "gaudy shapes" (6), and "hovering dreams / The fickle Pensioners of Morpheus train" (9–10). What Milton dismisses, Wordsworth dismisses: frivolous reveries such as those encouraged by Gilpin, who urged the tourist in quest of the picturesque to create and represent fanciful scenes inspired by bits and pieces of scenery. These amusements may be harmless, but they are too passive to be considered an exercise of poetic imagination. Wordsworth asks his reader for imaginative work, for energy corresponding to the poet's. The reader cannot "be borne along by slaves" ("Essay Supplementary" 410–411). Milton links to "sage and holy, / [. . .] divinest Melancholy" ("Penseroso" 11–12) a stronger order of imagination, not available to "our weaker view" (15). She must be properly understood, Milton insists, as the unmorbid muse of tranquility, as illumination of a different order than what is seen by ordinary eyes in garish light. Her appearance is deceptive; she is one

> Whose Saintly visage is too bright
> To hit the Sense of human sight;
> And therfore to our weaker view,
> Ore laid with black staid Wisdoms hue. (13–16)

Milton invokes Melancholy to make "Hell grant what Love did seek" (108). This beneficent contemplative power is consistent in aim and gravity with the "power to virtue friendly" that the pedlar will later claim for his melancholy tale (*Excursion* 34). Having motivated the Wanderer's proper use of melancholy by this allusion to "Penseroso," the poet's narrative will shortly return more explicitly to Milton, but not without first establishing that, for the young Wanderer, sacred literature and sacred nature have become interfused. They signify the same thing. Tending cattle "on the lonely mountain tops" (14), the young pedlar apprehended the immortality he had read about in the Bible and accepted on faith as "the written Promise" (14). But superior even to Scripture is the experience of nature:

> But in the mountains did he *feel* his faith;
> There did he see the writing; —all things there
> Breathed immortality, revolving life,
> And greatness still revolving; infinite. (14)

Nature brings sacred text to life. Having foregrounded the power of nature's immortal, revolving life, the poem returns again, as we have come to expect, to books.

The poet tells us that the young pedlar would browse in the bookstalls and pick up "The book that had most tempted his desires" (15) and read it out-of-doors. A desire for something to read outside suggests that nature alone is not enough for the pedlar and once again brings into question the narrator's claim about the pedlar's small need for books: "Among the hills," the young poet tells us, "He gazed upon that mighty orb of song, / The divine Milton" (15). At first "that mighty Orb of Song" seen in the hills seems to be a metaphor for the sun as celebrated in poetry. But the beginning of the next line also identifies the mighty orb with "the divine Milton." The phrase "divine Milton" startlingly reverses the emphasis of the "written promise" passage and now foregrounds the poet and his poetry as an emblem of natural illumination. The poet as orb inherits the properties of immortal, "revolving life" (14). In a single phrase echoing Milton's own "divinest Melancholy" ("Penseroso" 12), "divine Milton" fuses book and nature, "Penseroso" and "Wanderer," Milton and Wanderer, sacralized contemplative text and spontaneous visionary illumination. This fusion marks the end of the pedlar's adolescence and securely grounds the psychological integrity the pedlar comes to find in the exercise of his itinerant profession. It is clear at his point that we are meant to see the Wanderer as Thomas Gray's "mute inglorious Milton" ("Elegy " 59), and that Wordsworth will be returning a debt to the nature poetry of the eighteenth-century graveyard meditation by giving Gray's forgotten rural sage a voice.

And perhaps we should see even more. Graver suggests that the Wanderer may be modeled in part on the wise, unlearned speakers whom Cicero chose to rescue from oblivion in *De Oratore,* as Cicero explains at 2.2.7–8 ("Oratorical" 96–97). But the classical precedent surely goes further back than this: Wordsworth could hardly have failed to have in mind Plato's memorial portrait of Socrates, the sage who left no writings and led his pupils to wisdom while expressly denying that he possessed any wisdom of his own. The Wanderer must be understood as a Socratic figure, teaching his Mathetes, the poet, without offering much explicit instruction or claiming any explicit authority.

"In dreams, in study, and in ardent thought, / Thus [. . .] was he reared" (*Excursion* 18), the young man sums up. Before the pedlar was eighteen, he knew "the first virgin passion of a soul / Communing with the glorious Universe" (17), a sublime universe of scripture, poetry, and "the roar of torrents" (18). Overpowered by the "fever of his heart" (18), he often tried, and often failed, to find repose in the "stillness of abstracted thought" (17). But what most stabilized him, he felt, was breathing the "air of poverty, / And drinking from the well of homely life" (18). The young Wanderer's passionate solitary experiences produced a compensatory need for calm and intimate psychological engagement with people, and he fulfills that need not in the school-teaching career his parents intended for him but as an itinerant pedlar. Among the people he meets, he hears "a plainer language" while the "liberty of Nature" (20) calms his extreme emotions, and puts his "mind in a just equipoise of love" (21):

> His heart lay open; and, by Nature tuned
> And constant disposition of his thoughts
> To sympathy with Man, he was alive
> To all that was enjoyed where'er he went;
> And all that was endured. (21)

The discipline of patient travel and attendance upon his modest rural customers opens his heart and empties it of egotism and self-indulgent morbidity.

His compassion qualifies him to understand Margaret's struggle well enough to memorialize her life with beneficent effect. This accomplishment is no small feat, for to see Margaret in the truest light he has had to become an elderly prophet with the visionary eye of youth, "a Being made / Of many Beings," a skillful artificer of vision, memory, meaning, and foreknowledge (24. Time "had not tamed his eye"; rather, it had given him "wondrous skill" to discover "meanings which it brought / From years of youth" and "knowledge of all the years to come, / Human, or such as lie beyond the grave" (24).

The emphasis here, at the end of the biography, on visionary knowledge rather than the empirical visual eye, ironically brings the young man back to the actual cottage bench, but with a transformed vision of his own. The recollected history has been more than a temporary refuge, for memory alters the young man's perception and brings some life and subtle movement to the young man's apprehension of the place, despite his unrelieved physical fatigue. He sees the old man "Screened from the sun" with "The shadows of the breezy elms above / Dappling his face" (25). The once gloom-spreading elms now benignly "screen" rather than fully enclose. The "breezy dappling" revises the unmoved spots of the picturesquely dappled downs in the young poet's initial fancy; now a present participle enlivens a moribund image, just as the Wanderer had transformed pictured lines into the liveliness of dreams. What the young pedlar achieved through imagination the young poet is just beginning to achieve through acts of memory and loving memorialization.

A general freshening of the landscape marks the end of the poet's excursion into memory as well as the beginning of a productive Wordsworthian inspiration akin to the "one soft impulse" of "Yew-tree." The implication of man and elm in moving lights and shadows leads to another subtle and lively perception on the part of the poet, the small but significant moisture on the old man's hat, "as if the brim / Had newly scooped a running stream" (25). The word "brim" evokes something of the old man's capacity and generosity. His successful improvisational drinking, as if from a "running stream," reminds us of the old man's practical skill, and it puts us sufficiently in mind of the agricultural metaphor at the beginning of the young man's history that the running stream now evokes the flow of life to which the young man will gain more access through the old man's pure discourse. Although we are told early on that the two men have greeted each other, Wordsworth displaces the greeting by the pedlar's biography, postponing the young poet's first reported words for several hundred lines until the simple naturalistic words can acquire a more figurative resonance:

> "'Tis," said I, "a burning day;
> My lips are parched with thirst, but you, I guess,
> Have somewhere found relief." (25)

The parched lips identify the poet once again with the parched meadow to which he likened himself when speaking of his need for the old man's refreshing songs. The old man's relief once again attests to his superior skill, and he does in fact point the way to the long-awaited drink, from Margaret's well behind the fence. What the poet finds behind the fence contrasts sharply, however, with the physical relief of the spring. His description of the place conveys his perception of having trespassed into a "chearless spot" (26), a "garden-ground run wild" that showed the trespassing footprints of those whom the fruit "had tempted to o'erleap / The broken wall" (25–26). Such temptation is of course just what the thirsty poet has succumbed to.

The gesture domesticates the psychological pattern of Milton's Satan, who when he overleaped the wall of forbidden Eden, found no pleasure there because he carried Hell within his mind wherever he went and could not escape it. The poet at this moment is similarly trapped in a negative perception of this landscape. But when he withdraws from the cheerless well and returns to the Wanderer, his locus of spiritual refreshment, we begin to see a change in his fallen perception. The young man, now "standing, freely to respire" and cooling his "temples in the fanning air" (26), has already begun to feel life in this place, mainly through his excursion into memory. It has been an essential exercise for receiving the old man's tale. The Wanderer begins by plainly announcing his visionary eye: "I see around me here / Things which you cannot see" (26). The sentence is now believable to the Wanderer's audience. Water, having been established as a force of physical and spiritual life, is the transitional hinge that moves the poem from the Wanderer's biography to Margaret's.

Second Excursion: The Wanderer's Tale of Margaret

The Wanderer introduces Margaret by offering his own description of the well just visited by the poet. Unlike the poet, who describes himself as jumping into a cheerless spot to get a drink, the Wanderer has seen more fully into the life of it; the spring is, as Charles Lamb noted in his review, active, expressive, and responsive to the human hand that engages it. The Wanderer's empathy for the once-active spring is the same as his empathy for the woman whose hand had dislodged its "natural sleep" (27). The spring and Margaret are very nearly the same life-giving entity when the Wanderer remarks that

> the good die first,
> And they whose hearts are dry as summer dust
> Burn to the socket. Many a Passenger
> Hath blessed poor Margaret for her gentle looks,
> When she upheld the cool refreshment drawn
> From that forsaken Spring. (27–28)

The spring has recurred to its natural sleep (which should not be conflated with literal death), in the sense that it has been forsaken by the human lives that depended upon and participated in it. It was the center of Margaret's physical, spiritual, and communal life; but it seems important to the Wanderer to indicate to the poet the conditions under which its life can be felt. The two descriptions of Margaret's spring, the poet's and the Wanderer's, building as they do on the water imagery in the pedlar's biography, mark but one of many points of contact among Margaret's decline, the pedlar's growth, and the perceptual challenge that the young poet faces.

While the pedlar's biography presented stages of ideal growth of a fine mind from well-nurtured childhood to visionary maturity, the vignettes that make up Margaret's story chart an opposing process of psychological decay that begins in the full bloom of adulthood and ends in a despairing death. And while it is easy to see Wordsworthian autobiographical types in the Wanderer and the poet, it is not so easy to see until a bit later that Margaret, too, is an autobiographical type. She reappears at the beginning of book 2 in the guise of the despondent and aggrieved Solitary whose "cure" so to speak becomes the main didactic mission of *The Excursion* and sustains its theme of "Despondency" and "Despondency Corrected."[9] These are the titles of books 3 and 4 and the psychotherapeutic motive for telling the remaining stories. The contrasts and affiliations among the Wanderer, the poet, and Margaret develop in book 1 as an overture to the psychodrama as a whole. Kenneth R. Johnston points out that in 1809 Wordsworth conceived the Solitary as the

> inner antagonist whose contrary personality and counter-arguments provided the necessary opposing weight against which the rest of *The Excursion* balances [. . .]. The Solitary represents not only the type of disaffected intellectual activist [. . .] but also those solipsistic and desponding elements Wordsworth recognized in himself as the main obstacles [. . .] to the very writing of the poem itself. ("Reckless" 131–132)

Margaret is an early version of the Solitary, but without his intellectualizing defenses. All the characters in "The Wanderer," not just Wanderer and poet, are parts of Wordsworth's mind reflecting on its growth and vulnerability to decay. The flourishing Wanderer tells a "just-so" story of a woman with whom he feels an almost uncanny affiliation, but whose extinction could not be reversed by any of the forces—nature, reading, religion—that had nurtured and strengthened him (and, of course, Wordsworth). The fact that it took Wordsworth so many years to work through just how to meld the story of the pedlar as a developing poet to the story of Margaret as an extinguishing soul should encourage us to pay a great deal of attention to the resulting structure.

Margaret suffers a range of calamities, beginning with bad harvests and her husband's long illness and impoverishment. Eventually her unemployed and increasingly despondent husband secretly joins the army and leaves her with two small children and the conscription money. She dies heartbroken. The Wanderer is not particularly eager to tell this story in detail and stops himself early on, right after describing how demoralizing it was for Margaret to watch her unhappy husband tease the children: "'Every smile,' / Said Margaret to me, here beneath these trees, / 'Made my heart bleed'" (31). This moment when the story stops is also the first sign of contagious morbidity in Margaret. She seems to have caught it from her husband, just as when, much later on, we learn that "Her Infant Babe / Had from its Mother caught the trick of grief, / And sighed among its playthings" (43). Not wanting to feed and communicate his own morbid thoughts, the Wanderer breaks off to ask why one should turn away from "natural comfort" now, "while this multitude of flies"—the same "host" that had pestered the young man—"Is filling all the air with melody" (32). But the poet, as oblivious to melodious flies as before, has already caught something potentially morbid from the Wanderer's description: "The things of which he spake / Seemed present" (33). This morbid presence is in fact cold enough to send the poet back into the bright light, where he "stood / To drink the comfort of the warmer sun" (33). The poet senses that the only cure for his restless haunting by what "seemed present" is actually to hear the sad story, and he begs the Wanderer to continue. The Wanderer agrees, but not without admonishing against "vain dalliance" with misery "contented thence to draw / A momentary pleasure, never marked / By reason, barren of all future good" (33–34). The Wanderer immediately distinguishes this vain, unreasoned dalliance, so reminiscent of the "Yew-tree" Solitary's melancholy, from a different kind of thoughtful *gravitas* that we might call "Penseroso" melancholy: "But we have known that there is often found / In mournful thoughts, and always might be found, / A power to virtue friendly"(34). The rest of the story will test the poet's capacity for both kinds of melancholy, the "power to virtue friendly" and the self-indulgent but ultimately self-destructive sentiment.

 This is the central dilemma of the poem. We will be in a better position to further understand the difference between the two kinds of melancholy later, after examining Margaret's deepening melancholy as portrayed by the Wanderer and received by the poet. The Wanderer's successive descriptions of Margaret's abode, and his careful monitoring of the poet's reactions to both the story and the actual place, bring into sharper focus the right and wrong kinds of emotional contagion that the Wanderer introduced when he interrupted his own potentially pathogenic story.

 When Margaret tells the Wanderer that her husband has gone, she speaks "With fervent love, and with a face of grief / Unutterably helpless, and a look / That seemed to cling upon me" (35). The meager physical description is focused on Margaret's emotional expression and how it registers in the Wanderer. "A strange surprise and fear" comes to his heart, and he realizes that he has in a sense been rendered helpless by Margaret's helplessness (35). It is important to note how unobtrusively the Wanderer participates in Margaret's troubles. He has no advice. She does the talking, and for the moment her mood changes. He leaves her "busy with her garden tools" (36) in early spring. But this will be the last time he sees her occupied with the accustomed round of activities that keep her life and her cottage intact. The poem continues to encourage the view, introduced in the descriptions of Margaret's spring, that Margaret's well-being is secured by her reciprocal dialogue, her "bond / Of brotherhood" (27) with her rural plot.

When he returns in midsummer, she is not at home. While he waits "with sad impatience" (38), he notices that not much has come of the spring garden, and he describes the devolution of the garden economy in downward-moving, engulfing, and invasive terms that figure both the devolution of Margaret's mind and his own increasing alarm at her long absence. Weeds invade the cottage; cultivated plants either invade or perish. Bind-weed drags the peas to earth as Margaret, abandoned herself, in turn abandons the garden she loves:

> Carnations, once
> Prized for surpassing beauty, and no less
> For the peculiar pains they had required,
> Declined their languid heads—without support. (38)

Nature is subduing and encumbering nature, including Margaret's child, who "cried aloud; / Then, like a blast that dies away self-stilled, / The voice was silent" (38–39). In this gruesome situation, with an abandoned infant locked inside, the Wanderer suspends judgment and simply waits in increasing desolation for Margaret to return and unlock the door. Again, he lets her do the talking:

> I am changed;
> And to myself, said she, have done much wrong
> And to this helpless infant. I have slept
> Weeping, and weeping I have waked; my tears
> Have flowed as if my body were not such
> As others are; and I could never die. (40)

Margaret is as "changed" as the unusual weather that initiated her family's destruction. Her tears are so removed from the flow of life, earlier figured by the communicating spring, that not even her body is experienced "as others are." She has no energies with which to counter what is destroying her, and none come to her.

She has been wandering the fields, seeking consolation in a Wordsworthian manner, turning toward just the sort of "natural wisdom" the Wanderer has had access to; but she is as desperately unsuccessful as the Wanderer is calm and successful: "I wander," says Margaret, "knowing this / Only, that what I seek I cannot find. / And so I waste my time" (40). Wordsworthian nature therapy does not work for Margaret (or, later on, for the Solitary); ultimately it is unreliable for Wordsworth. The tenderly elegiac loss of the "Intimations" ode, the "splendour in the grass" (179), is here dramatized naturalistically as a brutal and tragic loss of life and sanity.

The Wanderer's commentary is uncompromising in two ways. He pulls no punches in displaying the damage Margaret does to herself and what she loves. It is one thing to abandon the carnations and the peas, another to leave the infant alone, locked in the cottage all day. But significantly, just when the reader or the poet might be most tempted to recoil from Margaret, the Wanderer pauses not only to praise her *goodness* but to reassert his affiliation with her. He loves her and "clings" to her, his bond of brotherhood unbroken, and the Wanderer succeeds in establishing this bond of compassion in the poet by reminding him that

> my spirit clings
> To that poor Woman:—so familiarly
> Do I perceive her manner, and her look,
> And presence; and so deeply do I feel
> Her goodness, that, not seldom, in my walks
> A momentary trance comes over me. (40–41)

His praise is unstinting, even as he describes her depression with clinical precision: the listless, subdued body, averted eyes, and almost motionless sighs, "The careless stillness of a thinking mind / Self-occupied; to which all outward things / Are like an idle matter" (41). Before leaving, the Wanderer wishes her well and exhorts her to pray, but to no effect. It will turn out that prayer offers no consolation either.

The next visit continues the pattern of decline, as the Wanderer's next description moves into the disheveled cottage, Margaret's intimate space, where she sits as "sad and drooping" (42) as her garden, now trampled and gnawed by distinctly unpicturesque sheep. Significantly, the emblem of Margaret's negligent housekeeping is the changed condition of her books, which dominates the brief description of the cottage interior. Her "small lot of books" that previously had been arranged "in seemly order" now "Lay with straggling leaves / Scattered here and there, open or shut, / As they had chanced to fall" (42–43). Books, a positive spiritual force in the Wanderer's education, have become barren for Margaret. Her straggling leaves precisely echo the straggling leaves of the young pedlar's books, and bring back to mind the dark content, the martyr's stories; but Margaret is now living a modern dark tale. Her story is supposed to have the same beneficent effect on the poet as a martyr's legend had on the Wanderer.

Like Margaret, who lost her interest and pleasure in books, the Babe finds no pleasure in toys: "Her infant Babe / Had from his Mother caught the trick of grief, / And sighed among its playthings" (43). On the last visit the Wanderer learns that the Babe has died. The word "trick," meaning "habit," strongly signals how complicit Margaret is in her depressive grief. The Wanderer develops this insight in a subtle way near the end of his tale, by drawing attention back to the bench, the central locus of the entire dialogue.

Third Excursion: Back to the Bench

The Wanderer describes second-hand a solitary habit of Margaret's that he has not observed directly. Margaret likes to sit, vainly imagining her husband's return. Even "if a dog passed by she still would quit / The shade, and look abroad" (45). The energy Margaret gives to her illusions rounds out the significance of the cottage bench. Margaret, like the Solitary of the "Yew-tree," is also exactly like the poet was in his initial mirage of Virgilian landscape; but while the poet woke up to reality, she made the debilitating cycle of mirage and disillusionment a self-destructive habit from which she could not escape:

> On this old Bench
> For hours she sate; and evermore her eye
> Was busy in the distance, shaping things
> That made her heart beat quick. (45)

Her fancies prompt repeated and futile inquiries about her husband. "Meanwhile her poor Hut / Sank to decay" (46). Margaret lived and died "reckless and alone," the "Last human Tenant of these ruined Walls!" (46)

In finally allowing the reader and the poet to see Margaret in this light, the Wanderer tactfully distances himself, reporting only what he has heard as he obliquely brings to light her ruinous psychological practice. Because he has never blamed or criticized Margaret, especially at moments when the reader or the poet is most tempted to recoil from her, but has on the contrary reasserted his love for her at just these problematic moments, the Wanderer's manifest and uncompromising compassion in this, his final description of

Margaret in her landscape, check the contagion of grief that the poet almost "catches" from hearing the tale.

It took years for Wordsworth to work out the last 50 or so lines that take the poet and Wanderer from the solitary desolation of the "Last human tenant of these ruined walls" to the secure public structure that quietly marks the end of the poem, "A Village-Inn,—our Evening resting-place" (49). Moreover, in 1850 he radically revised the 1814 ending in a way that points up the seriousness of the poetic challenge he faced.

In both versions, the poet "turned aside in weakness" (47) when the story was over, and began to review Margaret's sufferings: " it seemed / To comfort me," he says, "while with a Brother's love / I bless'd her—in the impotence of grief" (47). Finding pleasure or comfort in "the impotence of grief" is exactly what the Wanderer does not want the poet to take away from hearing the story; he was clearly warned earlier on against such vain dalliance with misery. But the poet does not seem to understand that this dangerous pleasure he is about to indulge contributed to Margaret's undoing, and so the Wanderer intervenes. When "fondly" (47)—meaning foolishly—the aggrieved poet starts toward the cottage, the Wanderer stops and rebukes him as follows, in the 1814 text:

> My friend! enough to sorrow you have given,
> The purposes of wisdom ask no more;
> Be wise and chearful; and no longer read
> The forms of things with an unworthy eye.
> She sleeps in the calm earth, and peace is here. (47)

The Wanderer, by way of urging the poet toward reading forms with a more worthy eye, tells how he revisioned the choking weeds as an active, beneficent presence:

> I well remember that those very plumes,
> Those weeds, and the high spear-grass on that wall,
> By mist and silent rain-drops silver'd o'er,
> As once I passed, did to my heart convey
> So still an image of tranquility,
> So calm and still, and looked so beautiful
> Amid the uneasy thoughts which filled my mind,
> That what we feel of sorrow and despair
> From ruin and from change, and all the grief
> That passing shews of Being leave behind,
> Appeared an idle dream [. . .]. (47–48)

The lines above are substantially the same in the 1850 text (1.942–52) up to this point, but the last sentence ends differently in the two versions. In 1814, we read "all the grief / [. . .] / Appeared an idle dream, that could not live / Where meditation was" (48). The Wanderer's apocalypse of consciousness is confident and complete: "I turned away / And walked along my road in happiness" (48). But in 1850, we read a more convoluted, less certain sentence that interpolates some religious fine print: "all the grief," the Wanderer explains,

> Appeared an idle dream, that could maintain,
> Nowhere, dominion o'er the enlightened spirit
> Whose meditative sympathies repose
> Upon the breast of Faith. I turned away,
> And walked along my road in happiness. (989–995)

"Like every modern reader I know of," writes Karl Kroeber, "I find the original infinitely more powerful and moving than the revision" (*Ecological* 50). This interpolation (however sincerely it may reflect Wordsworth's later religious conviction) spoils the Wanderer's lesson; which is, in Kroeber's words, "that nature never withdraws its fundamental beneficence," but that human beings are tragically "drawn into resisting what connects us to the beneficence of natural vitality" (50–51). The interpolation also disturbs the poem's careful preparation for the poet's apocalypse, which follows and matches the Wanderer's in its 1814 simplicity and immediacy.

In both versions, the poet's imagination finds a tranquil prospect from the bench where the Wanderer gives his last speech, and where Margaret's morbid fancy had endeared and cultivated the "torturing hope [. . .] / Fast rooted at her heart" (46). The poet sits down next to the Wanderer and simply sees the "things which you cannot see" (26), the Wanderer's announced topic at the beginning of his tale. The shared consciousness of poet and Wanderer, marked now by "we" and "us," perceives a genuine locus amoenus in the ruin, an illumined vision of the here and now:

> A slant and mellow radiance, which began
> To fall upon us, while, beneath the trees,
> We sate on that low Bench: and now we felt,
> Admonished thus, the sweet hour coming on.
> A linnet warbled from those lofty elms,
> A thrush sang loud, and other melodies,
> At distance heard, peopled the milder air. (48)

The two men are admonished not by faith or precept but by "A slant and mellow radiance." *Admonished* means both "warned," with a sense of the peril of Margaret's failure, and "put in mind of a thing forgotten, overlooked, or unknown," a milder Latin meaning, more current in English then than now. This sense of "admonished" resonates precisely with Wordsworth's avowed goal of reminding readers of "knowledge, as it lurks inoperative and unvalued in their own minds" (*Letters* 3:238), but not in the spiritually stunted vision that Lamb ascribes to the picturesque traveler or in the mere reproduction of Virgilian pastoral.

Picturesque travelers sit on benches and take in the prospect below. Here though, the radiant prospect from "that low Bench" (48) is anything but a picturesque ruin "out there," but rather an insight figured by turning away from the ruined place so as to better illuminate and see into the life of it. The bench on which Margaret used to sit has itself quietly accumulated symbolic significance; by supporting gestures of looking outward that are at the same time looking inward, it has become a figure for psychological prospect. It is now a complex *ethical* place, filled with the fluctuating human character of its former inhabitant and its visitors, all of whom are in dialogue with each other and with the environment. The "slant and mellow radiance" signifies the poet's assimilation of the lesson or goal he had merely fancied in the distant Virgilian landscape and then seen emblematically at closer range when, thirsty, restless, and pestered by the flies, he found the Wanderer at ease on the bench, "Recumbant in the shade, [. . .] / Beneath the shelter of these clustering elms" (5), echoing Virgil's "lying down under the shelter of a spreading beech" in the first line of the first *Eclogue*.

What then is "the power to virtue friendly" (34) in the melancholy tale? The Wanderer has activated the poet's imagination by describing his visits with Margaret, but in so doing he has made *himself* as much a character in Margaret's story as Margaret. The Wanderer, just as fearful as Socrates of emotional contagion, and just as appreciative of a positive mimetic effect, engages the poet's imagination with two contrasting mimetic models: (1) a description of Margaret's decline and (2) the Wanderer's own exemplary behavior in artfully relating the story and monitoring its effects. The "power to virtue friendly" in the Wanderer's melancholy tale is not Margaret's grief but the Wanderer's compassion for what Margaret, "whose stock / Of virtues bloomed beneath this lonely roof" (28), endured while the structure collapsed around her. The story of Margaret, a modern folktale vividly rendered, feeds the poet just as "Old songs—the product of his native hills" fed the Wanderer's young soul (6). The biography of the Wanderer and the dramatic interaction between poet and Wanderer (a poetic consciousness in two stages of development) is a kind of *Prelude* in two voices, articulating and implementing Wordsworth's "system" of mind, imagination, and nature.

H. W. Piper reminds us that Wordsworth's "system," or "metaphysics" as it came to be called, was assimilated by the next generation of English Romantic poets largely from the 1814 *Excursion*. The immediately influential parts, as Piper explains, "were those which asserted that there was an active principle in each natural form and in the whole of nature, that through the power of the Imagination the poet in contemplating the forms of Nature communes with this spirit" and that religion and mythology document "such imaginative experience of Nature" (Piper 147–149). The poet and the Wanderer, an unsung prophet of the Scottish soil, introduced these ideas dialogically in the first book of *The Excursion,* a work that permanently changed both Keats's and Shelley's conception of the poet's tasks and themes. It had a temporary effect on Byron, who learned some "metaphysics" from Wordsworth for his own unique locodescriptive figurations of mind, as worked out in *Manfred* and the last cantos of *Childe Harold's Pilgrimage*. The intensity of that temporary Wordsworthian effect has not been fully appreciated or examined. This is the topic of the next chapter.

CHAPTER 6

"Till the Place Became Religion": Byron's Coliseum

> Has not the Soul, the Being of your Life
> Received a shock of awful consciousness,
> In some calm season, when these lofty Rocks
> At night's approach bring down the unclouded Sky,
> To rest upon their circumambient walls.
> —Wordsworth, *The Excursion*

Byron's best-known responses to *The Excursion* are two passages in *Don Juan*, one in the author's own person in the dedication, the other from the mouth of his eponymous hero. The dedication excoriates Wordsworth who

> in a rather long "Excursion"
> (I think the Quarto holds five hundred pages)
> Has given a sample from the vasty Version
> Of his new System to perplex the Sages. (25–28)

Later on Don Juan seconds this uncharitable assessment with "A drowsy frowsy poem called the 'Excursion', / Writ in a manner which is my aversion" (3.847–48). The 1821 wit of *Don Juan* is an important part of Byron's response to Wordsworth, but like so much else in conflicted Byron, extravagant satire is only *part* of the story. Byron himself harbored grandiose desires to perplex the sages, as he wrote to Thomas Moore on 28 February 1817: "You will see that I shall do something or other—the times and fortune permitting—that, 'like the cosmogony, or creation of the world, will puzzle the philosophers of all ages'" ("*So late*" 177). Only a month ago, when Byron had written to Moore that he was "half mad [. . .] between metaphysics, mountains, lakes, love unextinguishable, thoughts unutterable" ("*So late*" 165), it was Wordsworth's "metaphysics" as communicated by *The Excursion* that was driving him half-mad enough to use such rhetoric at all. Although Byron publicly denounced *The Excursion*, it is clear that he was registering a complicated response, both in the psychodrama of *Manfred* (1817) and in *Childe Harold's Pilgrimage* 3 and 4 (1816–1818). Of particular interest are two similar locodescriptive set pieces depicting the Coliseum in an evening landscape. Byron's distinctive imaginative temperament deepens this most characteristic of ancient Roman places—and least Wordsworthian—into a Wordsworthian emblem of mind.

The Excursion gave Byron the notion that "contemplation of natural forms can mean communication with them and eventually communion with the greater life of which they are an expression" (Piper 122). Piper observes that while communication implies a shared language, in the sense that "the features of the landscape have qualities of human personality or human feeling to which the observer can respond," communication does not, however, necessarily imply communion: "Communion clearly depends on such a capacity as Wordsworth's for mystical experience." Moreover, the coherence of Wordsworth's "system depends equally on ideas as to what Nature is, and on the enriched experience which follows when such ideas are imaginatively grasped" (122). Piper and others have discussed Wordsworth's nature language in the nature spirit speeches of *Manfred* and in the Alpine descriptions from *Childe Harold* 3, but the questions of what "nature" and "mystical experience" are for Byron merit more attention. In *Manfred* and *Childe Harold* 4, half-mad Byron worked out not only an exposition of this madness but also an intimation of its cure.

My topic is the all-too-characteristically tortured Byronic hero in two moments of uncharacteristic tranquility, when he experiences what Stephen Cheeke has called an "intense communion with history and spirit-of-place" at the Coliseum (4).[1] I want to discuss each Coliseum description from several angles: how each functions within the individual poem, how they relate to each other, and how they document Byron's confrontation with Wordsworth's metaphysics and Wordsworth's transformation of the locodescriptive poem into the poem of the mind. *Childe Harold's* 18 Coliseum stanzas, an expansion of Manfred's Coliseum soliloquy, develop the same concerns found in the descriptive soliloquy and make more explicit certain ideas that were only latent in Manfred's description. Like Manfred, Harold finds a psychological balance point at the Coliseum; and, as in *Manfred,* the pilgrim's balance does not hold. For Byron/Manfred/Harold nature enfolds the old stones of the Coliseum, and the human history they embody, as assuredly as nature enfolds "the stationary rocks" (1850 *Excursion* 9.8) for Wordsworth. For Byron, the unexpectedly numinous Coliseum became, in Manfred's astonished and uncharacteristic term, "religion." The brief, strangely intrusive Coliseum in Manfred, and the amplified one in *Childe Harold* 4—by far the longest and most psychological place description in the *Pilgrimage*—reveal to what extent Byron could imagine and inhabit an active Wordsworthian universe.

Childe Harold's Pilgrimage becomes, in due course, a very Wordsworthian sort of poem, even if the melancholy and defiant narrator seems (like Manfred) a most un-Wordsworthian sort of individual. Following the powerful example of Wordsworth's *Excursion*, the last two cantos increasingly center their place descriptions in the traveler's consciousness. *Childe Harold* is a "variant of the Romantic quest [. . .] in which movement toward a paradise—even one unreached—gave way to a state of expiatory homelessness" (McFarland 19). Consider the following speech:

> No more of that; in silence hear my doom:
> A hermitage has furnished fit relief
> To some offenders: other penitents,
> Less patient in their wretchedness, have fallen,
> Like the old Roman, on their own sword's point.
> They had their choice: a wanderer must I go,
> The Spectre of that innocent Man, my guide.
> No human ear shall ever hear me speak;
> No human dwelling ever give me food,
> Or sleep, or rest: but, over waste and wild,
> In search of nothing, that this earth can give,
> But expiation, will I wander on—
> A Man by pain and thought compelled to live,
> Yet loathing life—till anger is appeased
> In Heaven, and Mercy gives me leave to die. (*Borderers*, act 5)[2]

As McFarland has observed: "The lines seem to be quintessential Byron, but are in fact Wordsworth's" (19).[3] Indeed this speech, which concludes Wordsworth's *Borderers* (written during the mid-to-late 1790s, but not published until 1842 in revised form) dates precisely from the period during which Wordsworth was struggling with the problem that he dramatized in the story of Margaret, the problem of the mind's complicity in its own ruin. Since *The Borderers* was not published until after Byron's death, there is no question of any direct influence upon Byron. It is therefore all the more remarkable how well Wordsworth's speech characterized the as yet unborn Byronic hero.[4] These "emblems of torn existence" (McFarland 20), not uncommon in Romantic poetry, are ubiquitous in Byron. Byron, unlike Wordsworth, rarely provides emblems of torn existence healed; Byron's Coliseum is a brilliant exception that proves the rule.

Byron's existence was comprehensively ruptured when Lady Byron permanently separated herself and their daughter, Ada, from Byron because of his allegedly incestuous affair with his half-sister, Augusta Leigh. During this painful domestic crisis, Byron set *Childe Harold* 3 in the places he visited: Belgium, the Rhine, the Alps, and the Jura, where the pilgrim begins to reflect seriously on nature and politics, and on his own mental states. Canto 4, set entirely in Italy, meditates on time and history, and deepens the more inwardly psychological trend established in canto 3. It was while writing this canto that Byron wrote to Moore that he was "half mad" with thinking about philosophy, natural landscapes, love, and the inexpressible—the very preoccupations that inform *Manfred* and *Childe Harold* 3. And just as the Coliseum description seems to emerge as a balance between Alpine grandiosity and despair for Manfred, so too does the fourth canto's Coliseum for the more frankly autobiographical Harold.

Cheeke observes in his stimulating study of Byron's places that in *Manfred* "the Coliseum is, as it were, an *antithetical figure* to that of the Alps" (87; my italics). Cheeke does not explain though how the Alps function as a figure and is even curiously at pains to undermine their figurative status. The reason for this discrepancy is clear: The assumption underpinning Cheeke's study is that human subjectivity is determined by specific locations and situations, an assumption that leads him to appreciate Manfred's Coliseum as a potent force redeeming Manfred "from the solipsism of the mind's own place"(87). Indeed, Cheeke reduces Milton's figure of the "mind's own place" to very nearly a solipsism in which acts of the mind have no appropriate role other than acquiescence to the determining place. Cheeke's provocative assumption that place determines (or properly ought to determine) mind makes Byron's Alps problematic for him because he finds them, so to speak, too much mind and not enough place. Byron, as Cheeke explains,

> does not offer detailed or precise descriptions of Alpine culture at all but rather invokes the mountains abstractly, as if "the Alps" are in fact a literary mode rather than a place, and as a literary mode (as in Orientalism) they readily translate into "psychological and metaphysical correlatives." This means not only that the Alps stand for a certain ideal model of the human mind: grand, free, soaring, solitary, etc.—these commonplaces are taken for granted; but that the very process of turning the Alps into a literary and psychological mode is in itself an assertion of the sovereignty of the mind over its determining places. (86)

Cheeke rightly points out that by Byron's time Alpinism was a "literary mode" akin to Orientalism. The existence of a mode of place description does not however constrain poets to use it in a slavishly imitative way that "asserts the sovereignty of mind"—mind understood as mere copying—"over its determining places."

When Cheeke charges Byron with privileging mind over place, he really means that Byron's Alps are mere rhetorical imitation: "The Alps disappear" into Alpinism; they are "not primarily a setting, nor even a metaphor; but a philosophical orientation" (86), as if setting, metaphor, and orientation are mutually exclusive notions. I have tried to show throughout this study that they are not. It would seem beyond dispute that (contrary to Cheeke) the Alps are manifestly *Manfred*'s setting; and when he writes that the Alps are a "philosophical orientation," he writes an instructive metaphor which actually deserves to be opened for further reflection. We would do well not to saddle Byron with a commonplace Alpinism that does not mesh well (as we shall see) with *Manfred*'s depiction of the Alps. Only by assuming a commonplace Alpinism do we find it problematic that "the relation between mental suffering and the Alps is not a straightforward one, as the mountains offer neither an unequivocal correlative for mental superiority, nor a clear image of mental breakdown" (Cheeke 89). The fact that Cheeke does not find any clear concept allegory in Byron's Alps is neither surprising nor alarming: indeed, it only enhances their evocative potential, just as it does in Dante's subtle allegories. Cheeke finds this evocative potential in Byron's Coliseum and praises how Harold's version "exhibits a kind of historical method, in which a strict literalism and material reality of place go hand in hand with a supernaturalism centred upon the notion of a 'magic spot'" (104).

One should note, however, that every feature of Cheeke's critique of Byron's Alps could, with even more justification, reduce the Coliseum to imitative neoclassicism or (more particularly) to yet another instance of the British meditation on Roman ruins that is as old as the earliest extant Anglo-Saxon verse.[5] If Byron's Alps are neither literal nor precise, so too are his depictions of the Coliseum.

Harold's Coliseum, even though it is more developed than Manfred's, tellingly avoids anything like "strict literalism." It is (like the Alps) a poetic image, a "magic circle" (4.1295) with a more perfect shape than the ellipse Byron literally experienced. Byron merges this perfect shape anachronistically with the head of Caesar, who was in no way literally associated with the building and who had been assassinated many decades before it was built. Whether Byron depicts the Alps or Rome, his sense of history and culture shows itself to be more antique than modern, more paradigmatic than literal. Byron evidently had little interest in the style of historiography that took firm hold later in the nineteenth century and entailed a strong desire to represent the past for its own sake and as it really was. In 1824, the year of Byron's death, the historian Barante was writing against the grain of prevailing practice when he declared: "We are sick of seeing history like a tame hired sophist lend herself to every proof that people want to draw from her. What we want of her is the facts" (qtd. in Bann 20). Byron did not want such "facts"; he wanted paradigms of general human behavior. In linking the conqueror of Gaul with the anonymous ghosts of slain gladiators, Byron was no more committed to the literal and material than was Dante when he depicted Caesar's assassin in a hell that contained a disproportionate sample of contemporary Florence.

This chapter attempts to clarify Byron's subtle figurations of mind and place, and, equally, to clarify how Byron's unusually systematic imagery establishes a deep rhetorical-psychological connection between mental suffering in disturbed Alpine landscapes and the relief experienced in the surprisingly calm Roman arena (which in *Manfred* is in no way part of the literal setting). Such rhetorical connections are, as my larger argument has tried to show, characteristic of classical place ecphrasis and its vigorous afterlife in figurative literary description.

Much of *Childe Harold*'s third canto, like *Manfred*, is devoted to Alpine suffering. It ends as it began, in personal despair, with an apostrophe to Byron's small daughter Ada Augusta. This explicitly autobiographical frame for the third canto's Alpine vicissitudes foreshadows canto 4 in two mutually reinforcing ways. First, in canto 4 Byron entirely drops the Harold persona that he had begun to shed with the autobiographical material of canto 3. He writes to his friend Hobhouse in the dedicatory preface to canto 4, "I recur from fiction to truth" (120). The author, says Byron, is "speaking in his own person. The fact is, that I had become weary of drawing a line [. . .]. It was in vain that I asserted, and imagined I had drawn, a distinction between the author and the pilgrim" (*Complete Poetical Works* 2:122). Byron had defended the raffish and unregenerate Childe Harold persona of the early cantos in an 1812 addition to the preface, as a sort of negative role model.[6] Harold, wrote Byron then,

> was never intended as an example, further than to show that early perversion of mind and morals leads to satiety of past pleasures and disappointment in new ones, and that even the beauties of nature, and the stimulus of travel [. . .] are lost on a soul so constituted, or rather misdirected. Had I proceeded with the Poem, this character would have deepened as he drew to the close [. . .].
> (*Complete Poetical Works* 2:6)

Later on Byron did of course proceed with the poem. Some four years later in the preface to canto 4, a deeper and more imaginative self than Byron was able to foresee in 1812 writes freely about how his poem connects him to the "magical and memorable abodes" described therein, "however short [the poetry] may fall of our distant conceptions and immediate impressions" (*Complete Poetical Works* 2:121). Byron's antithetical doublet, joining "distant conceptions" and "immediate impressions," suggests a distinctive quality of Byron's imagination: how at its most acute it could create an intimate and palpable poetic image from what would seem to be the most shopworn of sentimental materials, an ancient ruin in a landscape.[7] Byron's magical abodes are not ordinary places. Like Ovid's ethical abodes, they are dwellings inhabited by powers who determine their character.

It is one of the gentle ironies of Byron's self-presentation that the Harold of the early cantos had little sense of the transformative magic of his poetic abodes; actual Byron, having "recurred" to autobiographical truth, does. Early in canto 4, Byron declares:

> The Beings of the Mind are not of Clay;
> Essentially immortal, they create
> And multiply in us a brighter ray
> and more beloved existence. (4.37–40)

Byron insists that these beings are potent enough to regenerate a deadened inner world. For Fate, continues Byron,

> by these Spirits supplied
> First exiles, then replaces what we hate;
> Watering the heart whose early flowers have died,
> And with a fresher growth replenishing the void. (4.42–45)

It is clear from Byron's letters and journals that among the early flowers that had died was the prospect of a wife, a family, and a home; the loss of which preoccupied him throughout the trip that inspired *Manfred* and *Childe Harold* 3 and 4. Indeed at a purely formal level, the stanzas to Ada in canto 3 (stressing both loss as well as the harmonious blend of her father's elements) establishes a pattern for Manfred's near-twin Astarte and for many counterpart females of canto 4.

The landscape over which he traveled was often experienced in intimate relationship with his psychic interior, but not in ways prescribed by eighteenth-century Alpinism. On 23 September 1816, for example, he moves as quickly from Paradise to lifelessness as Manfred does, as he explains in the journal he wrote for Augusta Leigh:

> The whole of the day as fine in point of weather—as the day on which Paradise was made.—Passed *whole woods of withered pines—all withered*—trunks stripped & barkless—branchless lifeless—done by a single winter—their appearance reminded me of me & my family. ("*So late*" 102; Byron's italics)

On 29 September he writes in the journal that "recollections of bitterness" (104) and "home desolation" (104–105) have preyed upon him in the

Alps. Like Milton's Satan, who "Saw undelighted all delight" in the garden (*Paradise* 4.286), Byron is not nursed by nature:[8]

> Neither the music of the Shepherd—the crashing of the Avalanche—nor the torrent—the mountain—the Glacier—the Forest—nor the Cloud—have for one moment —lightened the weight upon my heart—nor enabled me to lose my own wretched identity in the majesty and the power and the Glory—around—above—& beneath me. ("*So late*" 105)

In Rome, however, Byron does for a moment lose his "wretched identity" and merge with a larger one, not in a meditation on the natural sublime, as he may have expected, but at the Coliseum, in a meditation in which the distant past becomes an immediate and unifying force. It is ironic that this meditation satisfies in fact a deep desire for identity, memory, and remembrance rather than the manifest longing for oblivion and loss of identity that Byron shares with Manfred. Since Manfred (unlike Byron) has no children and no social or political commitments, remembrance is not among his conscious concerns. For all his blustery Promethean angst, Manfred (unlike the beneficent Titan) has no gift at all for mankind. Byron does, or at least wants to. Like the autobiographical pilgrim, he wants to be "remembered in his line" (*Childe Harold* 4.77), wants a place in his daughter's memory, a place in social memory, and a place in the literary canon. In life, Byron of course succeeded on all three counts. Ada named her eldest son after him. He is still revered in Greece as a national hero. In *Childe Harold* he became "the bard of civilization, [. . .] freedom, noble aspiration, and heroic action" (Goldstein 208), without blinking at the catastrophic and inescapable suffering of anonymous and obscure individuals.

When Byron is most autobiographical, he actually facilitates temporal perspectives on both the personal and the cultural past. His immediate experiences and ongoing preoccupations motivate all his temporal excursions, giving the final canto a stronger overarching unity-in-diversity than the previous three. The fourth canto's distinctly different direction was apparent to one of its first reviewers, Sir Walter Scott. Scott's characterization of the last canto would have been entirely appropriate to a review of Wordsworth's *Excursion*:

> His descriptions of present and existing scenes however striking and beautiful, his recurrence to past actions however important and however powerfully described, become interesting chiefly from the tincture which they receive from the mind of the author. (228)

This new psycholgical tincture can be directly related to his just-completed work on what in 1821 Byron would call the "mental theatre" or "metaphysical drama" of *Manfred* ("*Born for Opposition*" 186–187, 205, 210).

Manfred's Drama of the Divided Self

In 1817 Byron called his experimental composition "a kind of poem in dialogue" ("*So late*" 170), just the sort of dramatic experiment Wordsworth outlined in the Preface to *The Excursion*. But while Wordsworth framed his dialogue by narrative, Byron built in acts, scenes, and stage directions—all the surface structure of a typical play. Byron's result looks much like a closet drama in the tradition of Milton's *Samson Agonistes* and also shares Milton's thematic concern with temptation, sin, and redemption. Byron's purpose in fusing lyric poetry with dramatic poetry was the same as Wordsworth's and Milton's before him: to express the self as in a lyric poem, but through many voices, as in a drama. What distinguishes Wordsworth and especially Byron from Milton is that their Romantic psychodrama is (like Dante's, for example) far more patently personal and autobiographical than Milton's treatment of a general spiritual problem. General spiritual problems for Wordsworth or Byron are grounded in and presented (with varying transparency) as the poet's personal experience. This is not to say that poetry is ever a literal transcript of any poet's life, only that the boundary is particularly complicated for avowedly autobiographical poets. Byron himself complained in a 5 July 1821 letter to Thomas Moore that he could "never get people to understand that poetry is the expression of *excited passion,* and that there is no such thing as a life of passion any more than a continuous earthquake, or an eternal fever" ("*Born for Opposition*" 146; Byron's italics). Byron's life, however, was marked by more earthquakes and fevers than most; and he substantiated them in locodescriptive poetry that became psychologically more complex in the course of his travels. Byron, like Wordsworth, was no "gentlemanly spy upon nature"; places affected him deeply. It was on this common ground that Byron could both assimilate and react against Wordsworth.

Manfred, read strictly as dramatic dialogue, evokes a bewildered response in keeping with its psychologically innovative structure: *Manfred* "has no action; no plot—and no characters," as Francis Jeffrey complained in his 1817 review (116). Jeffrey had not much more sympathy for Byron's adventures of the heart than he had for Wordsworth's: "Manfred merely muses and suffers from the beginning to the end" (116). If, however, we read the musing and suffering as Manfred in dialogue not with other people but with variously underdeveloped, idealized, or specialized pieces of himself, then it becomes clear that the very weakness of the work as drama brings success as a lyric of the disintegrating and integrating self.

In *A Mental Theater* Alan Richardson sums up Manfred's psychodrama of disintegration (43–58). Manfred's encounters

> represent Manfred's increasingly desperate attempts to find release from an intolerable, flawed self-consciousness, whether through oblivion or, in the

more complex encounters, through a scene of recognition that could render him psychically whole. All of Manfred's acts and desires emanate from his sense of psychic disintegration, and the emerging account of his past, with its seemingly obscure crime, is the story of how and why his psychic torment came about. (44)

Manfred's crime (driving his incestuous lover to suicide?) is never made fully explicit, but the psychic conflict correlative to it emerges through the rhetoric of his dramatic encounters in the first two acts. Just as the rhetoric of the first two acts communicates the conflict, the rhetoric of the third and final act communicates the forces of integration that may be available to counter Manfred's alienation from self and world.[9] Byron's experiment in "metaphysical" or "mental" theater subsumes physical action to the movements of the mind as it struggles to overcome a disintegrative process that has its source in a crime whose major victim (it would seem) is the protagonist himself. Goethe, a kindred spirit who admired Byron's adaptation of Faustian themes, immediately understood *Manfred* as "a wonderful phenomenon" distilling "the quintessence of the most astonishing talent born to be its own tormentor," even if "the gloomy heat of an unbounded and exuberant despair becomes at last oppressive to us" (Rev. of *Manfred* 119).

The poem aims for resolution, but not in ways that dramas normally achieve resolution—by, say, having the protagonist overcome his antagonists or the hero marry his beloved—but rather by bringing the conflicting pieces of the self into harmony without losing any of its complexity. Inasmuch as the poem does succeed, it succeeds by communicating integration and resolution rhetorically, by producing discordant images and then harmonizing them. The images and voices for the first version of *Manfred* emerged from the journal for Augusta Leigh, as Byron explained on 12 October 1817 in a letter to John Murray:

> The germs of Manfred may be found in the Journal which I sent to Mrs. Leigh [. . .] when I went over first the Dent de Jamant & then Wengeren [*sic*] or Wengeberg Alp & Sheideck and made the giro of the Jungfrau Schreckhorn &c. &c. shortly before I left Switzerland—I have the whole scene of Manfred before me as if it was but yesterday—& could point it out spot by spot, torrent and all.—Of the Prometheus of Aeschylus I was passionately fond as a boy—(it was one of the Greek plays we read thrice a year at Harrow) [. . .]. The Prometheus— if not exactly in my plan—has always been so much in my head— that I can easily conceive its influence over all or anything that I have written. ("*So late*" 268)

The germs of *Manfred* are thus a potent combination of Byron's incestuous love for Augusta (the model for Manfred's crime against Astarte), his passion for the tormented Prometheus, and an experience of the Alps that both assimilated and transcended the eighteenth-century gothic machinery of the fearsome natural sublime. Alpine extremes provide the outer physical and inner psychological environment for most of both *Manfred* and canto 3. Extreme moods so predominate these works that the occasional moment of harmony invites all the more scrutiny.

The greatest integration of Manfred's fragmented self is (formally) where the imagery is most securely integrated, and (dramatically) where the subject matter is for once not in an antagonizing relationship to Manfred: in his descriptive soliloquy recollecting the Coliseum. Significantly, the Coliseum was not in the first version of the poem; Manfred had simply exhausted himself and died, a conclusion that Byron described to John Murray on 14 April 1817 as

> d----d bad. It must on *no account* be published in its present state; —I will try & reform it—or re-write it altogether—but the impulse is gone—& I have no chance of making anything out of it [. . .]. I wonder what the devil possessed me. ("*So late*" 211–212)

Even Byron was confused and bewildered by this poem and could not begin revising until a trip to Rome rekindled his imagination. "You will find I think some good poetry in this new act," he wrote on 5 May to John Murray. In the same letter he provided his impressions of "Rome—the wonderful" where he had been doing nothing but sightseeing and revising the third act. "Rome has delighted me beyond everything since Athens—& Constantinople" (219), he exulted; and in another letter to Murray on 9 May he was even more enthusiastic:

> I am delighted with Rome—[. . .]—finer than Greece—[. . .]—*as a whole*— ancient and modern—it beats Greece—Constantinople—every thing—at least that I have ever seen—But I can't describe because my first impressions are always strong and confused—[. . .]—where there is much to be grasped we are always at a loss. (221–222; Byron's italics)

What Byron grasped in Rome and could not articulate in letters he did express in the revised third act of *Manfred* (and throughout the year in *Childe Harold* 4). The major revision, the "good poetry" he mentioned to Murray, is Manfred's remembrance of the Roman amphitheater.

The soliloquy presents the hero's recollection, both the act of remembering as well as its particular descriptive content, as a paradigm for integration. Such an act of integration is urgently needed at this point in the drama, which previously had been concerned almost exclusively with the psychological splitting of Manfred's personality. Elledge explains that Byron typically figures psychological splitting, as well as the efforts his characters make to reconcile the irreconcilable, through a preferred quartet of dialectical image patterns, the most important of which is the antinomy of fire and clay. For Byron, fire represents "variously passion, aspiration, freedom, motion, emotion, energy, infinity, and divinity," while clay represents variously "intellect,[10] frustration, bondage, ennui, sterility, finitude, and mortality" (8). This basic polarity is often supported by three additional contrasts: light against dark, organic against inorganic, and the self against the *doppelgänger*. Elledge's dialectical image patterns systematically inform the psychic projections that constitute *Manfred*'s antagonistic quasi characters and figure the oscillating emotional state arising from Manfred's fundamental contradiction and confusion: he experiences himself as alternately superman and doomed hero.

In the overall emotional dynamic of *Manfred*, extremes tend to engender their opposites, and equilibrium is fragile. Manfred oscillates very quickly from despair to grandiosity and back again to despair, as in this speech from the second act:

> In phantasy, Imagination, all
> The Affluence of my Soul, which one day was
> A Croesus in Creation, I plunged deep—
> But like an ebbing wave it dashed me back
> Into the Gulph of my unfathomed Thought. (2.2.142–46)

Images akin to this wave that dashes into unfathomed thought interlace Manfred's outer and inner landscapes, and they appear in nearly every scene. The general physical and psychological setting is the terrifying sublime. Heights and abysses and cosmic eternities with no human scale of time or space communicate Manfred's wildly oscillating moods. An almost physical law of compensation seems to order the transitions: a deep abyss (physical or psychological) calls for grandiosity, and vice versa.[11] An example particularly important to the psychodramatic image series is the attempted suicide on the Jungfrau, where Manfred experiences a "barrenness of spirit" that renders him his "own Soul's Sepulchre" (1.2.26–27). This diminished mental state produces in turn a soaring eagle overhead and a Promethean fantasy of being eaten by a bird of prey—a grander torment than is available to mere mortals (1.2.29–33). Significantly, Manfred proceeds to sum up the conflict, as if his rhetoric of conflicting images has taught him something. "We," he says—the plural pronoun confesses for once his participation in humanity—are constructed of unmediated opposites, "Half dust, half deity, alike unfit / To sink or soar, with our mixed essence make / A conflict of its elements" (1.2.40–42). He has a sense (albeit fleeting) that he shares his essence with someone other than the near-twin Astarte, an emblem of exactly what severs Manfred from humanity: his narcissistic and incestuous love for his idealized self. As Manfred explains to the Witch, there is but one person with whom he "wore the chain of human ties" (2.2.104), a markedly negative description of social participation. Astarte, he says,

> was like me in lineaments—her eyes
> Her hair, her features, all, to the very tone
> Even of her voice, they said, were like to mine,
> But softened all and tempered into beauty. (2.2.107–10)[12]

The resemblance ends there: "Her faults were mine—her virtues were her own" (2.2.118).

Byron took the name "Astarte," a variant of "Ishtar" and "Astoreth," the ancient fertility goddess and queen of heaven who was both wife and sister to the sun god, from a tale of incestuous siblings in Montesquieu's *Persian Letters* (Richardson, "Astarté"). Montesquieu's tale presents the lovers sympathetically, as victims of bigoted Islamic rulers who, as the brother-lover explains, forbid the "sacred unions, which are ordered rather than permitted by our religion, and which are the artless images of a union already formed by nature" (Montesquieu 112). Such an earnestly enlightened perspective would have appealed to Byron. The incongruously "Persian" name of the phantom sister who joins Manfred in a sacred and transgressive union embeds her into the play's Zoroastrian machinery of Arimanes and the Evil Principle, while the goddess's role as queen of heaven and daughter of the moon also gives the character Astarte a beneficent affinity with the quiet night sky that makes the Coliseum become "religion." Like the taciturn Night spirit who dwells in "the Shadow of the Night" (1.1.108) and is tortured by light, Astarte—the dramatic and psychological nexus of the play—has few words for Manfred and remains obscure until her phantom appears at the end of act 2 and exerts a powerful influence on him.

Manfred declares to Astarte's phantom, "I feel but what thou art" (2.4.133) and demands a response. She mirrors back his narcissistic identification with her by merely repeating his name (2.4.149). When he asks for more speech and in particular for forgiveness, saying he lives "but in the sound" of her voice, she reflects back a strong hint of *his* imminent death: his "earthly ills," she says, will end the next day (2.4.151–52). The disappearance of her voice from the play after this encounter does in fact accurately foreshadow his death, but it also foreshadows the (temporary) relief from narcissistic self-consciousness, self-alienation, and fragmentation he experiences before he dies. This bit of dialogue shows how rigorously the play foregrounds the psychic structures that underwrite Manfred's connection to the "person" he loves, rather than the purely social dimension of an actual human relationship. Astarte does not speak or act like a naturalistic lover, and certainly not like the victim of a crime; she mirrors Manfred, and her recognition of him relaxes his manic quest for relief. Manfred, believing that he will achieve the oblivion he seeks, thanks Nemesis for the "grace accorded" by this interview (2.4.167) instead of ranting at the inadequacy of the phantom's response. *Grace,* a markedly unusual word for Manfred, signals a profound shift in his mental state, this time into the completely new and unexpected emotional territory that irrupts in act 3, beyond the Alpine extremes and the Zoroastrian dark side that have formed his chaotic inner landscape.

The interview with Astarte has the effect of what Blackstone calls a "direct intervention of grace," a "little 'satori'" (234) that settles upon Manfred in the immediate aftermath. When act 3 begins, it is as if we are in a different play:

> There is a calm upon me,
> Inexplicable stillness, which till now
> Did not belong to what I knew of life.—
> If that I did not know Philosophy
> To be of all our Vanities the Motliest—
> The merest word that ever fooled the ear
> From out the Schoolmen's jargon—I should deem
> The golden secret, the sought "Kalon" found,
> And seated in my Soul. (3.1.6–14)

Manfred's "Kalon" (Greek "beautiful") almost seems to answer Shelley's request in the 1816 "Hymn to Intellectual Beauty":

> Thus let thy power, which like the truth
> Of nature on my passive youth
> Descended, to my onward life supply
> Its calm [. . .]. (Version A, 78–81)

Manfred's speech registers Byron's respect for Shelley's experience of nature, calm, and beauty, as well as his own more limited capacity for participating in it:

> It will not last;
> But it is well to have known it, though but once;

> It has enlarged my thoughts with a new sense,
> And I within my tablets would note down
> That there is such a feeling. (3.1.14–18)

When Byron has Manfred say that "such a feeling" exists, Manfred mirrors Byron's sincere observation that Shelley, as well as Wordsworth and Coleridge, had access to a religious sensibility that he lacks. Such feelings exist, but not for him.

Thomas Medwin recalls Byron saying the following about Wordsworth and Shelley in the fall of 1816:

> Shelley, when I was in Switzerland, used to dose me with Wordsworth physic even to nausea; and I do remember then reading some things of his with pleasure. He had once a feeling of Nature, which he carried almost to a deification of it:—that's why Shelley liked his poetry. (194)

Byron's medical metaphor is apt. Shelley *was* trying to cure Byron's darkest moods with "Wordsworth physic." If we take Byron at his word in his letters and journals, Byron's Wordsworthian nature poetry, in lines such as "High mountains are a feeling, but the hum / Of human cities—torture" (*Childe Harold* 3.682–83), reveals more of what he *wants* to feel than what he does feel. Manfred has found no authentic nurse in nature, either. During the first two acts, the flora are noted as absent, or, if present, almost completely bereft of vigor. It is typical of Manfred to discern "weeds of bitterness" (2.1.58) and "herbless Granite" (2.2.65), and he likens himself to "A blighted trunk upon a cursed root / Which but supplies a feeling to Decay" (1.2.68–69).

Wordsworth's or Shelley's sense of the world's beauty as a spiritual force does not belong to what Byron/Manfred normally knows of life. Byron's sincerity is such that even when he has his hero experience an epiphany of the lost Kalon, he cannot authentically give his protagonist the capacity to understand what such possibilities might imply about the powers of the universe—the very knowledge that Manfred sought in his tower, before his torments incapacitated him. Byron understands this limitation; he mounted on *Manfred* the epigraph: "There are more things in heaven and earth, Horatio, / Than are dreamt of in your philosophy" (*Hamlet* 1.5.175–76).

Byron gave Manfred, however, the yearning for more things that are dreamt of in his limited and fragmented self-consciousness. In the first act, he had mused:

> Oh that I were
> The viewless Spirit of a lovely sound,
> A living voice, a breathing harmony [. . .]! (1.2.52–54)

But he cannot submit to an experience unless he feels he has authored it himself, and neither "inexplicable stillness" nor "breathing harmony" are experiences Manfred knows how to produce at will. Instead, Manfred abandons the unbidden feeling, objectifies himself as his own experimental data, and makes note of himself as evidence that some such feeling exists. Manfred's active minimization of this calming experience is all the more bleakly pathological in light of his obsessive amplification of every grandiose and despairing impulse.

Manfred's Coliseum

The lost Kalon returns unbidden to Manfred once again, and with more authentic and naturalistic force, when Manfred remembers the Coliseum in the last scene of the play. Here Manfred honors "the language of another world" (3.4.7), albeit not quite a Wordsworthian nature language, but all the same a language that owes a great deal to the way Wordsworth dramatizes spiritual reawakening by acts of recollection. Byron has Manfred recall and amplify a Wordsworthian "spot of time" from the past to make its supreme value felt in the present. Like Wordsworth, Byron redeems at once lost time and lost self. But Manfred/Byron's time scale, unlike Wordsworth's, reaches into the distant past; and Byron's spiritual "spot" is a most un-Wordsworthian Coliseum.

Under the night sky, the amphitheater modulates all Manfred's extremes and integrates the opposites that tear him apart. Manfred's rhetoric fully embodies Manfred's potential ethos. His place description, as physical as it is psychological, picks up the pieces of all the usual antinomies, fusing them into an emblem of the integration Manfred might have achieved. In a full departure from the melodramatic rant, Manfred's description grounds the unaccustomed tone rehearsed in the Kalon soliloquy in a memory of an actual place that utterly absorbs and engages him.

The description of the place begins with yet another of the complicated echoes and mirrors that structure the poem: "The Stars are forth—the Moon above the tops / Of the snow-shining Mountains; Beautiful!" (3.4.1–2). The beautiful, in simple English, recurs to Manfred in a quiet way that immediately echoes the end of the previous scene, when his servant, Manuel, remembered a similar night: "'Twas twilight, as it may be now," Manuel had begun, "and the mountain snows / Began to glitter with the climbing Moon" (3.3.35–40). Manfred's description shares an uncharacteristically modest tone with that of the lowly Manuel, who, unlike the main male characters, not only has a proper name but shares Manfred's first syllable *Man*. Like Manuel, Manfred lingers with Nature and the benign night sky:

> I linger yet with Nature, for the Night
> Hath been to me a more familiar face
> Than that of Man. (3.4.3–5)

This familiar face, night personified as a companion, invites comparison with how Manuel had just recalled the prominence of Manfred's night companion, Astarte:

> Count Manfred was, as now, within his tower—
> How occupied, we knew not—but with him
> The sole companion of his wanderings
> And watchings—her, whom of all earthly things
> That lived, the only thing he seemed to love—
> As he indeed by blood was bound to do—
> The Lady Astarte, his— (3.3.41–47)

Manuel's story breaks off mid-sentence with the name, portentously declining to characterize the relationship. Manuel thus reestablishes Astarte, the nexus of Manfred's entire conflict and (as we now know) the agent of the grace that helps resolve it, as a specific dramatic context for the soliloquy to follow.

The conflation of Astarte with Manfred's night/Nature and dark, unnatural love and knowledge becomes more vivid when Manfred personifies the night as a woman. The figure, reminiscent of Byron's 1815 woman-as-night in "She walks in beauty, like the night / Of cloudless climes and starry skies" ("She Walks in Beauty" 1–2), places Manfred beyond the constricting world of his Astarte crime, and within the ethical abode of a more sacred Astarte, the mythical queen of heaven. Another remarkable change in the new third act provides further evidence of the turnaround. In the original version of act 3, a demon named Astoreth sings a taunting jingle celebrating her kinship with death and the raven (McGann's Commentary in *Complete Poetical Works* 4:467–68). The poet wrote Astoreth completely out of the new version. The new night/Nature persona, a positive Astarte figure who controls the emotional tone of the soliloquy, has been lovely and instructive and anything but demonic. Instead of jingling, Byron flashes into the real poetry he sustains throughout the soliloquy:

> and in her starry shade
> Of dim and solitary loveliness,
> I learned the language of another world. (3.4.5–7)

The character Astarte had been instructive as well through the boundary-crossing experience she stimulated in him, both in life and when she reappeared as a phantom. At the dramatic level of characters and actions, she is the play's clearest vehicle of "another world" of emotional and spiritual potency. Manfred was utterly isolated in that world with a mirror image of himself and with a crime whose intensity filled it. Here, however, the night sky is a benign and restorative spiritual force.

Like Wordsworth, Byron dramatizes the spiritual by the faint, the shifting, the least tangible, the just-out-of-view. (Recall the slant radiance and the barely audible sounds that people the air at the end of Wordsworth's "Wanderer."[13]) Compare Byron's gesturing trees, the quietly layered sounds of owls, watchdogs, and winds, and the starlight framed by ruins in the following lines. The lines are genuine Byron, not imitation Wordsworth:

> The trees which grew along the broken arches
> Waved dark in the blue Midnight—and the Stars
> Shone through the rents of Ruin—from afar
> The watch-dog bayed beyond the Tiber; and
> More near from out the Caesar's palace, came
> The Owl's long cry, and, interruptedly,
> Of distant Sentinels the fitful song,
> Begun and died upon the gentle wind. (3.4.12–19)

As the description continues, the diction domesticates the monumental architecture and gives it human scale and feeling. And—so uncharacteristically for *Manfred*—energy is figured by benignly vigorous plant life:

> Some Cypresses beyond the time-worn breach
> Appeared to skirt the horizon—yet they stood
> Within a bowshot, where the Caesars dwelt,
> And dwell the tuneless birds of Night, amidst
> A Grove which springs through levelled battlements,
> And twines its roots with the Imperial hearths;
> Ivy usurps the Laurel's place of growth. (3.4.20–26)

The cypresses *skirt* the horizon, giving the sky a human and feminine garment. *Hearths,* rather than any number of more grandiose artifacts, are the emblems of imperial domicile. The springing and twining grove is a welcome usurpation. Evergreen ivy, an ancient European symbol of eternal life, replaces the military victor's laurel and also suggests that the poet's laurel is a not-so-everlasting species of imperial self-assertion.

What does outlast the imperial ego is the Coliseum's "ruinous perfection," comprising even what is wrecked and bloody:

> But the Gladiators' bloody Circus stands—
> A noble wreck in ruinous perfection!
> While Caesar's chambers, and the Augustan halls,
> Grovel on earth in indistinct decay. (3.4.27–30)

The idea of history latent in these lines—an ordered succession of events in which something decays and something is perfected—is a new vehicle for psychological stability and continuity. Heretofore Manfred's temporal image of the world has mirrored his mental fragmentation. Manfred's days and nights have been "Endless, and all alike, as sands on the shore, / Innumerable atoms" (2.1. 54–55). In contrast, when he remembers the Coliseum, huge but still at a human scale, moon and stars descend and fuse with the ruins, perfecting and completing the space, repairing gaps in time. While the description is for the most part pure soliloquy, Manfred addresses one "thou," the moon (goddess Astoreth's celestial body), with an unprecedented tone of fulfillment and tenderness. He has no control over this powerfully restorative agent and desires none:

> And thou didst shine, thou rolling Moon! upon
> All this, and cast a wide and tender light,
> Which softened down the hoar austerity
> Of rugged desolation, and filled up,
> As 'twere, anew, the gaps of Centuries,
> Leaving that beautiful which was still so,
> And making that which was not, till the place
> Became Religion, and the heart ran o'er [. . .]. (3.4.31–38)

Manfred's heart opens involuntarily, without his having commanded the spirits to make it so. The desolation is comprehensively "soften'd down," "till the place / Became Religion, and the heart ran o'er"—as within, so without. At the level of the dramatic action, Manfred has given up his struggle to command the Spirits because he thinks he will soon get what he wants, oblivion; but ironically, Manfred gets an unexpected fringe benefit from the cessation of psychomachic hostilities: a memory that recapitulates what it is like to participate in the world with an unbroken psyche that wants awareness, not oblivion.

A powerful index of this psychological change is the poem's modulation of a single word: *wreck*. When Manfred describes the Coliseum as a "noble wreck in ruinous perfection" (3.4.28), the oxymoron signals that integration or resolution might possibly be underway. The term *wreck* has figured so prominently in describing Manfred that it immediately links the amphitheater to him. We have heard that his ruling star is a "burning wreck of a demolished World" (1.1.45). He has likened himself, "furrow'd o'er / With wrinkles ploughed by moments" to blasted pines, "Wrecks of a single winter" (1.2.67–72), and confessed that his actions have made his life a barren shore where "nothing rests save carcases and wrecks" (2.1.57). His confession has been mirrored in the speeches of destructive destinies who do the same thing: make unmitigated "wrecks," of a person (2.3.29) and a city (2.3.52). But the Coliseum, having sustained the same destructive destinies to become, like Manfred's star, the wreck of a demolished world, is somehow noble and perfect in spite of or because of all this.

This mental "place" is a sense of calm so profound that Byron—very uncharacteristically—elevates it to "religion," described as follows:

> and the heart ran o'er
> With silent worship of the Great of Old!—
> The dead but sceptered Sovereigns who still rule
> Our Spirits from their Urns. (3.4.38–41)

The ancestral urn, the last vivid image in the description, encapsulates Byron/Manfred's dominant antinomy of clay and fire, dust and deity, in one cohesive and overdetermined image. Here clay and fire doubly merge: The ceramic urn is literally fired clay, and its content ash is metaphorically the fired clay of the cremated body. Dust and deity merge as ashes of the still-potent past, as Manfred merges for a moment into the stream of human time.

But Manfred soon distances himself, suppressing the psychic integration figured by his rhetoric. His image of integration evokes a compensatory distancing or splitting. The cool detachment that ended the "Kalon" soliloquy recurs:

> 'Twas such a Night!
> 'Tis strange that I recall it—at this time—
> But I have found our thoughts take wildest flight,
> Even at the moment when they should array
> Themselves in pensive order. (3.4.42–46)

The conclusion is sadly ironic, for the irony is lost on Manfred but perhaps intended by Byron. The strangeness Manfred senses in his thoughts is the strangeness of sanity, a mind in dynamic equilibrium rather than in stalemate, "one desart, / Barren and cold" (2.1.55–56). Blackstone describes the Coliseum of Manfred as a "dynamic ideogram" (235), and as Byron recognized, the dynamic ideogram produced "some good poetry," in fact the most sustained arrangement of coherent reflection in the entire play. Of all Manfred's speeches, it is the worst possible candidate for "wildest flight." Manfred neither surges into space nor plunges into the abyss, but rather "lingers" on the ground, down to earth and in the stream of time, surrendering willingly to a well-regulated resurgence of personal and cultural memory that completes his present state, and indeed prepares him for death. Formally the description recapitulates patterns established by the discordant voices emanating from the play's Alpine landscapes and is in this sense the poem's imagistic nexus, the most sustained and harmonious integration of the antithetical images that embody Manfred's fragmented and conflicted self. But Byron has his character misinterpret and all too unwittingly fail to completely assimilate all this. Manfred's failure at this juncture is secured in part by the fact that Byron gave his isolated character these words in a soliloquy; no other character has the opportunity to respond in ways that might further stimulate Manfred's reflections. In the English dramatic soliloquy, the character reliably speaks the truth to the audience alone, normally an unpleasant truth that the character urgently needs to conceal. Byron follows the truth-telling tradition but turns the usual content on its head. Manfred reveals an innocent secret of imagined peace that, tragically, he cannot share with anyone.

Although Manfred does not fully enact the integration figured by the descriptive soliloquy, it does nevertheless have a slight but telling effect on the dramatic resolution. When Byron revised the play, he not only wrote out dark Astoreth and wrote in a more beneficent night. He also made the strictly dramatic resolution of the third act more consistent with the imagistic resolution achieved by the ethical description of the Coliseum, as if the main character had assimilated at least a bit of the character of the ancient place and could act accordingly. In the new version, Manfred who has so loudly and consistently protested his autonomy and separation from humankind does not actually die alone. Two changes mitigate Manfred's solitude. First, Byron now has Manfred's genius (along with some unnamed spirits) summon him to death (3.4.81–91), as if a spiritual trace of Rome extends from the Coliseum. Second, he has Manfred die in the beneficent company of the Abbot, whom he now respects.

The Abbot, the most complex human character besides Manfred, not only mirrors and intensifies Manfred's awareness of fragmentation but also figures Manfred's strong desire for reconciliation. Byron gives the Abbot intimate knowledge of Manfred and puts into the Abbot's mouth a concise summary of Manfred's psychological configuration at the end of act 3, scene 1:

> This should have been a noble creature. He
> Hath all the energy which would have made
> A goodly frame of glorious elements,

> Had they been wisely mingled; as it is,
> It is an awful Chaos—Light and Darkness—
> And Mind and Dust—and passions and pure thoughts
> Mixed, and contending without end or order—
> All dormant or destructive. (3.1.160–67)

The Coliseum embodies the potential that the Abbot discerns in Manfred: "a goodly frame of glorious elements." The place enfolds all the binaries the Abbot discerns in Manfred, but it keeps them "wisely mingled" and permanently configured into a " ruinous perfection" instead of an "awful chaos." The structure thus brings together in a single ethical unity all those characterological elements that, according to the Abbot, Manfred cannot unite within himself.

The genius who comes for Manfred is a significant renaming of the ruling star introduced in the first scene of the play, as if a Roman ancestor he worshipped the night before were guiding him—or trying to—from the urn that figures significantly in the Coliseum description. The Roman *genius* is the "male spirit of a *gens* [one's people] existing in his lifetime in the head of the family, and subsequently in the divine or spiritual part of each individual" (*OLD*). The Romans believed that this ancestral spirit controls one's character and finally leads one to death—the genius literally rules from the urn and summons to the urn. Such ideas would have been commonplace to Byron, and he uses them to reinforce the connection to the dead but vital past that Manfred found by meditating upon the Coliseum. But then he has Manfred arrogantly reject the (admittedly infernal) genius along with the other unnamed spirits: "Away! I'll die as I have lived—Alone" (3.4.90). Manfred, however, does not get to die alone.

In fact, the entire encounter with the spirits happens in the company of the unfearing Abbot. With a gesture significantly reversing his refusal of help from (say) the Chamois Hunter, Manfred asks the Abbot for support in his dying swoon:

> 'Tis over— —my dull eyes can fix thee not,
> But all things swim around me, and the Earth
> Heaves as if it were beneath me. Fare thee well—
> Give me thy hand. (3.4.145–48)

Manfred's uncharacteristically dependent gesture, a request to be steadied while the earth heaved beneath him, is all the more marked when set against his refusal of comfort during his previous encounter with the Abbot. Then, when the Abbot had tried to persuade Manfred that atonement and reconciliation were possible, Manfred had assumed the imperious persona of the dying Emperor Nero, who like Manfred was "the Victim of a self-inflicted wound" (3.1.89), and who rejected help from a mere soldier:

> The dying Roman thrust him back and said—
> Some empire still in his expiring glance—
> "It is too late—is this fidelity?"
> ABBOT: And what of this?
> MAN: I answer with the Roman
> "It is too late!"
> ABBOT: It never can be so,
> To reconcile thyself with thy own soul. (3.1.94–99)

Manfred's request for the Abbot's hand is Byron's largest single step (albeit too little too late) in developing the Abbot during act 3 as an actual character in relationship to Manfred, rather than as merely an intimate perspective on Manfred's mind. Heedless of Manfred's warnings, the Abbot has followed Manfred, seen and heard the spirits undaunted, and stayed to attend Manfred's death. For all that, Manfred's satanic grandiosity surges forth one last time. He wants to die with some of mad Nero's empire in his expiring glance: "Old Man! 'tis not so difficult to die" (3.4.151). These last words, as Byron wrote to Murray on 12 August 1817, produce "the whole effect & moral of the poem" ("*So late*" 257). But the words are spoken holding the Abbot's hand. Lone Manfred, in spite of himself, dies connected to present humanity and to a vital past, an image of Rome more spiritually complicated and integrated than the mad emperor he wants consciously to imitate. Although Manfred rejects the Abbot's religion, his behavior shows a partial assimilation of the "religion" represented by the Coliseum, its ancient Roman context and its modern, organic perfection. It is the amphitheater, then, so powerfully associated with the eve of death—"'Twas such a Night!" (3.4.42)—that speaks the language of another world and acts as a genuine deathbed comfort.

Manfred of the Coliseum description shares an imaginative quality with Byron, Byron's self-described *mobilité*. He defines it in a note to *Don Juan* 16.820 as "an excessive susceptibility of immediate impressions—at the same time without losing the past" (*Complete Poetical Works* 5:769). Mobilité extending into the personal and historical past is precisely the self-integrating drama of memory that Manfred undertakes. The Roman Coliseum, set against the sublime Alpine glaciers that dominate *Manfred's* setting and its hero's sublimely fragmented psyche, gave Byron exactly the vehicle he needed to figure Manfred's integrating self as a perfecting resurgence of the past into the present. The same drama of integration tenuously held would appear soon afterward in a more frankly subjective Coliseum, the best developed of the entire series of ethical place descriptions in *Childe Harold* 4.

Harold's Coliseum

In *Manfred* Byron began to develop the possibilities he had glimpsed—albeit through a lens darkened with disdain—in the psychological locodescriptive poetry of *The Excursion*. *Childe Harold* 4 takes up the same themes and employs basically the same techniques, but in a more leisurely and extended deployment of place description as a vehicle for exploring the complexities of the human psyche. Here the integrating drama of ego and counterpart personality, of personal and cultural memory and oblivion, becomes more complicated than in *Manfred*. Pilgrim Byron reflecting on his own life, fortunes, and artistic aspirations remembers much more of the personal and cultural past than Manfred does; and the personal and historical time perspectives become more finely interfused. Approaching Rome, Byron's past/present mobilité finds its most deeply implicating mood, and the reader begins to anticipate how complex Byron's perception and memory may become when he gets to this evocative place. This increased complexity, however, does not represent any fundamental change in the poet's tune; it is rather a brilliant riff on the basic melody already worked out at a smaller scale in *Manfred*.

At stanza 44, the pilgrim remembers wandering (as at the beginning of Manfred's Coliseum soliloquy) and retracing the ancient itinerary of a friend of Cicero's, Servius Sulpicius. Servius described the journey in a consolatory letter to Cicero upon the death of Tullia, Cicero's daughter and favorite child, a historical counterpart to Byron's "lost" daughter, Ada. Servius, hoping to give his friend some Stoic perspective on his devastating loss, described the war-ravaged towns of Aegina, Piraeus, Corinth, and Megara and drew an analogy between losing a city and losing a person. Byron partially translates the analogy (strikingly reminiscent of the wrecks of person and city at *Manfred* 2.3.29 and 2.3.52) in a note to stanza 44: "the carcases of so many noble cities lie here exposed before me in one view" (*Complete Poetical Works* 2:234).[14] The pilgrim "saw all these unite / In ruin" (4.395–96). Byron unites himself—"I in desolation"—to Servius' "dust and blackness" (4.412) and imagines dead Rome: "The skeleton of her Titanic form, / Wrecks of another World, whose ashes still are warm" (4.413–14), a vast Promethean enlargement of Manfred's Roman ancestors ruling from their funeral urns. From personal and cultural losses of the present and the distant past, Byron builds in three elegiac stanzas a complicated trace of personal and cultural memory that begins the work of integrating antiquity with the living present, an exercise in integrating himself with the world.

The wandering pilgrim travels over ground that becomes increasingly numinous as he approaches Rome, unlike Manfred, who experiences a sudden intrusive memory of Rome. Unlike Manfred, he never travels to metaphysical abodes such as the abode of the Evil Principle, but always to actual places that turn out to have more authentic spiritual meaning for Byron than Manfred's spiritual machinery. It is as if Byron is following the Chamois Hunter's advice to be the kind of hunter who stays close to the ground. The pilgrim's journey culminates not in some purely fictional place but in actual Rome, imaginatively engaged. Byron the exile addresses the place as a whole in his own full voice: "Oh Rome! my Country! City of the Soul! / The Orphans of the Heart must turn to thee" (4.694–5). At the Coliseum, he "evocates" not a ghost, as in *Manfred,* but the *genius loci.* The answer he will get is the poetry that the genius loci seems to write about itself when the place becomes a speaking emblem of mind.

The pilgrim's last stop before Rome is the fountain of the tutelary nymph Egeria. Mythological Egeria is consort and muse to Rome's legendary King Numa, who persuaded the Romans that he received political inspiration from trysts with Egeria in her sacred grove. When Numa died Egeria's grief was so profound that, in Ovid's account, she dissolved into perpetual tears that water the garden. While Byron's description of the place engages traditional materials from Livy, Ovid, and Juvenal, the sources and analogues do not begin to account for the power of this ethical place description. A primitive homeopathic strain in Byron's imagination engages Egeria and her grove and presents the place anew and whole, as an authentic poem of the mind.[15] Byron's Egeria, and the ethical garden in which she dwells, marks the recurrence of the same power, and the same challenge, that Astarte symbolized in *Manfred.* After a perfunctory one-line reference to the more famous Numa, Byron enthusiastically introduces Egeria as the dream of perfect love, set in a classical locus amoenus; but here the garden-as-woman figures unfulfillable desire. "Egeria! sweet Creation of some heart / Which found no mortal resting-place so fair / As thine ideal breast" (4.1027–29).

He finds the mosses of her fountain eternally watered. The face of the spring "Reflects the meek-eyed Genius of the place" (4.1039), a place "Haunted by holy Love—the earliest Oracle!" (4.1062). Like Astarte and the subject of "She Walks in Beauty," Egeria has a special affinity for night: "The purple Midnight veiled that mystic meeting / With her most starry canopy" (4.1057–58). But the dream has no earthly realization—dust and deity are completely sundered: "Oh Love! no habitant of Earth thou art— / An unseen Seraph, we believe in thee" (4.1081–1082). Love, like other gods, is fevered "into false creation" (4.1091) by desire:

> The mind hath made thee, as it peopled Heaven,
> Even with its own desiring Phantasy,
> And to a thought such shape and image given,
> As haunts the unquenched Soul–parched—wearied—wrung—and riven. (4.1086–89)

The encounter with Egeria follows the typical pattern for Byron's love fantasy: a gorgeous dream of narcissistic love—"Of its own beauty is the Mind diseased, / And fevers into false creation" (4.1090–1)—that ultimately leads to despair. The process here is figured by the decay of the well-watered garden into a wilderness of sinister plants. The garden turns against the gardener:

> Alas! our young Affections run to waste,
> Or water but the Desart! whence arise
> But weeds of dark luxuriance, tares of haste,
> Rank at the core, though tempting to the eyes,
> Flowers whose wild odours breathe but agonies,
> And trees whose gums are poison [. . .]. (4.1072–77)

Byronic dust completes the figure: "Few—none—find what they love or could have loved" (4.1117); for circumstance, says Byron, "turns Hope to dust,—the dust we all have trod" (4.1125). The pilgrim's despair is complete: "Our life is a false nature—'tis not in / The harmony of things [. . .] . / Disease, death, bondage" (4.1126–32) rain upon humanity. "And worse, the woes we see not [. . .] throb through / The immedicable Soul" (4.1133–34).

The despair and stasis into which the Egeria description resolves itself finally gives way to a one-stanza transition to the Coliseum. Some energy and courage begin to accumulate in the pilgrim's immedicable soul as he approaches the monument that will turn out to be his refuge:

> Yet let us ponder boldly—'tis a base
> Abandonment of Reason to resign
> Our right of Thought—our last and only place
> Of Refuge. (4.1135–38)

Reason, then, is Byron's refuge from Egeria's false creation, the "unreached Paradise of [. . .] despair" (4.1096). But a divine faculty that can bring forth true creation is figured heroically in stanza 127 by dark against light, beneficent shadow against harsh light, a reversal of the usual connotations, and by Prometheus against Zeus—familiar *Manfred* material. In *Manfred*, the night spirit had implored Manfred not to torture her with light (1.1.108–09). In canto 4 of *Childe Harold* night is akin to the more explicitly Promethean interior of the human *mind*, linked by the emphatic near-rhyme to the passage's final image of a dark *mine* lit by a beam:

> Our right of Thought—our last and only place
> Of Refuge; this, at least, shall still be mine:
> Though from our birth the Faculty divine

> Is chained and tortured—cabined, cribbed, confined,
> And bred in darkness, lest the Truth should shine
> Too brightly on the unprepared Mind,
> The Beam pours in, for Time and Skill will couch the blind. (4.1137–43)

One who has just read *Manfred* might guess a trace of Manfred's therapeutic moon in the beam pouring in. The guess would be borne out in the next stanza which repeats not only the *-ine* rhyme scheme but the words *mine divine shine;* for the pilgrim has arrived at the Coliseum, an "exhaustless Mine [mind?] / Of Contemplation" (4.1150–51):

> the Moonbeams shine
> As 'twere its natural torches—for divine
> Should be the light which streams here, to illume
> This long-explored but still exhaustless Mine
> Of Contemplation. (4.1147–51)

If Manfred's Coliseum is at least a latent image of historic continuity and psychic wholeness, the pilgrim's Coliseum evokes nothing less than the exhaustless interior of the self. So begin the 18 Coliseum stanzas (128–145), by far the longest treatment of any place in canto 4.

The deep Coliseum mind, figured next as deep sky, seems to start producing its own poem when the last line of stanza 128 enjambs the next, and "the deep Skies assume / Hues which have words" (4.1152–1153). This refraction of moonlight into hues is a figure for the poet articulating his unitary impression into words, a unitary impression of eternity perfected by time. Time "broke his scythe" on the place and gave it "a Spirit's feeling [. . .] a power / And Magic" (4.1157–59). In the next eight intensely psychological stanzas (130–137), Byron first invokes both Time and Nemesis as his muses. As a poet, he craves a gift *for*—not from—Time as "Beautifier of the dead" (4.1162), comforter, healer, avenger, and sole philosopher. As he merges with the ruin he asks to be heard—to be able to speak—so that the wreck of his life might be redeemed by poetry:

> Amidst this wreck, where thou hast made a shrine
> And temple more divinely desolate,
> Among thy mightier offerings here are mine,
> Ruins of years. (4.1171–74)

He asks Time to hear him only if he has not been "too elate" (4.1175), a dangerous fate-tempting proposition for the inflation-prone Byronic hero. After ending this apostrophe to Time on a very low note—"let me not have worn / This iron in my Soul in vain" (4.1178–1179)—he then immediately oscillates toward the grandiose in his invocation of Nemesis. The invocation sounds like magisterial Manfred's voice in act 1, but now it is the pilgrim who says: "I call thee from the dust! / Dost thou not hear my heart?—Awake! thou shalt, and must" (4.1187–88). When Byron dedicates his blood to Nemesis, "To thee I do devote it—*thou* shalt take / The vengeance" (4.1194–95; Byron's emphasis), his melodramatic words put the actual destruction of gladiators in its cultural context as theater where plays were also performed:

> Here, where the Ancient paid thee homage long—
> Thou, who didst call the Furies from the abyss,
> And round Orestes bade them howl and hiss [. . .]. (4.1182–84)

The pilgrim wants both Time the avenger and Nemesis to adjudicate the tragic outcome; but unlike Manfred, he gives up his authority gladiator-style to the attending spirits, as if the Furies howling and hissing around Orestes were a howling and hissing circus audience.

Byron, the most popular of the great English Romantic poets in his own time, has in fact throughout *Childe Harold* been making a spectacle of his pain for a mass audience. "My domestic destruction," he wrote to Moore on 28 February 1817, "was a fine opening for all the world, of which all, who could, did well to avail themselves" ("*So late*" 177). The pilgrim asks for justice for the "Ancestral faults" (4.1190) he has incurred, and imagines himself avenged by "a far hour," by Time, that much larger audience, "the Corrector where our Judgements err" (4.1165), that is by readers. He craves his place in the canon; he wants to rule from his own urn:

> Though I be ashes; a far hour shall wreak
> The deep prophetic fullness of this Verse,
> And pile on human heads the Mountain of my Curse! (4.1204–06)

If Byron's verse will be a curse that fulfills itself in time, it is an ironic curse that shows Byron gaining some perspective on his histrionic anger. "That Curse shall be Forgiveness," (4.1207) he hastens to assure us and himself. Moreover, he reflects that he has "not lived in vain: / My Mind may lose its force, my Blood its fire, / And my Frame perish even in conquering pain" (4.1225–27). In accepting that he will lose *both* his fire and his clay frame, he overcomes his dominant antinomy for a moment, the antinomy he had believed embraced everything. Outside the antinomy, something endures that Byron figures forth in a simile likening titanic strength to a soft tone.

The resulting image of eternal Promethean energy unites the opposites of strength and softness: "that within me which shall tire / Torture and Time, and breathe when I expire" (4.1228–29), *like* something soft and actively softening: "Like the remembered tone of a mute lyre," sinking on "softened Spirits" to "move / In hearts all rocky now the late remorse of Love" (4.1231–33).

From the quiet he finds in the Coliseum, Byron invokes the genius loci, "thou dread Power / Nameless, yet thus omnipotent, which here / Walk'st in the shadow of the midnight hour," (4.1234–36) with a religious attitude: "With a deep awe, yet all distinct from fear" (4.1237). The place has, in Manfred's words, become religion. The pilgrim's next image of the place, an image of death rearing life, figures his own emergence from dust:

> Thy haunts are ever where the dead walls rear
> Their ivy mantles, and the solemn scene
> Derives from thee a sense so deep and clear
> That we become a part of what has been,
> And grow unto the spot—all-seeing but unseen. (4.1238–42)

That the dead walls should *rear* ivy animates and personifies the ancient wall as intent on nurturing the living present. The enlivening wall figures exactly how the depressed and emotionally inert pilgrim begins to come to life enmeshed with the Coliseum and its human history. The human beings of Byron's distant genial past are ashes and dust, like the wall. Byron's spiritual and artistic awakening here is as alive and present but as dependent and reciprocally related to the past as the ivy growing into the spot, becoming part of what has been. This "solemn scene" may not be purely sylvan, but the animating presence of the ivy connects it with the tradition of the woody theater inaugurated by Virgil. Its vitality derives in part from its participation in the verdant growth covering it and in part from its character as an actual theater where the most characteristically Roman of all spectacles were held. Although Cheeke contends that the Coliseum "was the place to go in ancient Rome not for aesthetic pleasure, but to enjoy the experience of seeing a man killed" (5), there was in ancient Rome no simple disjunction between aesthetic pleasure (however defined) and the pleasures afforded by the Coliseum. Diverse spectacles were staged there, from naval battles and wild beast hunts to plays in which condemned criminals were actually executed in elaborately produced fictional worlds.

The most important human participants in those spectacles were, for Byron, the sacrificed gladiators whose blood had literally fed the spot. Gladiators had made only a cameo appearance in *Manfred,* but in a crucial passage: "But the Gladiators' bloody Circus stands— / A noble wreck in ruinous perfection" (3.3.27–28). The figure of the gladiator flourishes in *Childe Harold* 4 (stanzas 139–142) as the main character of the Coliseum meditation, a slave-superstar uniting deity and dust in a theatrical persona who is "Butchered to make a Roman holiday" (4.1267). The gladiator passage develops and intensifies the process of acceptance underway in stanzas 137–138. The gladiator, a second and more vivid image of union than the wall-reared ivy, empowers the poet's voice just as the wall had, and by a similar process. The gladiator, like the death-accepting pilgrim in stanzas 137—138, "Consents to death, but conquers Agony" (4.1254). The gladiator, like the wall, is dead but potent in the present. His thundering blood is audible in the pilgrim's voice and footsteps:

> And through his side the last drops, ebbing slow
> From the red gash, fall heavy, one by one,
> Like the first of a thunder-shower; and now
> The arena swims around him—he is gone. (4.1256–59)

"But here," Byron adds a few lines later, "where Murder breathed her bloody steam,"

> My voice sounds much—and fall the stars' faint rays
> On the Arena void—seats crushed—walls bowed—
> And Galleries, where my steps seem echoes strangely loud. (4.1270–78)

When the pilgrim experiences an animated genius loci as an active fragmentary structure securing its autonomous life, the pilgrim and the genius speak as one voice. It is this merger of genius loci and narrator that makes Byron's Coliseum such a powerful emblem of *his* mind and such a distinctively Romantic and vividly ethical place description.

Byron, now in the fully amplified voice of the place, concludes the description with three stanzas that complete the development of the Coliseum as an emblem of mind. Stanza 143 personifies the wall once again, this time as a titanic skeleton that recapitulates Servius's cadaverous towns and counters the finality of their destruction. The eternally productive cadaverous structure, the exhaustless mine of contemplation we met at the beginning of the passage, is an eternally active and productive ancestral genius. The Coliseum, the poet's genius, rears grand progeny—the major artifacts of civilization:

> A Ruin—yet what Ruin! from its mass
> Walls—palaces—half-cities, have been reared;
> Yet oft the enormous Skeleton ye pass

> And marvel where the spoil could have appeared.
> Hath it indeed been plundered, or but cleared? (4.1279–83)

Byron's psychological insight here is that the Coliseum's very ruin is inextricable from its development into a stable structure: "Alas! developed, opens the decay, / When the Colossal Fabric's form is neared" (4.1284–85). The decay-opened fabric, in dynamic equilibrium with all forces that impinge upon it, fills with well-modulated illumination in a final image of psychic and cultural integration. At stanza 144, the Coliseum's round structure is Caesar's head, a psychic space in which once again we find oppositional image pairs resolved. Light versus dark modulates, as in Manfred's soliloquy, into moonlight and starlight. This modulated light is, as in *Manfred,* the essential illumination, the gap-filling plenum, a figure for meaning and value:

> But when the rising Moon begins to climb
> Its topmost arch, and gently pauses there;
> When the Stars twinkle through the loops of Time,
> And the low Night-breeze waves along the air
> The Garland-forest, which the grey Walls wear,
> Like Laurels on the bald first Caesar's head;
> When the light shines serene but doth not glare—
> Then in this magic circle raise the dead:
> Heroes have trod this spot—'tis on their dust ye tread. (4.1288–96)

The soft "Garland-forest" waving in "the low Night-breeze" recalls the mute and sinking lyre-tone of stanza 137. The air is in motion about the Coliseum in a peculiarly Romantic way, as a "property of landscape, but also a vehicle for radical changes in the poet's mind" (Abrams, "Correspondent" 26). Abrams's observation applies particularly well here, for this feature of Romantic rhetoric adds yet another dimension to an already overdetermined emblem of mind. The gently moving organic/inorganic wall, the mine of contemplation now likened to Caesar's laurel-crowned imperial head, has accumulated so many layers of signification that it figures nothing less than a magic circle within which civilization is made and unmade, permanently contained, and literally raised from the dead. Within the magic circle dust and deity merge as the alive-in-death gladiator, the quintessential performance artist who made a cameo appearance in *Manfred.* Harold's Caesar-Coliseum is the most complete expression of Manfred's ancestors ruling from the urn.

In 1816, when Shelley was "dosing" him with Wordsworth, Byron wrote these wistful lines:

> When elements to elements conform,
> And dust is as should be, shall I not

> Feel all I see—less dazzling—but more warm?
> The bodiless thought? the Spirit of each Spot?
> Of which, even now, I share at times the immortal lot?
> (*Childe Harold* 3.702–06)

Byron's "Spirit of each Spot" is Wordsworth's "Spirit that knows no insulated spot," the "*active* principle:—howe'er removed / From sense and observation," that is assigned to "every Form of Being" (*Excursion* 387; Wordsworth's italics). Instead of finding Wordsworth's active principle as Manfred tried to do when he imperiously summoned it—"Mysterious Agency!" (1.1.28)—Byron finds the mysterious agency when it comes unbidden through mobilité, a perceptual artistry that, by his own account, integrates the past with the surge of present sensation. Mobilité recalled and amplified the Coliseum, interfusing its unity and permanence with the imagination that perceived it. Its ruin redeemed Manfred's ruling star, the "burning wreck of a demolished World" (*Manfred* 1.1.45)—Byron's darkest sense of both self and history—into a unifying classical-romantic "scene" of psychic and cultural cohesion. The place became religion, both magical abode and pious attachment. Like all the ethical places that watered Harold's heart and replenished the void, it "came like Truth—and disappeared like dreams" (*Childe Harold* 4.56).

Byron's treatment of the Coliseum directly echoes Wordsworth's depiction of Margaret's cottage. Indeed, if modern editors could publish a section of *Excursion* 1 under the title "The Ruined Cottage," one could just as legitimately excerpt the Coliseum section of *Childe Harold* 4 under the title "The Ruined Amphitheater." In each case the poet attempts to place a decayed building in its historical, geographical, and moral contexts. One might want to argue that Byron's interest in his building is more "historical" than Wordsworth's in his, in that the Coliseum is world famous whereas the cottage is known only locally. But it would be a mistake to do so. Wordsworth's interest in Margaret's cottage is as historical as Byron's in the Coliseum; the difference is primarily that Bryon could expect his reader to know already much of the historical context of the Coliseum. Wordsworth had to devote many lines of the poem to a thorough account of this particular cottage's history, though he could expect his reader to know already the general historical context of Margaret's misfortune.

Byron learned from Wordsworth how to make a ruined building into an emblem of a complex and tragic personal history. Byron is careful in his depiction of the Coliseum to allude only to those historical facts that are germane to his own personal history, and when necessary he even distorts history—as when he places Julius Caesar in the Coliseum—to strengthen the personal connection. But this concern with the personal is by no means solipsistic. Byron had discovered in *Excursion* 1 the technique whereby a place ecphrasis could forge a link between the personal and the public: Margaret's story is not about her alone; it is about all those who have to deal with overwhelming grief; and it is presented as a lesson given by the wandering pedlar to his young friend.

Even self-absorbed Byron realized that, in a similar fashion, the Coliseum offered a way to link his personal griefs to those suffered by countless other orphans of the heart. It was not only Byron, after all, whose anguish had become the material for public entertainment. Byron found in Wordsworth's *Excursion* the model for using a ruined building in a landscape as a kind of intersection between the private and the public, the individual and the community. As Byron doubtless realized, the Coliseum was perhaps even better suited to this purpose than Margaret's cottage. It is, after all, the most public of all public places, a location that has been visited by millions and been famous for millennia. And it fuses the human artifact into its natural landscape even better than a cottage into a garden that is beginning to encroach upon it. The Coliseum had become over the centuries its own quite stable garden, bedecked with greenery of all sorts securely rooted into its very walls. Byron takes pains to depict the building as enfolding cosmic nature: it is filled with moonlight and stars shine among its arches, as if the vault of heaven were somehow contained within the vaults of its Roman architecture. It would be hard to argue that this Byron is any less a poet of the natural landscape than the Wordsworth of Margaret's overgrown cottage. In both cases, the poems blur the boundary between the natural and the artificial, though Byron went perhaps even further than his predecessor in obliterating it altogether.

No doubt Byron considered *The Excursion* to be a "drowsy frowsy" piece of work. But he paid careful attention to it all the same, and he learned from it how to do something he could not otherwise have done: to find a way back from his Alpine loneliness into the community of all those who dwell in damaged circumstances. The Coliseum and the cottage are richly complex places in which buildings situated in a dramatically human-altered landscape offer moving emblems of human ruin and recovery.

Epilogue: Immediacy

> Description is revelation. It is not
> The thing described, nor false facsimile.
> —Wallace Stevens,
> "Description without Place"

My topic has been the imagined place in European literature, illustrated by a necessarily restricted selection of examples. I have emphasized the self-conscious psychological valency that place description took on for the British Romantics, but I would not like to leave readers with the false impression that the poetics of immediacy that is so well developed in descriptions of significant places is either uniquely European or that it died out with a last efflorescence during the Romantic period.

In her aesthetic manifesto, "Modern Fiction," Virginia Woolf declared: "Life is not a series of gig-lamps symmetrically arranged; life is a luminous halo, a semi-transparent envelope surrounding us from the beginning of consciousness to the end" (150). Woolf's conviction that the purpose of fiction is to convey this luminosity, "this varying, this unknown and uncircumscribed spirit, whatever aberration or complexity it may display, with as little admixture of the alien and external as possible" (150), reminds us that the aspirations of classical ecphrasis remained a part of European literary culture well into the twentieth century. A modernist project like Woolf's—or Kafka's, Proust's, or Hemingway's—was in fact governed by an intense desire to make the reader "as if present" and emotionally engaged; to move the reader to experience life through the poet's art; to say, as Odysseus said about the artistry of the bard Demodocus: "How true to life, all too true [*kata kosmon*]" (8.489; Fagles trans.).

This ancient and enduring goal of rhetorical immediacy gave rise to a number of assumptions about what is integral to a literary work, as opposed to what might be considered an "admixture of the alien and external," as Woolf puts it. The story of classical ecphrasis and its heritage has therefore entailed a story about unity—or, to be more precise, about at least three kinds of unity. There is, first, the unity of the work, considered sometimes as a discrete passage, sometimes as an independent opus, sometimes as the totality of an author's production, or sometimes even as the entire cultural output of a community; then, second, the unity of the psyche, whether that of the author, of the characters depicted in his works, or (for a poet like Wordsworth or Byron) a merger of both; and, third, the unity of the mind and the world in experience, so that the thing experienced and the person doing the experiencing are joined together as a single spiritual unit. If the historical development of classical place ecphrasis—from the primitive homeopathic union of person and place in Homer's descriptions to the creative place perception of Milton's Satan or Wordsworth's *Excursion* characters and on to what Robert Alter has aptly called the "urban pastoral" of *Mrs. Dalloway*'s humanly embodied London (103)—if all this could be sketched in one broad stroke, at least one clear feature would emerge: an increasing urgency, in Romantic and modernist art, to achieve integrity as fully as possible on all three of these levels, but especially to inscribe the unity of mind and place in experience. When Alter calls Clarissa Dalloway's London an "allegorical figure of human existence both in its pulsing vitality and its ultimate destiny of decay," and a "theater of vitality and transience" (120), he invokes a long tradition of ethical place description that includes such theaters of human existence as Virgil's tragic Carthage and Byron's Coliseum.

It is commonly recognized that notions of unity, along with related notions of a shareable life that could be apprehended and imaginatively conveyed in literature, met with a particularly intense wave of skepticism as modernism waned in the mid-to-late twentieth century. But the importance of place description did not diminish with the decline of the modernist aesthetic. On the contrary, postmodernism has become closely identified with the very question of the human significance of places. Consider Fredric Jameson's influential ecphrasis of "a full-blown postmodern building" (38), architect John Portman's Westin Bonaventure Hotel:

> The descent is dramatic enough, plummeting back down through the roof to splash down in the lake. What happens when you get there is something else, which can only be characterized as milling confusion, something like the vengeance this space takes on those who still seek to walk through it. Given the absolute symmetry of the four towers, it is quite impossible to get your bearings in this lobby [. . .]. I will take as the most dramatic practical result of this spatial mutation the notorious dilemma of the shopkeepers on the various balconies: it has been obvious since the opening of the hotel in 1977 that nobody could ever find any of these stores, and even if you once located the appropriate boutique, you would be most unlikely to be as fortunate a second time; as a consequence,

the commercial tenants are in despair and all the merchandise is marked down to bargain prices. (43–44)

Jameson's ecphrasis frames the issue of postmodern aesthetics in terms of a problematic relationship between the human mind and the spaces in which human bodies are located. It is a traditional, if not archetypal, way of proceeding. As a pendant to what turns out to be a self-consciously allegorical description, Jameson offers a moral: "my principal point here," he writes, is

> that this latest mutation in space—postmodern hyperspace—has finally succeeded in transcending the capacities of the individual human body to locate itself, to organize its immediate surroundings perceptually, and cognitively to map its position in a mappable external world. (44)

Jameson's postmodern hyperspace is an original take on a traditional topos: hell as spatial disorientation, as the place where it is impossible to find one's way.

Even the postmodern cinema is still earnestly concerned with the implications of Milton's observation that "the mind is its own place." Nothing could illustrate this concern more vividly than the 1999 film *Being John Malkovich*, written by Charlie Kaufman and directed by Spike Jonze. The premise of the plot is that the hero, Craig Schwartz (John Cusack), discovers behind a file cabinet an extraordinary portal, a noir version of the wardrobe that takes the children to Narnia. This gateway, however, leads not into a magical kingdom of lions and witches but into the consciousness of the actor John Malkovich. Craig finds that he can remain inside the mind of the actor and experience the world as Malkovich does for around 15 minutes at a time. When the quarter hour is up, he finds himself just as mysteriously dumped in a ditch beside the New Jersey Turnpike. The film develops by exploring the implications of one person's moving into the space of another person's mind. The film critiques the notion of immediacy in its own wacky fashion, but it never departs from the basic assumption that a perfect sharing of experience is possible. It does, however, raise serious questions about the desirability of such sharing.

Postmodernism thus remains very interested in the way in which the configuration of places reflects the structure of the human psyche, though in a somewhat more skeptical manner (as we might expect) than that of modernism. The postmodern place tends to be characterized not only by acute spatial discomfort of various kinds but by inauthenticity, artificiality, or Disneylandish separation from reality. The Westin Bonaventure as Jameson describes it has something quintessentially phony about it, and it is that cruel and lavish phoniness that marks its congruence with late capitalist culture. Even the John Malkovich who plays the role of John Malkovich in the film turns out to be curiously inauthentic: the credits list the actor playing the role as "John Horatio Malkovich," though the actor we know from such films as *Dangerous Liaisons* and *The Portrait of a Lady* is named John Gavin Malkovich. The Westin Bonaventure and the mind of John Malkovich thus turn out to be less "actual" places than representations of places, and the depictions of such places are, like the art ecphrasis theorized by the twentieth century, representations of cultural representations.

Postmodernism has been fascinated by the excessive, the superficial, and the meaningless. Modernism, on the other hand, had fought the recurring battle against excessive, superficial, or meaningless description that, as this book has shown, had been fought in various ways by ancient rhetoricians and Romantic poets. In its modernist form, it was James's battle against the novel as "loose baggy monster" (*Art* 84) or Woolf's against the "gig-lamps symmetrically arranged." The technical virtuosity with which modernists broke through the shell of the older realism into the newer produced, as Colin Falck points out, an unintended theoretical by-product: "the widely accepted view that art need not be in any sense 'realist.'" When coupled with the notion that language does not somehow relate to or express the language-using animal's apprehension of its environment, the view that art need not be realist "was effortlessly transformed into the view that there is no such thing as 'realist' for art to be" (150). Falck is surely right to insist that on the contrary a "genuine realism of the imagination has always been—and has widely been recognized to have been—a defining characteristic of literature, whether before, during, or after the modernist period" (151). It is just this sort of imaginative realism that makes a bizarre postmodern comedy such as *Being John Malkovich* possible.

In light of postmodern skepticism about the possibility of authentic representation, it is perhaps not surprising that critics of the late twentieth century steadfastly ignored the classical definition of ecphrasis and substituted their own, in which vivid immediacy was replaced by definitions such as Hollander's "mimesis of mimesis" (*Gazer's 6*) that imply the pure play of representational mediation. Radical redefinition of this sort not only answered the particular philosophical and critical concerns of the late twentieth century; it also exploited a connection between these concerns and Romantic ideas about art. The Romantic work of art—organic, autonomous, and growing by its own principles—was imagined later in the nineteenth century as no longer a paradigm for the natural processes of an active universe but rather as an object detached from the world, without any secure relationship at all to its human author or its audience. The position taken by critics such as Hamon who conceptualize ecphrases as detachable fragments of the texts in which they reside is, as Ruth Webb remarks, "not so far away from the 'art for art's sake' of the previous [nineteenth] century" (18).

The same historical process that opened the mimetic abyss between description and narrative, art and life, author and work, audience and work, signifier and signified—the list of mimetic ruptures could be extended—made the very notion of representation itself appealingly problematic. "Contemporary critical discourses tend to focus on representations or obviously mediated forms of expression," as Mario Klarer explains:

> Claude Levi-Strauss' Structural Anthropology, Derridean Deconstruction, Jean Baudrillard's simulation theory and the "representationalism" of New Historicism find, despite their idiosyncrasies, a common denominator in the emphasis on "representation." (2)

Some extrapsychic or supraindividual power named "language" or "ideology" or the "political unconscious," and so forth, became the mysterious agency of all this representational production, leaving human beings, theoretically, with no effective "self" or "subject" or "imagination" with which to engage such daunting powers.

In a theoretical climate that privileges notions of representation that entail radical scepticism about both the human subject and the allegedly real world,[1] it is "no wonder," writes Klarer, "that the majority of investigations in this field [ecphrasis] reproject a poststructuralist theoretical grid onto texts of periods whose representational concepts and practices are often diametrically opposed to late twentieth-century notions" (2). One who has resisted the urge to shoehorn the critical concepts and cultural practices of the past into the pigeonholes of contemporary theory is Steven J. Halliwell, from whose historically sensitive book *Aesthetics of Mimesis* I have borrowed the concept of "ethical form" as an aid to explaining ethical place description. Halliwell's work aligns well with Klarer's provocative suggestion that ecphrasis,

> a seemingly postmodern word-and-image hybrid [. . .], be wrenched away from the conceptual frameworks of late twentieth-century theorizing and examined, instead, as a vehicle through which we can reconstruct dominant concepts of representation in specific cultures and periods. (2)

Klarer acknowledges—having appreciated Ruth Webb's essay on ecphrasis—that representational theorizing, as practiced in the late twentieth century, "draws attention to the dichotomies of 'art' versus 'nature' and 'word' versus 'image.'" He points out that "degrees of difference between these oppositions vary in each period and culture, thus offering an indirect look at central mimetic concepts of the time" (2). Convinced that there is a problem here, Klarer remains refreshingly open to revising a theoretical framework that he himself embraces in his own work. Certainly Klarer was not speaking in opposition to further discussions of representation; he was instead advocating a more nuanced and historically informed discussion. My inquiry has been undertaken in that spirit, in an effort to lay open to view the best-developed genre of classical ecphrasis, and the only genre to have an English name, Wordsworth's coinage *locodescriptive.* From the *Odyssey* to the *Aeneid* to *The Excursion* to *Being John Malkovich,* places have always been crucial to any genuine realism of the imagination that expresses the felt experience of attunement, of being alive in a (not always pleasant) world that is at least in part a world of our own making.

Attunement and disharmony of mind and place are not merely features of European languages and cultures. Indeed J. E. Malpas founded his 1999 philosophical study, *Place and Experience,* on the following observation:

> The same basic idea of human life as essentially a life of location, of self-identity as a matter of identity found in place, and of places themselves as somehow suffused with the "human," is common to the work of poets and novelists from all parts of the globe and in relation to all manner of landscapes and localities." (6)

Malpas instances Aboriginal Australian and Maori beliefs about person and place (2–4) as well as a long list of nineteenth- and twentieth-century authors for whom "the exploration of character and event, of life and love, of culture and idea is one and the same with the exploration, and often the rediscovery, of landscape, countryside and place" (7). Malpas takes such notions seriously—as neither mere literary conceits nor the testimony of the ignorant or sentimental. Much could be learned from such true multiculturalism.

When the ethnographer Keith H. Basso asked Dudley Patterson, an Apache renowned for his exceptional wisdom, to explain the Apache notion of wisdom, Patterson replied: "Wisdom sits in places" (121). Basso's patient attempt to understand the answer led to his distinguished monograph on language and landscape among the Western Apache. Basso concludes that *both* language and landscape are figurative—a revelation that came to Wordsworth through direct experience—and that cultural ecologists ignore at their peril the symbolic complex of a particular place, its name, and the objects and events it enfolds. Tribal history is not so much temporal as spatial, a "path" or "trail" with "footprints" found at various significant locations in Apache country: "What matters most to Apaches is *where* events occurred, not when, and what they reveal about the development and character of Apache social life" (31). After completing his guided tour of these significant locations, Basso concludes that "the country of the past—and with it Apache history—is never more than a narrated place-world away. It is thus very near [. . .] and can be easily brought to life at any time" through stories told, usually in the present tense, by a skilled place maker in spoken Apache (32). In these performances "a type of historical theater" strips away the "'pastness' of the past and long-elapsed events are made to unfold as if before one's eyes" (33). We have seen that the Greco-Roman progymnasmata called exactly this sort of narrative *ekphrasis* and distinguished it from ordinary narrative (*diegesis*).

There are even more important parallels between the paradigmatic place-worlds of Apache history, the classical sense of historical places such as Carthage, and the sense of history implicit in (say) Wordsworth's ruined cottage or Byron's Coliseum. In Virgil's poem, Carthage is of course a part of history, a significant location from the Roman past; but for Virgil (as for the Apache) the past only matters as a paradigm for the present and future. Carthage and the personal tragedy that takes place there is the paradigm of the rise and fall of the mighty, and therefore a cautionary emblem for the nascent Roman Empire and the temptations to which it is and will inevitably be exposed. Virgil, like an Apache place maker who freely invents the details of the place he makes, depicts Carthage in his own distinctive way so as to make the paradigm alive for his audience.

Virgil depicted the mountains framing the Carthaginian harbor as a woody theater suitable for both happy and sad actions—a fit setting for the opening scene in a drama that will seem at times like a the celebration of a triumph, at other times like a memorial service for the dead. Virgil's ecphrasis depends for its effectiveness on assuming a unity of the external, natural world and the fates of Rome and Carthage with the internal, psychological landscape of his characters. Though Ruskin attacked this unity as a "pathetic fallacy," it has been the basis of many of the most admired literary works from the *Aeneid* onward. It is precisely this merger of the mind with the world "out there" that enables a Romantic place description to take on complex ethical color from the personages who interact with a significant place.

Indeed we continue to speak so freely of "interacting" with the "outer" world, including the worlds that others conjure for us by their words, that it is easy to forget that *perception* names the process by which what is "out there" becomes our own inner experience—and that this process remains not at all well understood. Elaine Scarry, a literary scholar unusual for her appreciation of such cognitive-perceptual problems, devoted *Dreaming by the*

Book to the question: "By what miracle is a writer able to incite us to bring forth mental images that resemble in their quality not our own daydreaming but our own (much more freely practiced) perceptual acts?" (6–7). Strikingly reminiscent of Quintilian's wonder at discourses that make us "seem to ourselves not to be dreaming but acting" (435; 6.2.30), such questions point toward pathways that remain as open for exploration in the twenty-first century as they were in the first.[2]

Such pathways are fenced off by attempts to abolish "self," "nature," and so forth, by rhetorical fiat. Iterations of "representation" only further obscure these pathways, and in that spirit it is easy to understand the strategic attraction of so-called notional ecphrasis, the description of purely fictive representations. But the problem of representation is not solved by moving the locus of mimesis from the boundary between the world and its representation to another boundary between one representation and another.

An anecdote told by Wendy Doniger illustrates why we might not want to let matters rest where they are. Her story concerns an actual place (an academic conference on methodology) and a colleague's dream story about an imagined place: a pretentious restaurant controlled by a cruel waiter, a modern ethical abode of the sort Kafka might have created. It is also precisely the sort of establishment we might expect to find in Jameson's monumentally pretentious Westin Bonaventure. The florid menu—an ecphrastic text whose function, purpose, and conventions we all understand and participate in—inscribes what is to be experienced there:

> Once, while David Shulman and I sat through a conference on methodology in the history of religions, he had a dream; he dreamed that we were in a restaurant, and the waiter brought the menu, which we perused hungrily; but when we began to order (I ordered fresh oysters and Peking duck and mangoes), the waiter interrupted: "I'm sorry, Madam," he said, "but in this restaurant you eat the *menu*." (168; Doniger's italics)

The dream suggests at least two choices for the hungry diners: getting up and leaving in search of the absent food described in the mouth-watering menu; or sitting through dinner, chewing on the menu itself in the abyss that the waiter's revelation has opened for them.

Doniger's readers can be entertained by her story only because it appeals to a cascade of resemblances and contrasts: between dream and reality, between menu and food, between the conference setting and the dream restaurant, between the waiter's words and the words spoken by scholars to their audiences, between Doniger's food choices and what the reader may know about her South Asian scholarship, between Shulman the dreamer and

Doniger the character-turned-narrator, and so forth. But its most powerful appeal is to the reader's belief that if textual mangoes are in fact hungrily perused—even in a setting that reeks of inauthenticity, as a restaurant in Jameson's allegorical hyperspace certainly would—the tantalizing experience must necessarily be grounded somehow in the sensuous pleasures of real food. The grapes on Clitophon's blushing wine-bowl may be ecphrastic representations, but their effectiveness in Achilles Tatius's novel depends on the reader's belief that there are, somewhere out there in the world, such things as genuine vineyards, real nourishment, and true love.

Notes

Introduction: Ecphrasis, Description, and the Imagined Place

1. Literary scholars do not follow a consistent English spelling. I adopt the Latinized spelling "ecphrasis," unless I am directly citing the Greek lexeme, *ekphrasis*.
2. See for example Krieger; Heffernan; Grant F. Scott; Hollander; and Putnam.
3. I thank Clayton Koelb for this translation.
4. For English translations see Kennedy, *Progymnasmata* 33, 64, 90, 128. Unless otherwise noted, all translations of the progymnasmata are cited by page number in Kennedy. The sections on ecphrasis in the Greek progymnasmata are in Spengel as follows: Hermogenes, 2.16–17; Aphthonius, 2.46–49; Theon, 2.118–220; Nicolaus, 3.49193.
5. The *OED* cites only two older usages.
6. Still standard French. Michel Patillon's 1997 French translation of Theon's *Progymnasmata* gives "La description" as the title for Theon's "Ekphrasis" (66).
7. For weather and medicine in France, see Gillispie (226–230).
8. Philip Hardie calls it a "quasi-ekphrastic description" (239).
9. For more on the ethical meaning of mountains, see Koelb (forthcoming, 2007).

Chapter 1: As If Present: Classical Ecphrasis

1. "Presence" took on a heavy burden in the late twentieth century and became associated, through the work of Jacques Derrida, with a metaphysics that some considered outmoded: what Terence Cave, in his study of *enargeia*, calls the "fallacy of presence" (5). Cf. Falck (86–114).
2. Cf. Wordsworth, 1814 *Excursion* IX (408):

   in what vivid hues
   His mind gives back the various forms of things,
   Caught in their fairest, happiest attitude!
   While he is speaking I have the power to see
   Even as he sees.

3. See Becker on simile and ecphrasis (49–50).

4. See Cave (6, n. 2).
5. Heffernan cites 1715 (without quoting Kersey's definition) as the moment ecphrasis enters English ("Ekphrasis" 297), but Kersey's definition does not authorize Heffernan's take on ecphrasis as art description.
6. Herodotus does not use the Greek term *ekphrasis*. It is Theon who cites the passage as an example of ecphrasis.
7. The crocodile is at 2.68, the hippopotamus at 2.71.
8. For a rejoinder to Ruskin, see Hecht.
9. Cf. Piehler, *Visionary*. He observes that Socrates' dialogue in the grove and the dialogue of Aeneas and Anchises in Elysium anticipate medieval dream visions in their use of visionary authority, dialogue, and landscape (84).
10. Cf. Parry (3).
11. One could easily enumerate the six charms in Keats's "To Autumn," a Romantic locus amoenus in which Keats clearly draws upon—and utterly renews—the European ecphrastic tradition. Cf. Blake's season poems in *Poetical Sketches*, which are markedly *not* in this tradition. See Piehler's discussion of rhetoric and archetype ("Allegories" 7–14).
12. Ovid's ethical topography thrives in the Renaissance. When Shakespeare's Lavinia tries to tell her father, Titus, that she has been raped in the woods, she draws his attention to Ovid's tale of Philomela (*Metamorphoses* 6). Titus asks the rhetorical question, "Lavinia wert thou thus surpriz'd sweet gyrle?" For the "vast and gloomie woods," he explains, "Patternd by that the Poet here describes, / By nature made for murthers and for rapes" (*Titus Andronicus* 4.1.1450–56).
13. Plutarch, "Mark Antony" (293; Ch. 26); Ovid, *Metamorphoses* (4–5;1.36–44); Florus, *Epitome* (208–13; 1.40); "How to depict justice," in Gellius, *Attic Nights* (3:36–39; 14.4); Cacus in *Aeneid* 8.190ff.; Diodorus (1:162–67; 1.46); Apuleius, *Metamorphoses* (196–205; 4.35–5.3); Gellius quotes volcanoes of Pindar, *Pythian Ode* (1.21ff.) and Virgil, *Aeneid* (3.570ff.).

Chapter 2: Unity, Form, and Figuration

1. For a detailed investigation of Horace's actual rhetorical context, see Trimpi.
2. For primary sources on interart comparison in sixteenth-century Italy, in English translation, see Klein and Zerner. Lessing and other eighteenth-century writers lumped "visual arts" into one coherent group, unlike typical Renaissance writers. Leonardo, for example, argued for the superiority of painting over sculpture (as well as music, poetry, and mathematics). These writings were dubbed *Paragone* (It. "comparison") by a nineteenth-century editor of Leonardo. *Paragone* has come to mean "polemical writings on the comparison of the visual arts regardless of period," although "Leonardo himself could not have used the word in any semblance of its modern denotation" (Farago 8–9). Mitchell, indebted more to Lessing's verbal–visual oppositionalism than to Leonardo (who took on various arts, but was mainly concerned to assert his intellectual superiority over his *visual* rivals, the sculptors), assumes a specialized definition that accords with

a twentieth-century preoccupation with word and image as opposites: "The *paragone* or debate of poetry and painting is never just a contest between two kinds of signs, but a struggle between body and soul, world and mind, nature and culture" (*Iconology* 49).
3. For a comparative study of serial form in poetry and music, see Paula Johnson.
4. Lessing does not mention Dio in *Laocoön*, but among his posthumous papers is a complaint that refers to Dio's orations (Howard xxvi). Iconoclastic Lessing would pointedly disapprove of Phidias's Zeus and might even urge its destruction. See Mitchell, *Iconology* (112–115).
5. Cf. Cicero, *De Legibus* (325; 1.8.24–25) for a similar notion of the innate conception of God.
6. For discussions of how British painting expands its narrative potential, see Kroeber, *British Romantic Art*, and Meisel for later nineteenth-century art.
7. A signal event in the splitting that eventually produced Coleridge's distinction between allegory and symbol (as lower and higher forms of figuration) is Du Bos's 1719 distinction between "complete" and "incomplete" allegory. The lower "complete" form merely personifies abstract qualities. The higher "incomplete" form "animates and gives speech to nature," as in the psalm "When Israel came out of Egypt" (1:176–77; ch. 25). When Coleridge deprecated allegory, "allegory" meant Du Bos's complete allegory.
8. For a bibliography and defense of twentieth-century expansions of allegory, see Kelley, *Reinventing*. For a spectrum of theoretical takes on allegory as a medieval genre, see Russell, *Allegoresis*.
9. Quintilian does not consider "o navis" personification because the ship does not talk back. See Quintilian 9.2.35. But, since an inanimate object is thought of as alive, the figure fits modern definitions of personification. See Jon Whitman (269–272) for a history of the terms *prosopopoeia* and *personification*. See Quilligan for a discussion of the problematic relationship between personification and literary allegory.
10. For a monograph devoted to *Leucippe and Clitophon*, see Morales, *Vision and Narrative*. See Doody (160–212) for a discussion of religious allegory in the ancient novel and its influence on medieval fiction.

Chapter 3: A Sylvan Scene

1. The episode comes at the halfway point in the epic and constitutes a "restart" of Odysseus's adventures. Virgil uses a very similar device in the *Aeneid*, creating a new beginning of his poem after Aeneas emerges from the underworld through the gates of ivory. Cf. Porphyry's reading of the Phorcys description as a Neoplatonic allegory of the soul taking on material form.
2. In 1960 R. D. Williams wrote an influential essay on Dido's murals that is as important to the modern theory of ecphrasis as it is to modern readings of the *Aeneid*. When Williams wrote that the murals show "Virgil's ability to use a traditional device (*ekphrasis* [not transliterated]) in such a way as to strengthen and

illuminate the main themes of his poem" (145), he was not only using the term in its modern sense, as description of a work of art, he was concisely setting forth the thesis upon which Putnam would build in all his essays on art ecphrasis in the *Aeneid*.
3. G. Williams notes that Virgil rather originally gives the harbor description completely to a narrator who uses present tenses to convey, intimately and directly, "facts that need not be known to the characters" (640).
4. "Tum silvis scaena coruscis / desuper, horrentique atrum nemus imminet umbra."
5. See for example the plan of Pompey's theater as reconstructed in the Renaissance (Bieber 181). Even clearer is the three-dimensional model of the similar theater at Herculaneum (Bieber 186), which conveys a vivid sense of the how the *versurae* projected toward the audience from the plane of the *scaenae frons*.
6. The word Virgil and Ovid choose is *saxum*, which means "rock," in the sense of a building material or something made from rock such as a stone knife. The earth once held both building materials, rafters and rock, living by the root.
7. The passage occurs in Achaemenides' account of his perilous escape from the cave of the Cyclops, after having been abandoned by Odysseus: "Past Pantagia's mouth with its living rock I voyage—past the Megarian bay and low-lying Thapsis" (*Aeneid* 3.688–69; Fairclough trans.).
8. *Metamorphoses* 14.713.
9. Compare the terrifying "selva oscura" in which the pilgrim finds himself in the opening lines of Dante's *Inferno*.
10. For *Paradise Lost* as religious masque, see John G. Demaray, *Milton's Theatrical Epic*.
11. Cf. Milton's "hairy sides / With thicket overgrown" with Virgil's shuddering/bristling shade, "horrenti umbra."
12. Cf. Don Cameron Allen's *Harmonious Vision*.
13. As Lewalski points out, and few would disagree: "*Paradise Lost* is preeminently a poem about knowing and choosing" (79).
14. "Almost every sentence of the "Prospectus" rings with echoes of Milton's voice in *Paradise Lost*" (Abrams, *Natural* 21).

Chapter 4: The Universe Dead or Alive: Gilpin, Wordsworth, and the Picturesque

1. For a survey of other major British positions on the sublime, the beautiful, and the picturesque, see Hipple. For picturesque tourism, see Andrews.
2. The definition is not quite as circular as it sounds. Landscape is not necessarily picturesque but can be represented that way.
3. In what follows, all italics in quotations from Gilpin are his own, unless otherwise noted.
4. When Gilpin tries to imagine a landscape painting consisting of smooth mountains and a smooth plain, "the very idea is disgusting" (*Three Essays* 19).
5. Burke contrasts the emotionally evocative potential of verbal description, to the detriment of visual art: "On the other hand, the most lively and spirited verbal

description I can give, raises a very obscure and imperfect *idea* of such objects; but then it is in my power to raise a stronger emotion by the description than I could do by the best painting. [. . .]. The proper manner of conveying the affections of the mind from one to another, is by words" (55–56; 2.4).
6. I am indebted to Joseph S. Viscomi for this observation.
7. Wayne Shumaker writes that nonrational psychic states are not only "impregnated with feeling" but "that their dynamic structure is largely determined by it. When the mind does not stand coolly off from experience to conceptualize it, but instead flows into it undivided and whole, as among children and savages, the resulting image of the world derives in considerable part from the patterns of the affections themselves" (263).
8. More's letter is not precisely dated. Andrews discusses it in *Search* (239), but somewhat out of context so that it reads as a simple disavowal of Gilpin.
9. Burke's "great" in this context parallels Addison's category of the Great, discussed above.
10. Gilpin composes landscape the way Zeuxis is supposed to have composed Helen, from bits and pieces of the most beautiful women.
11. Wordsworth was acutely aware of the socioeconomic forces at work bringing about enormous changes in the character of cottage life, as these citations clearly indicate. There is no need to resort to allegorical readings, as Alan Liu does, to uncover Wordsworth's encounter with history. As John O. Hayden remarked in his review of *Wordsworth: The Sense of History*, "It is a pity Liu did not devote his time to describing and analyzing Wordsworth's explicit political and social views in the context of the time" (249).
12. Wordsworth's note is to line 346, 1793 text, "The mountains, glowing hot, like coals of fire."
13. For Coleridge on imagination and fancy, see *Biographia Literaria* 1, chapters 4, 10, and 13. For Wordsworth's response, see Preface to *Poems* (1815), 381–385.
14. Piper cites Robinet, *Considérations philosophiques de la graduation naturelle des formes d'être* (1768). For more on Robinet, see Roger (642–651).
15. Not all fancy is pathological, but its instability and subjectivity can easily isolate the distempered mind. In contrast, imagination is always beneficial because it connects and communicates. In Preface to *Poems* (1815), Wordsworth holds that both imagination and fancy are necessary to the poet (373).
16. Much recent discussion of Wordsworth, Gilpin, and the picturesque has contrasted "Tintern Abbey" with Gilpin's description of Tintern Abbey in *Observations on the River Wye* (31–38). Critics have been at pains to focus attention on how far Wordsworth acknowledges poverty, industry, and pollution in the Wye Valley. See McGann, *Romantic Ideology*; Marjorie Levinson, "Insight"; and K. R. Johnston, "Politics."
17. As an elegy, it is a strange specimen whose figurations displace most of the generic topics of grief. It may be contrasted with a more explicitly generic romantic elegy such as Shelley's "Adonais." See Race 86–117.
18. Because "picturesque" in British thought covers the whole gray scale between the sublime and the beautiful, and because nothing is purely one or the other,

the door was always open in actual practice for applying the term to all kinds of things; such imprecision has doomed it as a technical term.
19. The main critical problem with the poem has to do with interpreting the "power." I am arguing that the term be understood as part of the constellation of rhetoric identified by Piper.

Chapter 5: The Visionary Eye: Wordsworth's Antipicturesque *Excursion*

1. According to Francis Jeffrey's review: "Imitations of Cowper, and even of Milton [. . .], engrafted on the natural drawl of the Lakers—and all diluted into harmony by that profuse and irrepressible wordiness which deluges all the blank verse of this school of poetry" (1).
2. For studies of Romantic naturalization of visionary experience, see Abrams, *Natural*; Kroeber, *Ecological*.
3. Cf. Kroeber, *Ecological* 123–124.
4. All citations of *The Excursion* are from the 1814 edition, unless the 1850 edition is specified. While references to the 1850 edition are to line numbers, the 1814 edition is cited by page only, as there are no line numbers in the 1814 text.
5. The history of the text is complicated. One or another manuscript version of the poetry Lamb heard in 1797 is frequently anthologized for twentieth-century readers as two separate poems, "The Pedlar" and "The Ruined Cottage." "The Pedlar" was first published as a separate poem under that title in 1979 (Hayden, Notes 552). The story of Margaret told by the Wanderer (the Pedlar's name in *The Excursion*) has since 1949 been published separately under the picturesque title, "The Ruined Cottage." For more on "The Pedlar" and "The Ruined Cottage" see Butler.
6. See Johnston, *Wordsworth and 'The Recluse.'*
7. *Mathetes* (Greek "pupil") is the joint pseudonym of John Wilson and Alexander Blair, whose letter to Coleridge's *Friend* prompted a reply from Wordsworth.
8. Heffernan observes a tendency in eighteenth-century art and poetry "to domesticate or appropriate outdoor space" (*Re-Creation* 108).
9. Cf. Abrams's provocative account of Victorian despondencies corrected by reading Wordsworth (*Natural* 134–140).

Chapter 6: "Till the Place Became Religion": Byron's Coliseum

1. For a neo-Marxist celebration of Byronic despair as antidote to ideology, see McGann: "As Baudelaire was the first to appreciate fully, Byron's despair, along with the entire range of his negative emotions, is the source of his greatness as a poet and his importance for the (programmatically hypocritical) reader" (*Romantic* 127). See Praz for the classic monograph on the phenomenon noted by Baudelaire.
2. Compare the 1797–1799 *Borderers* (5.3.264–75) in the Cornell Wordsworth for another early version of this same speech.

3. McFarland quotes an elided version of lines 2312–21 from the published 1842 text, but without citation. His observation applies with equal force to both versions.
4. Hazlitt's observation has been echoed for two centuries: "The Giaour, the Corsair, Childe Harold, are all the same person, and they are apparently all himself [Byron]" (qtd. in McFarland 20).
5. For an Anglo-Saxon poem about the Roman ruins at Bath, see Michael Alexander 27–29; for descriptions of Italy in English poetry since the Renaissance, see Mead.
6. The addition was published in 14 September 1812 in the fourth edition, only six months after the first.
7. See Aubin for the immediate predecessors.
8. I thank Paul Piehler for this observation.
9. See Richardson's *Mental Theater* for an indispensable introduction to Romantic psychodrama. He rightly emphasizes that "although dramatic interest centers on the history of a protagonist's consciousness" (1), the genre (and *Manfred* in particular) is "less a celebration of isolated subjectivity than a critique of the false assumptions behind psychic autonomy" (5). I support Richardson's general thesis, but my take on the Coliseum as an integrating experience nearly opposes Richardson's. He writes, for example, that the "image of the dead ruling over the living intimates Manfred's deep awareness of his disintegration" (58).
10. At first glance *intellect* seems out of place on the list. Intellect for Byron induces *Weltschmerz*: "Sorrow is knowledge" (1.1.10), says Manfred/Faust, whence frustration, ennui, et cetera.
11. For a compassionate discussion of Byron's manic-depressive illness, see Kay Redfield Jamison (149–190).
12. Cf. the lines to Ada at *Childe Harold* 3: 1094–98.
13. Cf. Wimsatt 32.
14. "Uno loco tot oppidum cadavera proiecta iacent" (Cicero, *Thirty-five Letters* 61).
15. Cf. Beaty, whose illuminating essay discusses Byron's reliance on Mangan's translation and commentary of Juvenal. I cannot go all the way with Beaty, though, in dismissing Livy and Ovid (344, n. 23). It seems clear enough that Mangan's remarks about Egeria (qtd. in Beaty 344) transparently draw on precisely the Livy and Ovid that Beaty cites, and that Mangan was attempting to blend all the classical sources into a coherent account. And of course Byron knew Livy and Ovid well enough without Mangan.

Epilogue: Immediacy

1. For a famous example see Liu who, after abolishing self, nature, and imagination, declares: "What there 'is' is history," with "history" defined as "absence," "the very category of denial" (39).

2. While the poets studied in this book achieved the goals of classical ecphrasis, it is important to remember that these goals have been vitally important not only to poets but also to those practicing law or statecraft. The abiding interest ancient writers such as Quintilian had in the notion of ecphrasis derived at least as much from the need to train skillful orators for careers in public life as from an interest in literary texts, and it is for that reason that the progymnasmatic syllabus was concerned mainly with descriptions of such real things as people, places, and actions. It is no surprise, then, that artworks as a distinct category of ecphrastic subjects appeared on the program only late and only rather marginally. The ability to set forth matters of urgent human concern has always had a higher social priority than the ability to create eloquent verbal depictions of paintings.

Works Cited

Note: All definitions of English words are taken from the *Oxford English Dictionary*, and definitions of Latin words are from the *Oxford Latin Dictionary*. These sources are usually not cited explicitly in the text.

Abrams, Meyer Howard. "The Correspondent Breeze: A Romantic Metaphor." *The Correspondent Breeze: Essays on English Romanticism*. New York: Norton, 1984. 24–43.

———. *A Glossary of Literary Terms*. Fort Worth: Harcourt Brace, 1993.

———. *Natural Supernaturalism: Tradition and Revolution in Romantic Literature*. New York: Norton, 1971.

Achilles Tatius. *Leucippe and Clitophon*. Trans. Tim Whitmarsh. Oxford: Oxford UP, 2001.

Addison, Joseph. *The Spectator*. Ed. Donald F. Bond. Vol. 3. Oxford: Clarendon P, 1965.

Alexander, Michael, ed. and trans. *The Earliest English Poems*. 2nd ed. New York: Penguin, 1982.

Allen, Don Cameron. *The Harmonious Vision: Studies in Milton's Poetry*. Enlarged ed. Baltimore: Johns Hopkins UP, 1970.

Alter, Robert. *Imagined Cities: Urban Experience and the Language of the Novel*. New Haven: Yale UP, 2005.

Andrews, Malcolm. *The Search for the Picturesque: Landscape Aesthetics and Tourism in Britain, 1760–1800*. Stanford: Stanford UP, 1989.

Aphthonius. *Aphthonii Sophistae Progymnasmata, partim à Rodolpho Agricola, partim à Joanne Maria Catanaeo Latinitate donata / cum luculentis & utilibus in eadem scholiis Reinhardi Lorichii Hadamarii*. Lugduni: Apud Antonium Vincentium, 1555.

Apuleius. *The Golden Ass: Being the Metamorphoses of Lucius Apuleius*. Trans. W. Adlington (1566). Rev. S. Gaselee. Loeb Classical Library. Cambridge: Harvard UP, 1958.

Aristotle. *Aristotle, On Rhetoric: A Theory of Civic Discourse*. Trans. George A. Kennedy. Oxford: Oxford UP, 1991.

———. *Poetics (Aristotle XXIII)*. Trans. S. Halliwell. Loeb Classical Library. Cambridge: Harvard UP, 1995. 28–141.

Arnheim, Rudolph. "Unity and Diversity of the Arts." *New Essays on the Psychology of Art.* Berkeley: U of California P, 1986.
Atkins, John William Hey. "Progymnasmata." *Oxford Classical Dictionary.* 1949.
Aubin, Robert Arnold. *Topographical Poetry in XVIII-Century England.* New York: MLA, 1936.
Bachelard, Gaston. *The Poetics of Space.* Trans. Maria Jolas. Boston: Beacon P, 1994.
Bann, Stephen. *Romanticism and the Rise of History.* New York: Twayne, 1995.
Barfield, Owen. *History in English Words.* Barrington: Lindisfarne Books, 1976.
———. "The Rediscovery of Meaning." *The Rediscovery of Meaning, and Other Essays.* Middeltown: Wesleyan UP, 1977. 11–21.
———. *Speaker's Meaning.* Middeltown: Wesleyan UP, 1967.
Barthes, Roland. "The Reality Effect." Trans. R. Carter. *Realism.* Ed. Lilian R. Furst. London: Longman, 1992. 135–141.
Bartsch, Shadi. *Decoding the Ancient Novel: The Reader and the Role of Description in Heliodorus and Achilles Tatius.* Princeton: Princeton UP, 1989.
Basso, Keith H. *Wisdom Sits in Places: Landscape and Language Among the Western Apache.* Albuquerque: U of New Mexico P, 1996.
Beaty, Frederick L. "Byron's Imitation of Juvenal and Persius." *Studies in Romanticism* 15 (1976): 333–355.
Beaujour, Michel. "Some Paradoxes of Description." *Towards a Theory of Description. Yale French Studies* 61 (1981): 27–59.
Becker, Andrew Sprague. *The Shield of Achilles and the Poetics of Ekphrasis.* Lanham: Rowman & Littlefield, 1995.
Bertrand, Edouard. *Un Critique d'art dans l'antiquité: Philostrate et son école.* Paris: E. Thorin, 1881.
Bialostosky, Don H., and Lawrence D. Needham. *Rhetorical Traditions and British Romantic Literature.* Bloomington: Indiana UP, 1995.
Bieber, Margarete. *The History of the Greek and Roman Theater.* Princeton: Princeton UP, 1961.
Blackstone, Bernard. *Byron: A Survey.* London: Longman, 1975.
Blair, Hugh. *Lectures on Rhetoric and Belles Lettres.* 1819. Rpt. Pelmar: Scholars' Facsimiles & Reprints, 1993.
Blake, William. *The Marriage of Heaven and Hell,* copy C, plate 6. *The William Blake Archive.* Ed. Morris Eaves, Robert N. Essick, and Joseph Viscomi. 14 March 2004. http://www.blakearchive.org/.
———. *Poetical Sketches.* New York: Payson & Clarke, 1927.
———. "Two Letters on Sight and Vision." *The Norton Anthology of English Literature.* Ed. M. H. Abrams. Vol. 2. 7th ed. New York: Norton, 2000. 88–91.
Bougot, Auguste. *Philostrate l'ancien: une galérie antique.* Paris: Librairie Renouard, 1881.
Burke, Edmund. *A Philosophical Enquiry into the Origin of our Ideas of the Sublime and Beautiful.* Ed. Adam Phillips. Oxford: Oxford UP, 1997. 188–320.
Butler, James A. Introduction. *The Ruined Cottage and the Pedlar.* By William Wordsworth. 3–35.

———. Preface. *The Ruined Cottage and the Pedlar.* By William Wordsworth. ix–xii.
Butler, James A., and Karen Green. Introduction. *Lyrical Ballads.* By William Wordsworth. 3–33.
Byron, George Gordon Lord. *"Born for Opposition": Byron's Letters and Journals.* Ed. Leslie A. Marchand. Vol. 8. Cambridge: Harvard UP, 1978.
———. *Childe Harold's Pilgrimage.* Canto 3. Ed. Peter Cochran. 3 Nov. 2005. http://www.internationalbyronsociety.org/pdf_files/childe3.pdf.
———. *Childe Harold's Pilgrimage.* Canto 4. Ed. Peter Cochran. 3 Nov. 2005. http://www.internationalbyronsociety.org/pdf_files/childe4.pdf.
———. *The Complete Poetical Works.* Ed. Jerome J. McGann. 7 vols. to date. Oxford: Clarendon P, 1980– .
———. *Don Juan.* Canto 3. Ed. Peter Cochran. 3 Nov. 2005. http://www.internationalbyronsociety.org/pdf_files/don_juan3.pdf.
———. *Don Juan.* Preface and Dedication. Ed. Peter Cochran. 3 Nov. 2005. http://www.internationalbyronsociety.org/pdf_files/don_juan_preface.pdf.
———. *Manfred.* Ed. Peter Cochran. 3 Nov. 2005. http://www.internationalbyronsociety.org/pdf_files/manfred.pdf.
———. "She Walks in Beauty." *Hebrew Melodies.* Ed. Peter Cochran. 3 Nov. 2005. http://www.internationalbyronsociety.org/pdf_files/hebrew_melodies.pdf.
———. *"So late into the night": Byron's Letters and Journals.* Ed. Leslie A. Marchand. Vol. 5. Cambridge: Harvard UP, 1976.
Cave, Terence. "*Enargeia:* Erasmus and the Rhetoric of Presence in the Sixteenth Century." *L'Esprit créateur* 16.4 (1976): 5–19.
Cheeke, Stephen. *Byron and Place: History, Translation, Nostalgia.* New York: Palgrave Macmillan, 2003.
Cicero. *De legibus. De re publica, De legibus (Cicero XVI).* Trans. C. W. Keyes. Loeb Classical Library. Cambridge: Harvard UP, 1928. 289–519.
———. *Thirty-five Letters of Cicero.* Ed. David Stockton. Oxford: Oxford UP, 1991.
Clark, Donald Leman. *John Milton at St. Paul's School.* New York: Columbia UP, 1848.
———. *Rhetoric in Greco-Roman Education.* New York: Columbia UP, 1957.
Clay, D. "The Archaeology of the Temple to Juno in Carthage." *Classical Philology* 83 (1988): 155–205.
Coleridge, Samuel Taylor. *Biographia Literaria. Collected Works* 7.
———. *The Collected Works of Samuel Taylor Coleridge.* Ed. James Engell and W. Jackson Bate. 16 vols. Princeton: Princeton UP, 1983.
———. "Dejection: An Ode." *Selected Poems* 179–183.
———. "Essays on the Principles of Genial Criticism." *Collected Works* 11: 353–386.
———. *Selected Poems.* Ed. Richard Holmes. New York: Penguin, 1994.
———. *The Statesman's Manual; or The Bible the Best Guide to Political Skill and Foresight. Lay Sermons.* Ed. R. J. White. *Collected Works* 6: 1–114.
Curtius, Ernst Robert. *European Literature and the Latin Middle Ages.* New York: Pantheon, 1953.

Dante. *Inferno.* Trans. Allen Mandelbaum. New York: Bantam, 1980.
Demaray, John G. *Milton's Theatrical Epic: The Invention and Design of "Paradise Lost."* Cambridge: Harvard UP, 1980.
Denniston, John Dewar. "Ekphrasis." *Oxford Classical Dictionary.* 1949.
Dickinson, Emily. *The Complete Poems of Emily Dickinson.* Boston: Little, Brown, 1924.
Diderot, Denis. *Diderot's Early Philosophical Works.* Ed. and trans. Margaret Jourdain. Chicago: Open Court, 1916.
———. *Lettre sur les sourds et les muets.* Ed. Paul Hugo Meyer. *Diderot Studies* 7. Ed. Otis Fellows. Geneva: Droz, 1965.
Dio Chrysostom. "The Twelfth, or Olympic, Discourse: On Man's First Conception of God." *Dio Chrysostom II.* Trans J. W. Cohoon. Loeb Classical Library. Cambridge: Harvard UP, 1932.
Diodorus. *The Library of History of Diodorus of Sicily.* Trans. C. H. Oldfather. 12 vols. Loeb Classical Library. Cambridge: Harvard UP, 1933.
Dionysius of Halicarnassus. *Rhetoric. Dionysii Halicarnasei opuscula.* Ed. Hermanus Usener and Lodovicus Radermacher. Vol. 2. Lipsiae: Teubner, 1904–1929. 372–373.
Dockhorn, Klaus. "Wordsworth and the Rhetorical Tradition in England." Trans. Heidi I. Saur-Stull. Bialostosky and Needham 265–280.
Doniger, Wendy. *Other People's Myths: The Cave of Echoes.* New York: Macmillan, 1988.
Doody, Margaret Anne. *The True Story of the Novel.* New Brunswick: Rutgers UP, 1996.
Du Bois, Page. *History, Rhetorical Description, and the Epic.* Cambridge: D. S. Brewer, 1982.
Du Bos, Jean-Baptiste. *Critical Reflections on Poetry, Painting, and Music.* Trans. Thomas Nugent. 5th ed. 3 vols. 1748. Rpt. New York: AMS P, 1978.
Durant, Geoffrey. "The Elegaic Poetry of *The Excursion.*" *The Wordsworth Circle* 9 (1978): 155–161.
Elledge, W. Paul. *Byron and the Dynamics of Metaphor.* Nashville: Vanderbilt UP, 1968.
Engels, Friedrich. "Engels an F. Mehring." *Karl Marx, Friedrich Engels: Studienausgabe in 4 Bänden.* Ed. Iring Fetscher. Frankfurt : Fischer, 1997. Vol. 1: 229–231.
Erbse, Hartmut, ed. *Scholia Graeca in Homeri Iliadem.* Berlin: Walter de Gruyter, 1977.
Falck, Colin. *Myth, Truth, and Literature: Towards a True Postmodernisim.* 2nd ed. Cambridge: Cambridge UP, 1994.
Farago, Claire J. *Leonardo da Vinci's "Paragone": A Critical Interpretation with a New Edition of the Text in the Codex Urbinas.* Leiden: Brill, 1992.
Flaubert, Gustave. *Madame Bovary.* Ed. Leo Bersani. Trans. Lowell Bair. New York: Bantam, 1989.
———. "A Simple Heart." *Three Tales.* Trans. Robert Baldick. London: Penguin, 1961.
Fletcher, Angus. *Allegory: The Theory of a Symbolic Mode.* Ithaca: Cornell UP, 1964.
Florus, Lucius Annaeus. *Epitome of Roman History.* Trans. Edward Seymour Forster. Loeb Classical Library. Cambridge: Harvard UP, 1984.

Friedländer, Paul. *Johannes von Gaza und Paulus Silentiarius: Kunstbeschreibungen Justinianischer Zeit.* Leipzig: Teubner, 1912.

Gellius. *The Attic Nights of Aulus Gellius.* Trans. John C. Rolfe. 3 vols. Loeb Classical Library. Cambridge: Harvard UP, 1952.

Gill, Stephen. *Wordsworth and the Victorians.* Oxford: Clarendon P, 1998.

Gillispie, Charles Coulston. *Science and Polity in France at the End of the Old Regime.* Princeton: Princeton UP, 1980.

Gilpin, William. *An Essay upon Prints: Containing Remarks upon the Principles of Picturesque Beauty; the Different Kinds of Prints; and the Characters of the Most Noted Masters.* 2nd ed. London: Robson, 1768.

———. *Observations on the River Wye, and Several Parts of South Wales, &c. Relative Chiefly to Picturesque Beauty; Made in the Summer of the Year 1770.* London: Blamire, 1782. Rpt Oxford: Woodstock Books, 1991.

———. *Three Essays: on Picturesque Beauty; on Picturesque Travel; and on Sketching Landscape: to which is added a poem, on Landscape Painting.* 2nd ed. London: Blamire, 1794.

———. *Two Essays: One, on the Author's Mode of Executing Rough Sketches; the Other, on the Principles on which They are Composed.* London: Cadell and Davies, 1804.

Goethe, J. W. Rev. of *Manfred*, by Lord Byron. Rutherford 119–120.

Goldstein, Laurence. *Ruins and Empire: The Evolution of a Theme in Augustan and Romantic Literature.* Pittsburgh: U of Pittsburgh P, 1977.

Graver, Bruce E. Introduction to "Translation of Virgil's *Aeneid.*" *Translations of Chaucer and Virgil.* By William Wordsworth. 155–174.

———. "The Oratorical Pedlar." Bialostosky and Needham 94–107.

———. "Wordsworth's Georgic Beginnings." *Texas Studies in Literature and Language* 33.2 (1991): 137–159.

Gray, Thomas. "Elegy Written in a Country Churchyard." *The Complete Poems of Thomas Gray.* Ed. H. W. Starr and J. R. Hendrickson. Oxford: Clarendon P, 1972. 37–43.

Hagstrum, Jean H. *The Sister Arts: The Tradition of Literary Pictorialism and English Poetry from Dryden to Gray.* Chicago: U of Chicago P, 1958.

Halliwell, S. *The Aesthetics of Mimesis: Ancient Texts and Modern Problems.* Princeton: Princeton UP, 2002.

Hamon, Philippe. Introduction. *La Description littéraire de l'antiquité à Roland Barthes: une anthologie.* Paris: Macula, 1991. 5–12.

———. "The Rhetorical Status of the Descriptive." *Towards a Theory of Description. Yale French Studies* 61 (1981): 1–26.

Hardie, Philip. Rev. of *Virgil's Epic Designs: Ekphrasis in the Aeneid,* by Michael C. J. Putnam. *Journal of Roman Studies* 90 (2000): 239–240.

Hayden, John O. Notes. *Selected Poems.* By William Wordsworth. New York: Penguin, 1994. 503–579.

———. Rev. of *Wordsworth: The Sense of History,* by Alan Liu. *Nineteenth-Century Literature* 45.2 (1990): 245–249.

Hazlitt, William. "Character of Mr. Wordsworth's New Poem, *The Excursion.*" *The Examiner* (21 August 1814; 28 August 1814; 2 October 1814). Rpt. *The Selected*

Writings of William Hazlitt. Ed. Duncan Wu. London: Pickering & Chatto, 1998. Vol. 2: 325–340.

Hecht, Anthony. "The Pathetic Fallacy." *Yale Review* 74.4 (1985): 481–499.

Hedrick, Charles W. "Conceiving the Narrative: Colors in Achilles Tatius and the Gospel of Mark." *Ancient Fiction and Early Christian Narrative*. Ed. Ronald F. Hock, J. Bradley Chance, and Judith Perkins. Atlanta: Scholars Press, 1998. 177–197.

Heffernan, James A. W. "Ekphrasis and Representation." *New Literary History* 22.2 (1991): 297–316.

———. *Museum of Words: The Poetics of Ekphrasis from Homer to Ashbury*. Chicago: U of Chicago P, 1993.

———. *The Re-Creation of Landscape: A Study of Wordsworth, Coleridge, Constable, and Turner*. Hanover: UP of New England, 1984.

Herodotus. *The Histories*. Trans. Robin Waterfield. Oxford: Oxford UP, 1998.

Hickey, Alison. *Impure Conceits: Rhetoric and Ideology in Wordsworth's* Excursion. Stanford: Stanford UP, 1997.

Hipple, Walter John, Jr. *The Beautiful, the Sublime, and the Picturesque in Eighteenth-Century British Aesthetic Theory*. Carbondale: Southern Illinois UP, 1957.

Hollander, John. *The Gazer's Spirit: Poems Speaking to Silent Works of Art*. Chicago: U of Chicago P, 1995.

Homer. *The Iliad*. Books 1–12. Trans. A. T. Murray. Loeb Classical Library. Cambridge: Harvard UP, 1924.

———. *The Iliad*. Books 13–24. Trans. A. T. Murray. Rev. William F. Wyatt. Loeb Classical Library. Cambridge: Harvard UP, 1999.

———. *The Iliad*. Trans. Alexander Pope. London: Penguin, 1996.

———. *The Odyssey*. Trans. Robert Fagles. New York: Viking, 1996.

———. *The Odyssey*. Books 1–12. Trans. A. T. Murray. Rev. George E. Dimock. Loeb Classical Library. Cambridge: Harvard UP, 1995.

———. *The Odyssey*. Books 13–24. Trans. A. T. Murray. Loeb Classical Library. Cambridge: Harvard UP, 1919.

Horace. *Ars Poetica. The Art of Poetry*. Trans. D. A. Russel. *Ancient Literary Criticism: The Principal Texts in New Translations*. Ed. D. A. Russel and M. Winterbottom. Oxford: Oxford UP, 1972. 279–291.

Horsfall, Nicholas. *A Companion to the Study of Virgil*. Leiden: Brill, 2000.

Howard, W. G. Introduction. *Laokoon: Lessing, Herder, Goethe: Selections*. New York: Holt, 1910.

Hunt, John Dixon, and Peter Willis, ed. *The Genius of the Place: The English Landscape Garden 1620–1820*. Cambridge: MIT P, 2000.

James, Henry. *The Art of the Novel: Critical Prefaces*. Ed. Richard P. Blackmur. New York: Scribner's, 1934.

———. "The Figure in the Carpet." *Complete Stories 1892–1898*. New York: Library of America, 1996.

———. "Miss Prescott's 'Azarian.'" *Notes and Reviews*. Cambridge: Dunster House, 1921. Rpt. Freeport: Books for Libraries P, 1968. 16–32.

Jameson, Fredric. *Postmodernism, or, The Cultural Logic of Late Capitalism*. Durham: Duke UP, 1991.

Jamison, Kay Redfield. *Touched With Fire: Manic-depressive Illness and the Artistic Temperament.* New York: Free Press, 1993.
Jeffrey, Francis. Rev. of *The Excursion,* by William Wordsworth. *Edinburgh Review* 24 (1814): 1–30.
———. Rev. of *Manfred,* by Lord Byron. *Edinburgh Review* 28 (1817). Rutherford 98–118.
———. Rev. of *Poems, in Two Volumes,* by William Wordsworth. *Edinburgh Review* 21 (1807): 241–231.
Jenkyns, Richard. *Virgil's Experience: Nature and History: Times, Names, and Places.* Oxford: Clarendon P, 1998.
Johnson, Francis R. Introduction. *The Foundacion of Rhetorike,* by Richard Rainolde. 1563. New York: Scholars' Facsimiles & Reprints, 1945. iii–xxii.
Johnson, Paula. *Form and Transformation in Music and Poetry of the English Renaissance.* New Haven: Yale UP, 1972.
Johnson, Samuel. *Dictionary of the English Language.* Facsimile of *A Dictionary of the English Language,* 1755. Harlow: Longman, 1990.
Johnson, W. R. *Darkness Visible: A Study of Vergil's Aeneid.* Berkeley: U of California P, 1976.
Johnston, Kenneth R. "The Politics of 'Tintern Abbey.'" *The Wordsworth Circle* 14 (1983): 6–14.
———. *Wordsworth and "The Recluse."* New Haven: Yale UP, 1984.
———. "Wordsworth's Reckless Recluse." *The Wordsworth Circle* 9 (1978): 131–144.
Kant, Immanuel. *The Critique of Judgment.* Trans. James Creed Meredith. Oxford: Oxford UP, 1989.
Keats, John. *Complete Poems.* Ed. Jack Stillinger. Cambridge: Harvard UP, 1978.
———. "Ode on a Grecian Urn." *Complete Poems* 282–283.
———. "To Autumn." *Complete Poems* 360–361.
Kelley, Theresa M. *Reinventing Allegory.* Cambridge: Cambridge UP, 1997.
Kennedy, George, trans. *Progymnasmata: Greek Textbooks of Prose Composition and Rhetoric.* Atlanta: Society of Biblical Literature, 2003.
Kermode, Frank. *The Genesis of Secrecy: On the Interpretation of Narrative.* Cambridge: Harvard UP, 1979.
Klarer, Mario. Introduction. *Word & Image* 15.1 (1999): 1–4.
Klein, Robert, and Henri Zerner. *Italian Art, 1500–1600: Sources and Documents.* Englewood Cliffs: Prentice-Hall, 1966.
Koelb, Janice Hewlett. "'This Most Beautiful and Adorn'd World': Nicolson's *Mountain Gloom and Mountain Glory* Reconsidered." *ISLE: Interdisciplinary Studies in Literature and Environment* (forthcoming, 2007).
Krieger, Murray. *Ekphrasis: The Ilusion of the Natural Sign.* Baltimore: Johns Hopkins UP, 1992.
Kroeber, Karl. *British Romantic Art.* Berkeley: U of California P, 1986.
———. *Ecological Literary Criticism: Romantic Imagining and the Biology of Mind.* New York: Columbia UP, 1994.
———. *Retelling/Rereading: The Fate of Storytelling in Modern Times.* New Brunswick: Rutgers UP, 1992.

Lamb, Charles. *The Letters of Charles and Mary Anne Lamb.* Ed. Edwin W. Marrs, Jr. Vol. 3. 1809–1817. Ithaca: Cornell UP, 1978.

———. Rev. of *The Excursion,* by William Wordsworth. *Quarterly Review* 23 (October 1814): 100–111.

Lessing, Gotthold Ephraim. *Laocoön: An Essay on the Limits of Painting and Poetry.* Trans. Edward Allen McCormick. Baltimore: Johns Hopkins UP, 1962.

Levinson, Marjorie. "Insight and Oversight: Reading 'Tintern Abbey.'" *Wordsworth's Great Period Poems: Four Essays.* Cambridge: Cambridge UP, 1986. 14–57.

Lewalski, Barbara Kiefer. "The Genres of *Paradise Lost.*" *The Cambridge Companion to Milton.* Ed. Dennis Danielson. Cambridge: Cambridge UP, 1997. 79–95.

Lewis, C. S. *A Preface to "Paradise Lost."* London: Oxford UP, 1961.

Liu, Alan. *Wordsworth: The Sense of History.* Stanford: Stanford UP, 1989.

Longinus. *On the Sublime (Aristotle XXIII).* Trans. W. H. Fyfe, Rev. Donald Russell. Loeb Classical Library. Cambridge: Harvard UP, 1995. 160–307.

Lucan. *The Civil War.* Trans. J. D. Duff. Loeb Classical Library. London: William Heinemann, 1928.

Lucretius. *On the Nature of Things.* Trans. W. H. D. Rouse and Martin F. Smith. Loeb Classical Library. Cambridge: Harvard UP, 1992.

Macpherson, James. *Fragments of Ancient Poetry, 1760.* Los Angeles: William Andrews Clark Memorial Library, UC, 1966.

Malpas, J. E. *Place and Experience: A Philosophical Topography.* Cambridge: Cambridge UP, 1999.

Marmontel, Jean François. *Élements de littérature.* 3 vols. Paris: Firmin-Didot, 1892.

———. "Descriptif." *Élements de littérature.* 1: 441–443.

———. "Description." *Élements de littérature.* 1: 443–450.

McFarland, Thomas. *Romanticism and the Forms of Ruin: Wordsworth, Coleridge, and the Modalities of Fragmentation.* Princeton: Princeton UP, 1981.

McGann, Jerome J. *"Don Juan" in Context.* Chicago: U of Chicago P, 1976.

———. *The Romantic Ideology: A Critical Investigation.* Chicago: U Chicago P, 1983.

Mead, Willaim Edward. "Italy in English Poetry." *PMLA* 23.3 (1908): 421–470.

Medwin, Thomas. *Medwin's Conversations with Lord Byron.* Ed. Ernest J. Lovell, Jr. Princeton: Princeton UP, 1966.

Meisel, Martin. *Realizations: Narrative, Pictorial, and Theatrical Arts in Nineteenth-Century Britain.* Princeton: Princeton UP, 1983.

Merivale, John Herman. Rev. of *The Excursion.* By William Wordsworth. *Monthly Review* 76 (1815): 123–136.

Milton, John. "Il Penseroso." *The Oxford Book of English Verse.* Ed. Sir Arthur Thomas Quiller-Couch. Oxford: Clarendon P, 1919; Bartleby.com, 1999. 3 Feb. 2006. http://www.bartleby.com/101/.

———. *Paradise Lost. The Complete Poems of John Milton.* Ed. Charles W. Eliot. New York: P. F. Collier & Son, 1909–1914; Bartleby.com, 2001. 26 Jan. 2006. http://www.bartleby.com/4/.

Mitchell, W. J. T. *Iconology: Image, Text, Ideology.* Chicago: U of Chicago P, 1986.

Montesquieu, Charles de Secondat. *Persian Letters*. Trans. C. J. Betts. Baltimore: Penguin, 1973.

Morales, Helen. Introduction. *Leucippe and Clitophon*. By Achilles Tatius. vii–xxxii.

———. *Vision and Narrative in Achilles Tatius' "Leucippe and Clitophon."* Cambridge: Cambridge UP, 2004.

Moran, Richard. "Metaphor." *A Companion to the Philosophy of Language*. Ed. Bob Hale and Crispin Wright. Oxford: Blackwell, 1999. 248–268.

Muecke, Frances. "Foreshadowing and Dramatic Irony in the Story of Dido." *American Journal of Philology* 104 (1983): 134–155.

Nicolson, Marjorie Hope. *Mountain Gloom and Mountain Glory: The Development of the Aesthetics of the Infinite*. Seattle: U of Washington P, 1997.

Nuttall, A. D. *Why Does Tragedy Give Pleasure?* Oxford: Clarendon P, 1996.

Ovid. *Metamorphoses*. Trans. Frank Justus Miller. Loeb Classical Library. 2nd ed. Cambridge: Harvard UP, 1984.

Parry, Adam. "Landscape in Greek Poetry." *Yale Classical Studies* 15 (1957): 3–29.

Patterson, Annabel. "Wordsworth's Georgic: Genre and Structure in *The Excursion*." *The Wordsworth Circle* 9 (1978): 145–154.

Patillon, Michel, ed. and trans. *Aelius Théon: Progymnasmata*. Paris: Belles Lettres, 1997.

Percy, Victoria, and Gervaise Jackson-Stops. "Exquisite Taste and Tawdry Ornament: The Travel Journals of the First Duchess of Northumberland—II." *Country Life* 7 Feb. 1974: 150–153.

Perkell, Christine. "*Aeneid* 1: An Epic Programme." *Reading Vergil's "Aeneid": An Interpretive Guide*. Ed. Christine Perkell. Norman: U of Oklahoma P, 1999. 29–49.

Piehler, Paul. "Allegories of Paradise." *Toward a Definition of Topos: Approaches to Analogical Reasoning*. Ed. Lynette Hunter. London: Macmillan, 1991. 1–16.

———. "Allegory without Archetype." *Petrarch's Triumphs: Allegory and Spectacle*. Ed. Konrad Eisenbichler and Amilcare A. Iannuci. U of Toronto Italian Studies 4. Toronto: Dovehouse Editions, 1990. 97–112.

———. *The Visionary Landscape: A Study in Medieval Allegory*. Montreal: McGill-Queen's UP, 1971.

Piggott, Stuart. *Ruins in a Landscape: Essays in Antiquarianism*. Edinburgh: Edinburgh UP, 1976.

Pindar. *Pythian Odes (Pindar 1)*. Trans. William H. Race. Loeb Classical Library. Cambridge: Harvard UP, 1997. 209–381.

Piper, H. W. *The Active Universe*. London: Athlone P, 1962.

Plato. *Collected Dialogues of Plato, Including the Letters*. Ed. Edith Hamilton and Huntington Cairns. New York: Pantheon, 1963.

———. *Phaedrus*. Trans. Alexander Nehemas and Paul Woodruff. Indianapolis: Hackett, 1995.

———. *Republic*. Trans. Paul Shorey. *Collected Dialogues* 576–844.

———. *Republic X*. Trans. S. Halliwell. Warminster: Aris and Phillips, 1989.

Plutarch. "Mark Antony." *Makers of Rome: Nine Lives by Plutarch*. Trans. Ian Scott-Kilvert. New York: Penguin, 1965. 272–349.

Pope, Alexander. *The Iliad of Homer.* Ed. Steven Shankman. Trans. Alexander Pope. New York: Penguin, 1996.
———. Poetical Index. *Iliad* 1162–1180.
———. Preface. *Iliad* 3–22.
———. "Summer. The Second Pastoral, or Alexis." *The Poems of Alexander Pope.* Ed. John Butt. Reduced version. New Haven: Yale UP, 1963. 129–132.
Porphyry. *On the Cave of the Nymphs.* Trans. Robert Lamberton. Barrytown: Station Hill P, 1983.
Porter, Charles A. "Voltaire, Diderot, Rousseau and the *Encyclopédie.*" *The Cambridge History of Literary Criticism.* Vol. 4: The Eighteenth Century. Ed. H. B. Nesbit and Claude Rawson. Cambridge: Cambridge UP, 1997. 489–521.
Pöschl, Viktor. "Basic Themes." *Virgil: A Collection of Critical Essays.* Ed. Steele Commager. Englewood Cliffs: Prentice-Hall, 1966. 164–182.
Praz, Mario. *The Romantic Agony.* Trans. Angus Davidson. 2nd ed. Oxford: Oxford UP, 1988.
Price, Martin. "The Picturesque Moment." *From Sensibility to Romanticism.* Ed. Frederick W. Hilles and Harold Bloom. New York: Oxford UP, 1965. 259–292.
Putnam, Michael C. J. *Virgil's Epic Designs: Ekphrasis in the Aeneid.* New Haven: Yale UP, 1998.
Quilligan, Maureen. *The Language of Allegory: Defining the Genre.* Ithaca: Cornell UP, 1979.
Quintilian. *Institutio Oratoria: Books 1–2 (Quintilian I).* Trans. Donald A. Russell. Loeb Classical Library. Cambridge: Harvard UP, 2001.
———. *Institutio Oratoria: Books 4–6 (Quintilian II).* Trans. H. E. Butler. Loeb Classical Library. Cambridge: Harvard UP, 1921.
———. *Institutio Oratoria: Books 7–9 (Quintilian III).* Trans. H. E. Butler. Loeb Classical Library. Cambridge: Harvard UP, 1921.
———. *Institutio Oratoria: Books 9–10 (Quintilian IV).* Trans. Donald A. Russell. Loeb Classical Library. Cambridge: Harvard UP, 2001.
Race, William H. *Classical Genres and English Poetry.* London: Croom Helm, 1988.
Randel, Don Michael, ed. *The New Harvard Dictionary of Music.* Cambridge: Belknap-Harvard, 1986.
Richards, I. A. *The Philosophy of Rhetoric.* London: Oxford UP, 1936.
Richardson, Alan. "Astarté: Bryon's *Manfred* and Montesquieu's *Lettres persanes.*" *Keats–Shelley Journal* 40 (1991): 19–22.
———. *A Mental Theater: Poetic Drama and Consciousness in the Romantic Age.* University Park: Penn State UP, 1988.
Roberts, W. Rhys, ed. and trans. *Dionysius of Halicarnassus on Literary Composition.* London: Macmillan, 1910.
Roger, Jacques. *Les sciences de la vie dans la pensée française du xviiie siècle; la génération des animaux de Descartes à l'encyclopédie.* Paris: Colin, 1963.
Rudy, John G. *Wordsworth and the Zen Mind: The Poetry of Self-Emptying.* Albany: SUNY P, 1996.

Ruskin, John. "Of the Pathetic Fallacy." *Selected Writings.* Ed. Dinah Burch. Oxford: Oxford UP, 2004. 68–81.

Russell, J. Stephen, ed. *Allegoresis: The Craft of Allegory in Medieval Literature.* New York: Garland, 1988.

Rutherford, Andrew. *Byron: The Critical Heritage.* New York: Barnes and Noble, 1970.

Scarry, Elaine. *Dreaming by the Book.* Princeton: Princeton UP, 1999.

Scott, Grant F. *The Sculpted Word: Keats, Ekphrasis, and the Visual Arts.* Hanover: UP of New England, 1994.

Scott, Sir Walter. Rev. of *Childe Harold's Pilgrimage: Canto 4,* by Lord Byron. *Quarterly Review* 19 (April 1818): 215–232.

Seneca. *Epistles III.* Trans. Richard M. Gummere. Loeb Classical Library. Cambridge: Harvard UP, 2001.

Shakespeare, William. *Hamlet. The Riverside Shakespeare 1183–1245.*

———. *The Riverside Shakespeare.* Ed. G. Blakemore and J. J. M. Tobin. 2nd ed. Boston: Houghton Mifflin, 1997.

———. *Titus Andronicus. The Riverside Shakespeare* 1069–1100.

Shelley, Percy Bysshe. "Hymn to Intellectual Beauty" (Version A). *The Oxford Book of English Mystical Verse.* Ed. D. H. S. Nicholson, and A. H. E. Lee. Oxford: Clarendon P, 1917; Bartleby.com, 2000. 27 Jan. 2006. http://www.bartleby.com/236/.

Shumaker, Wayne. *Literature and the Irrational: A Study in Anthropological Backgrounds.* Englewood Cliffs: Prentice-Hall, 1960.

Spengel, Leonard von. *Rhetores graeci.* 3 vols. Frankfurt: Minerva, 1966.

Spitzer, Leo. "The 'Ode on a Grecian Urn,' or Content vs. Metagrammar." *Comparative Literature* 7 (1955): 203–225. Rpt. *Essays on English and American Literature.* Ed. Anna Hatcher. Princeton: Princeton UP, 1962. 67–97.

———. Rev. of Curtius's *Europäische Literatur und lateinisches Mittelalter. American Journal of Philology* 70.4 (1944): 425–431.

Stevens, Wallace. "Description without Place." *The Collected Poems of Wallace Stevens.* New York: Vintage Books, 1982. 339–346.

Thomson, James. *Spring. The Seasons.* Ed. James Sambrook. Oxford: Clarendon P, 1981. 2–57.

Tiberianus. "Amnis ibat." Trans. J. Wight Duff and Arnold M. Duff. *Minor Latin Poets.* Vol. 2. Loeb Classical Library. Cambridge: Harvard UP, 1934. 558–561.

Trimpi, Wesley. "The Meaning of Horace's Ut Pictura Poesis." *Journal of the Warburg and Courtauld Institutes* 36 (1973): 1–34.

Trott, Nicola, and Duncan Wu. "Three Sources for Wordsworth's *Prelude* Cave." *Notes and Queries* NS 38 (1991): 298–299.

Tuve, Rosamond. *Elizabethan and Metaphysical Imagery.* Chicago: U of Chicago P, 1947.

Virgil. *Aeneid 1–6 (Virgil II).* Trans. H. R. Fairclough. Rev. G. P. Gould. Loeb Classical Library. Cambridge: Harvard UP, 2000. 261–597.

———. *Aeneid.* Trans. Robert Fitzgerald. New York: Vintage, 1990.

———. *The Aeneid of Virgil.* Trans. Allen Mandelbaum. New York: Bantam, 1981.

———. *Aeneis. Virgil's Aeneid*. Trans. John Dryden. Ed. Frederick M. Keener. London: Penguin, 1997.
———. *Eclogues*. Trans. Guy Lee. London: Penguin, 1984.
Walpole, Horace. *Horace Walpole's Correspondence with Hannah More, et al. The Yale Edition of Horace Walpole's Correspondence*. Vol. 31. Ed. W. S. Lewis, Robert A. Smith, and Charles H. Bennett. New Haven: Yale UP, 1961.
Webb, Ruth. "Ekphrasis Ancient and Modern: The Invention of a Genre." *Word & Image* 15.1 (1999): 7–18.
Webb, Ruth, and Weller, Philip. "Descriptive Poetry." *The New Princeton Encyclopedia of Poetry and Poetics*. Ed. Alex Preminger and T. V. F. Brogan. Princeton: Princeton UP, 1993. 283–288.
Webster's Third New International Dictionary of the English Language. 1993.
Whitman, Jon. *Allegory: The Dynamics of an Ancient and Medieval Technique*. Cambridge: Harvard UP, 1987.
Williams, Gordon. *Tradition and Originality in Roman Poetry*. Oxford: Clarendon P, 1968.
Williams, R. D. "The Pictures on Dido's Temple." *Classical Quarterly* 10 (1960): 145–151.
Wimsatt, W. K. "The Structure of Romantic Nature Imagery." *English Romantic Poets*. Ed. M. H. Abrams. Oxford: Oxford UP, 1975. 25–35.
Wolff, Samuel Lee. *The Greek Romances in Elizabethan Prose Fiction*. New York: Columbia UP, 1912.
Woodring, Carl. *Wordsworth*. Cambridge: Harvard UP, 1968.
Woolf, Virginia. "Modern Fiction." *The Common Reader*. Ed. Andrew McNeillie. London: Harcourt, 1984. 146–154.
Wordsworth, Jonathan. Introduction. *The Excursion*. 1814. By William Wordsworth. Unpaginated.
Wordsworth, William. "The Baker's Cart." *The Ruined Cottage and The Pedlar* 463.
———. *The Borderers. William Wordsworth: The Complete Poetical Works*. London: Macmillan and Co., 1888; Bartleby.com, 1999. 3 Feb. 2006. http://www.bartleby.com/145/.
———. *The Borderers*. Ed. Robert Osborn. Ithaca: Cornell UP, 1982.
———. "Description of the Scenery of the Lakes." *Selected Prose* Ed. John O. Hayden. New York: Penguin, 1988. 9–75.
———. *Descriptive Sketches*. Ed. Eric Birdsall. Ithaca: Cornell UP, 1984.
———. "Elegiac Stanzas Suggested by a Picture of Peele Castle, in a Storm, Painted by Sir George Beaumont." *Selected Poems* 209–210.
———. "Essay, Supplementary to the Preface." *Selected Prose* 387–413.
———. "Essays Upon Epitaphs." *Selected Prose* 322–371.
———. *An Evening Walk*. Ed. James Averill. Ithaca: Cornell UP, 1984.
———. *The Excursion*. 1850. *The Complete Poetical Works*. London: Macmillan and Co., 1888; Bartleby.com, 1999. 27 Jan. 2006. http://www.bartleby.com/145/.
———. *The Excursion*. 1814. Rpt. Oxford: Woodstock Books, 1991.
———. "Incipient Madness." *The Ruined Cottage and The Pedlar* 468–469.

———. "Lines Composed a Few Miles Above Tintern Abbey." 1798. *Selected Poems* 66–70.

———. "Lines Left upon a Seat in a Yew-tree, which stands near the Lake of Esthwaite, on a desolate part of the shore, commanding a beautiful prospect." *Selected Poems* 18–20.

———. *Lyrical Ballads, and Other Poems, 1897–1800*. Ed. James Butler and Karen Green. Ithaca: Cornell UP, 1992.

———. "Ode: Intimations of Immortality." *Selected Poems* 139–145.

———. Preface. *The Excursion*. 1814. vii–xiv.

———. Preface to *Lyrical Ballads*. *Selected Prose* 278–302.

———. Preface to *Poems*.1815. *Selected Prose* 372–386.

———. *The Prelude: The Four Texts (1798, 1799, 1805, 1850)*. Ed. Jonathan Wordsworth. New York: Penguin, 1995.

———. Prospectus. *The Excursion*. 1814. x–xiv.

———. "Reply to Mathetes." *Selected Prose* 107–126.

———. *The Ruined Cottage and The Pedlar*. Ed. James Butler. Ithaca: Cornell UP, 1979.

———. *Selected Poems*. Ed. John O. Hayden. New York: Penguin, 1994.

———. *Selected Prose*. Ed. John O. Hayden. New York: Penguin, 1988.

———. "The Sublime and the Beautiful." *Selected Prose* 263–274.

———. "The Tables Turned; An Evening Scene on the Same Subject." *Lyrical Ballads* 108–109.

———. "There Was a Boy." *Lyrical Ballads* 139–141.

———. "Tintern Abbey." See "Lines Composed [. . .] ."

———. "To M. H." *Selected Poems*. 105.

———. "Translation of Virgil's *Aeneid*." *Translations of Chaucer and Virgil*. 181–271.

———. *Translations of Chaucer and Virgil*. Ed. Bruce E. Graver. Ithaca: Cornell UP, 1988.

Wordsworth, William and Dorothy. *The Letters of William and Dorothy Wordsworth*. Vol.1. *The Early Years 1787–1805*. Ed. Ernest de Selincourt. Rev. Chester L. Shaver. 2nd ed. Oxford: Clarendon P, 1967.

———. *The Letters of William and Dorothy Wordsworth*. Vol. 3. *The Middle Years, part II, 1812–1820*. Ed. Ernest de Selincourt. Rev. Mary Moorman and Alan G. Hill. Oxford: Clarendon P, 1970.

———. *The Letters of William and Dorothy Wordsworth*. Vol. 5. *The Later Years, part II, 1829–1834*. Ed. Alan G. Hill. Oxford: Clarendon P, 1979.

Index

aboriginal Australian places, 194
Abrams, Meyer Howard, 121, 185, 202 n. 14, 204 n. 2, 204 n. 9 (ch. 5)
Achaemendides, 202 n. 7
Achilles
 at Patroclus's funeral pyre, 4, 35–36
 scepter of, 52–53
 shield of, 1, 23, 24–26: *see also* ecphrasis of battle; *pragmata*
Achilles Tatius, 56
 Leucippe and Clitophon, 3, 11, 22, 54–55, 64–67, 197
Addison, Joseph, 98–99, 108, 109, 203 n. 9
Aeneas, *see* Virgil, *Aeneid*
aesthetic categories, eighteenth-century, 98–101
 see also Addison; Burke; Gilpin; Kant; Lessing
Agamemnon
 scepter of, 52–53
Agricola, 21
Alexander, Michael, 205 n. 5
allegory, 57, 59–64, 201 nn. 7–10
 and description, 72, 190–92, 197
 as tenorless vehicle, 61–63
 as term of abuse, 52, 54
 see also Coleridge; Du Bos; Piehler; Quilligan; Russel
Allen, Don Cameron, 202 n. 12
Alpinism, 156, 158–59, 161, 187
Alps, 14, 104, 158–59, 164, 165, 177

Alter, Robert, 190
Andrews, Malcolm, 101, 201 n. 1, 202 n. 8
Anglo-saxon verse, ruins in, 159, 205 n. 5
animism, in Wordsworth, 130, 138
 see also forms as living agents; descriptions, ethical; ethical form
Aphthonius, 3, 20–25, 31, 34, 39–42, 72, 199 n. 4 (intro.)
Apuleius, Love's palace in, 40, 200 n. 13
Aristotle, 43, 45, 46
 On Rhetoric, 33, 57
 Poetics, 33, 48–49
Arnheim, Rudolph, 50–51
"as if present" motif, 19–21, 30–33, 43, 147, 189, 199, n.2 (ch.1)
 see also "before the eyes" motif; immediacy; vividness
astonishment (*ekplexis*), 29, 98, 109–10
Astoreth, 167, 171, 175
Atkins, John William Hey, 2
Aubin, Robert Arnold, 205 n. 7
Augustine, *Confessions*, 93
Austen, Jane, picturesque in, 107

Bachelard, Gaston, 3, 12
Balzac, Scotland in, 103
Bann, Stephen, 159

222 • Index

Barante, Amable-Guillaume-Prosper Brugière, baron de, 159
Barfield, Owen, xii, 29
Barthes, Roland, 6–8, 9, 10
  see also reality effect
Bartsch, Shadi, 3, 22, 23, 55, 56, 64–67, 73
Basso, Keith H., 194–95
Baudelaire, Charles, 204 n. 1 (ch. 6)
Beaty, Frederick L., 205 n. 15
Beaujour, Michel, 5–6, 45
Beaumont, Sir George, 118, 119
Becker, Andrew Sprague, 199 n. 3 (ch. 1)
"before the eyes" motif, 23, 28, 29, 33, 199 n. 2 (ch. 1)
  see also "as if present" motif; immediacy; vividness
Beethoven, Ludwig van, 74, 83
Bertrand, Edouard, 3, 5, 24
Beautiful, as aesthetic category, 98–100, 103–06, 127, 203 n. 18
  see also aesthetic categories, eighteenth-century; *Kalon*; Burke; Gilpin; Wordsworth, "The Sublime and the Beautiful"
Being John Malkovich, 191–92, 194
Bible, 142
Bieber, Margarete, 79–80, 202 n. 5 (ch. 3)
Blackstone, Bernard, 168, 174
Blair, Hugh, 19–20
Blake, William, 15, 51, 108
  Marriage of Heaven and Hell, 107–08
  Poetical Sketches, 200 n. 11
  "Two Letters on Sight and Vision," 92
Boccaccio, Giovanni, 67
Bougot, Auguste, 3, 5
Brower, Reuben A., 56
Burke, Edmund, 85, 99–100, 104–05, 107–10, 202–03 n. 5 (ch. 4), 203 n. 9
Butler, James A., 139, 204 n. 5

Byron, George Gordon Lord. 9, 17, 97, 104, 190, 195, 204 n. 1 (ch. 6)
  capacity for mystical experience, 168–70
  dialectical image patterns in, 166: see also psychodrama and rhetoric
  works:
    Childe Harold's Pilgrimage, 15–16, 154, 156–62, 165, 178–87, 205 n. 12
    Don Juan, 126, 155, 177
    Letters and Journals, 155, 161–62, 163, 164–65, 169
    Manfred, 15, 68, 154, 156–62, 163–77, 178, 183–85, 205 nn. 9, 10
    "She Walks in Beauty," 171, 179
  Byronic hero, 156–57, 181

Cacus, house of, 40, 200 n. 13
Caesar Augustus, 79, 159–60, 172, 185–86
Carthage, 42, 77–78, 81, 82, 190, 195
Carthaginian harbor, xi, 13, 14–15, 68, 69–85, 73–83, 136, 195, 202 n. 3
  see also history as paradigm
Carthaginian wars, see Punic wars
Cataneo, 21
Cave, Terence, 199 n. 1 (ch. 1), 200 n. 4
caves, 13, 14, 39, 69–70, 73, 77, 135, 202 n. 7
Cervantes, Miguel de, 67
Chaucer, Geoffrey, 141
Cheeke, Stephen, 156, 158–59
Cicero, 29, 30, 142
  De legibus, 291 n. 5
  Letters, 178, 205 n. 14
Clark, Donald Leman, 20, 21
Claude Lorrain, 15, 91
Clay, D., 71
Cleopatra, 40

Coleridge, Samuel Taylor, 92, 131, 132, 140, 169, 202 n. 7, 204, n. 7
  imagination and fancy in, 110, 114: *see also* fancy; imagination; *phantasia*
  works:
    Biographia Literaria, 94, 203 n. 13
    "Dejection: An Ode," 108
    "Essays on the Principles of Genial Criticism," 108
    The Statesman's Manual, 54
Coliseum, Roman, 16, 68, 155–87, 190, 195, 205 n. 9
configural understanding, 49–64 *see also* retrospective form
Cowper, William, 204 n. 1 (ch. 5)
  "The Task," 84
creative perception, 16, 73, 86–94, 142, 144–45, 152–53, 186, 190, 195
  see also fancy; imagination; memory; *mobilité*
Curtius, E. R., 13, 37, 38
Cyclops, 202 n. 7

Dante Alighieri, 38, 39, 159, 160, 163, 202 n. 9
Darwin, Charles, 128
definitions, as organs of perception, xii
Demaray, John G., 202 n. 10
Denniston, John Dewar, 2–4
depression, 149, 160, 183
  and mania, 166–70, 180
  compare fancy as pathological; Milton, "Il Penseroso"
Derrida, Jacques, 199 n. 1 (ch. 1)
descriptio, 1–2, 5, 10, 20, 26–27
  compare ekphrasis
  see also description(s)
description(s)
  as detachable fragments, 55, 70, 193: *see also* Hamon
  devaluation of, 5–11, 17, 26–28, 44, 45, 66–67: *see also* Lessing
  ethical, defined, 14
  hermeneutic, 65–68, 71, 73, 77–78, 136: *see also* Bartsch; configural understanding; descriptions, opening; hermeneutics; retrospective form; serial form
  high valuation of, 9–11, 17, 26–27, 65–68, 202–03 n. 5 (ch. 4)
  as interdependent allegories, 83: *see also* retrospective form
  as life force, 5–6, 9–10: *see also logos* as force of nature
  and music, 50–52, 74–75: *see also* serial form
  and narrative, 4, 24–27, 71–72: *see also* Lessing
  opening, 7, 73–74, 134–37
  place, *see under* place descriptions
  and *phantasia*, 29–31: *see also* "as if present" motif; emotion; immediacy; intersubjectivity
  and Romantic poetics, 8–9, 16–17, 85, 97–98
  as tenorless vehicles, 64–68: *see also* allegory
  and unity, 8–9, 10–11, 16, 43–68
  see also allegory, ecphrasis; *ekphrasis*
dialogue and landscape, *see under* landscape and dialogue
Dickens, Charles, 39
Dickinson, Emily, 51
Diderot, Denis, 122–23
  Lettre sur les sourds et les muets, 9–10, 32
Dido, 77
  as tragic heroine, 71, 76, 81–82, 86: *see also* Virgil, *Aeneid* 1
Dido's temple, xi, 4, 70, 71, 72, 82, 202 n. 2
  see also Carthaginian harbor; Virgil, *Aeneid* 1
Dio Chrysostom, 201 n. 1
  Olympic Discourse, 46–47: *compare* Lessing
Diodorus, 40, 200 n. 13
Dionysius of Halicarnassus, 27–29

Disneyland, 191
displacement, 16
Dockhorn, Klaus, 28
Doniger, Wendy, 196–97
Doody, Margaret Anne, 201 n. 10
drama, metaphysical, *see under* psychodrama
dramatic irony, 78
dramatic soliloquy, conventions in, 175
Dryden, John, 14–15
  Aeneis, 83, 84–85, 86
Du Bois, Page, 4
Du Bos, Jean-Baptiste, 201 n. 7
Durant, Geoffrey, 126

ecphrasis, xi, 17, 19–42, 57, 189, 199 nn. 1, 4 (intro.)
  of animals, 3, 23, 33–34, 42, 72
  of art, xi, xii, 1–5, 19–20, 23, 25, 40–41, 43–44, 71, 76, 118–20, 206 n. 2
  of battle, 4, 23, 71–72, 76
  in lawsuits, 27–30
  and narrative, 4, 24–27, 71–72
  of places: *see under* place descriptions; *see also* locodescriptive
  of *pragmata* (things done or made), 2, 23–26 : *see also* Achilles, shield of; Lessing; Pope
  as "speaking out," xi, 8, 34, 71
  of storms, 27–28, 71–72
  subject matter defined, 23
  and terseness, 34–36
  as topos of stillness, 71: *see also* ecphrasis of art; Lessing
  twentieth-century definitions, xi, xii, 8, 16–17
  virtues of, 33–34, 189
  see also description(s); *ekphrasis*; *phantasia*
Eden, 14, 15, 86–93, 103, 125, 134
Egeria, 179–80, 205 n. 15
ekphrasis, xi, 1–2, 4, 5, 10, 19, 20, 22, 24–25, 27–29, 56, 71, 195, 199 n. 1 (intro.), 200 n. 6, 201 n. 2
  see also ecphrasis; *descriptio*; description
elegy, conventions in, 120, 203 n. 17
Eliot, George, 128
Elledge, W. Paul, 166
Elysium, 200 n. 9
emotion, 23, 35–36, 73, 81
  aroused by representations, 47–49
  contagion of, 28–32, 47, 150–53, 189
  in Greco-Roman rhetorical theory, 28–32, 125, 138
  in Romantic poetics, 49,125, 138: *see also* Wordsworth
  see also aesthetic categories, eighteenth-century; *phantasia*
enargeia (vividness), 20, 23, 30–34
  and *energeia*, 33
  see also vividness
Engels, Friedrich, 16
Ennius, 77
Erasmus, Desiderius, 21
Erbse, Hartmut, 35
ethical form, 46–49,53,193
  see also Halliwell; Wordsworth, forms in
evidentia, 20

Falck, Colin, 192, 199 n. 1 (ch. 1)
false consciousness, 16
  see also creative perception; self-delusion
fancy, 109–11, 114, 129, 136, 203 n. 13
  as pathological, 15, 116–122, 144, 152, 203 n. 15
  see also creative perception; imagination; *phantasia*
Farago, Claire J., 200 n. 2
Favorinus, 40
Flaubert, Gustave, 9, 75
  Madame Bovary, 67
  "A Simple Heart," 6–9, 10, 11
Fletcher, Angus, 60
Florus, Lucius Annaeus, 40, 200 n. 13

form
  ethical, *see under* ethical form
  progressive, 45–46, 51–52
  retrospective, 45, 51–54, 64–68, 75–77
  serial, *see under* serial form
forms, as living agents, 115, 127, 151, 154
Fox, Charles James, 138–39
French Revolution, 103, 114
Friedländer, Paul, 3

Gellius, 200 n. 13
Gill, Stephen, 128, 130
Gillispie, Charles Coulston, 199 n. 7 (intro.)
Gilpin, William, 15, 99–101, 108, 119, 121–23, 125, 126, 135, 136, 137, 141, 203 nn. 8, 10, 16
  An Essay upon Prints, 103
  Observations on the River Wye, 84, 110, 203 n. 16
  Three Essays, 104–07, 109–11, 112, 202 n. 3, 202 n. 4 (ch. 4)
  Two Essays, 101, 104
  see also picturesque aesthetics; picturesque tourism
gladiators, 173, 182–84
Godwinism, 116
Goethe, J. W., 91, 164
Goldstein, Laurence, 162
Grand Tour, 103, 104
Graver, Bruce E., 14, 85, 126, 138, 142
Gray, Thomas, 125, 142
Great, as aesthetic category, 98, 203 n. 9
Green, Karen, 139

Hadamard, description of school in, 41
Hagstrum, Jean H., 25, 56
Halliwell, Stephen J., 30, 35, 45, 46, 47, 48, 193
Hamilton, William Rowan, 49
Hamon, Philippe, 6, 8, 9, 11, 70, 193

Hardie, Philip, 199 n. 8 (intro.)
Hayden, John O., 118, 134, 203 n. 11
Hazlitt, William, 126, 128, 130, 205 n. 4
Hecht, Anthony, 200 n. 8
Hedrick, Charles W., 54–55, 56, 64–66
Heffernan, James A. W., 19, 199 n. 2 (intro.), 200 n. 5, 204 n. 8
Hemingway, Ernest, 19, 189
Heracles, shield of, 24
Herculaneum, 202 n. 5 (ch. 3)
hermeneutic description, *see under* description, hermeneutic
hermeneutics, 61–62
Hermes, 13
Hermogenes, 3, 20, 21, 23, 24, 26, 34, 199 n. 4 (intro.)
Herodotus, 23, 33–34, 200 n. 6
Hesperides, 92
Hickey, Alison, 129
Hipple, Walter John, Jr., 202 n. 1
historiography, nineteenth-century, 159–60
history, 127
  in Byron, 178–87
  as fact, 159–60
  as paradigm, 195
  as theater, 195
  as "what there is," 205 n. 1; *see also* Liu
Hollander, John., 192, 199 n. 2 (intro.)
Homer, 1, 19, 38, 46, 92, 190
  Iliad, 4, 24–25, 34–36, 43, 52, 54
  Odyssey, 13, 30–31, 36–37, 43, 69–70, 83, 189, 194, 202 n. 1
Horace, 17, 62–63, 64, 65, 70, 200 n. 1
  Ars poetica, 43–45
  see also locus amoenus
Horsfall, Nicholas, 74
Howard, W. G., 46, 91, 202 n. 4
Hunt, John Dixon, 79
Hutchinson, Mary, 117

ideology, 193
　see also false consciousness
　imagination, 5–6, 9–10,15, 92,
　　98–99, 106–117, 122–23, 127,
　　135, 140–41, 144, 152–54,
　　156, 160, 165–66, 179, 186,
　　190, 192–96, 203 nn. 13, 15
　see also creative perception; fancy;
　　phantasia
　imagined places, and literal settings,
　　159–60, 196–97
　see also place descriptions
　immediacy, 4, 5, 35, 136, 152–53,
　　160–61, 189–97
　see also "as if present" motif; "before
　　the eyes" motif; vividness
　intersubjectivity, of artist and audience,
　　141, 152–53, 199 n. 2 (ch. 1)
　see also emotion
Italy, 104
　in English poetry, 205 n. 5
　see also Byron, *Childe Harold's
　　Pilgrimage*

Jackson-Stops, Gervaise, 102
James, Henry, 39
　The Art of the Novel, 9, 192
　"The Figure in the Carpet," 55, 65
　"Miss Prescott's 'Azarian,'" 125
Jameson, Fredric, 190–92, 196–97
Jamison, Kay Redfield, 205 n. 11
Jeffrey, Francis, 129–30, 132, 139, 163,
　　204 n. 1 (ch. 5)
Jenkyns, Richard, 73–74, 77, 80, 81,
　　85
John of Sardis, 20–21
Johnson, Francis R., 21
Johnson, Paula, 201 n. 3
Johnson, Samuel, 121–22
Johnson, W. R., 75–76, 83
Johnston, Kenneth R, 129, 202 n. 16,
　　204 n. 6
Jonze, Spike, 191
Juno, 70, 74, 76, 77–78, 82
Juvenal, 179, 205 n. 15

Kafka, Franz, 189, 196
Kalon (the beautiful), as redemptive
　　force, 168–69, 170, 174
　compare aesthetic categories,
　　eighteenth-century; Beautiful, as
　　aesthetic category; Wordsworth,
　　"Prospectus," "The Sublime and
　　the Beautiful"
Kalypso, 13–14, 36–37
　see also nymphs
Kant, Immanuel, 105–06, 108
Kaufman, Charlie, 191
Keats, John, 126, 128, 130, 154
　"Ode on a Grecian Urn," 1–2
　"To Autumn," 200 n. 11
Kelley, Theresa M., 201 n. 8
Kennedy, George, progymnasmata
　　translations, 199 n. 4 (intro.)
　see under Aphthonius; Hermogenes;
　　Nicolaus; Theon
Kermode, Frank, 61–62, 65, 132
Kersey, John, usage of *ecphrasis*, 200 n. 5
Klarer, Mario, 193–94
Klein, Robert, 200 n. 2
Knight, Richard Payne, 99
Koelb, Clayton, 199 n. 3
Koelb, Janice Hewlett, 199 n. 9 (intro.)
Krieger, Murray, 71, 199 n. 2 (intro.)
Kroeber, Karl, 12–13, 52, 152, 201
　　n. 6, 204 n. 2, 204 n. 3 (ch. 5)

La Fontaine, Jean de, 22
Lamb, Charles, 126, 128, 130–31, 133,
　　137, 145
landscape
　and dialogue, 163: *see also* Byron,
　　Manfred; Piehler; Plato,
　　Phaedrus; psychodrama;
　　Wordsworth, *Excursion* (1814)
　painting, and visual culture, 88,
　　93–95, 98: *see also* Claude;
　　Gilpin; picturesque aesthetics
　six charms of, *see* Libanius
　and theater, 69–95
　Virgilian, 14–15, 135–37, 150, 153

Leigh, Ada Augusta (Byron's half-sister), 157, 161–62, 164–65
Leonardo da Vinci, 200–01 n. 2
Lessing, Gotthold Ephraim, 4, 8, 9–10, 24, 25, 55, 72, 107, 201 n. 4
  and allegory, 52–54
  and binary oppositionalism, 98, 200–01 n. 2: *compare* Addison; Burke; picturesque aesthetics; Pope
  Laocoön, 45–46, 49–54, 69
  see also Achilles, shield of; ecphrasis, subject matter defined; description and narrative; *pragmata* (things done or made)
Levinson, Marjorie, 203 n. 16
Lewalski, Barbara Kiefer, 202 n. 13
Lewis, C. S., 90
  see also Narnia
Libanius, 3, 13–14, 33, 88, 200 n. 11
Liu, Alan, 16, 127, 203 n. 11, 205 n. 1
Livy, 179, 205 n. 15
locodescriptive, coined by Wordsworth, 125, 194
locodescriptive poetry, 97–98, 156, 163
  see also place descriptions; picturesque tourism; picturesque aesthetics
locus amoenus, 13–14, 36–39, 44, 87, 91, 120–21, 135, 152, 179–80, 200 n. 11
London, in Virginia Woolf, 190
logos, as force of nature, 49
  see also animism; forms as living agents; description as life force; Wordsworth on education
Longinus, 19, 28–29
Lorich, Reinhold, 21, 31, 34, 39–42, 72
Lovelace, Ada King, Countess of (Byron's daughter), 157, 161–62, 178, 205 n. 12
Lucan, 42
Lucretius, 122

Macpherson, James, 102–03
Malpas, J. E., 194
Mann, Thomas, 75
Maori places, 194
Mark Antony, 40
Marmontel, Jean François, 35, 88
McFarland, Thomas, 157, 205 nn. 3, 4
McGann, Jerome J., 16, 171, 203 n. 16, 204 n. 1 (ch. 6)
Mead, William Edward, 205 n. 5
Medwin, Thomas, 169
Meisel, Martin, 201 n. 6
Melancholy (personified), *see* Milton, "Il Penseroso"
  compare depression; fancy as pathological
Melville, Herman, *Moby-Dick*, 1, 11
memory
  in Byron, 162, 163, 165, 170, 178: *see also mobilité*
  as paradigm for psychic intergration, 165–70, 173, 174, 178
  in Wordsworth, 133, 134, 137, 143–44, 170
Merivale, John Herman, 129
metaphor, 56–60
  compare allegory
Mill, John Stuart, 128
Milton, John, 20, 21, 22, 70, 93, 100–01, 122, 125, 134, 139, 204 n. 1 (ch. 5)
  aesthetic diction in, 89–93
  "Il Penseroso," 140–42, 147
  Paradise Lost, 4, 12, 14, 15, 69, 84, 85–93, 103, 191, 202 nn. 10, 11, 13, 14
  Samson Agonistes, 163
mimesis, 43, 44, 48, 153: *see also* Halliwell
  and classical theory of art, xi, 17, 35, 45
  and ethical form, 45–49
  as expression, 47
  and postmodernism, 192–94, 196
Mitchell, W. J. T., 200–01 n. 2, 201 n. 4
mobilité, and Byron's imagination, 160–61, 177, 178

modernism, 189–90, 192
Montesquieu, Charles de Secondat, 167
Mont Ventoux, 93
Moore, Thomas, 155, 158, 163, 182
Morales, Helen, 66, 67
Moran, Richard, 58–59
More, Hannah, 108–09, 203 n. 8
motival development, 74–75, 83
Mount Snowdon, 93
Muecke, Frances, 78
Murray, John, 164, 165, 177

Napoleon Bonaparte, 14
Napoleonic wars, 95, 103
Narnia, 191
narrative and description, *see under* description and narrative
nature as protoartificial, in Virgil, 79–83
　compare picturesque aesthetics; representation of representation
Naiads, 69
　see also nymphs
Neoplatonism, 115, 201 n. 1
Nero, 177
New Criticism, poem as artifact in, 5
Newton, Sir Isaac, 114
Nicolaus, 3, 4, 20, 23, 199 n. 4 (intro.)
Nicolson, Marjorie Hope, 93–94
Nicostratus, 2–3
Northumberland, Elizabeth Seymour Percy, Duchess of, 101–03
nostalgia, 12–13, 83
Numa, 179
Nuttall, A. D., 47
nymphs, 69–70, 77, 80
　see also caves; Egeria; Kalypso; *locus amoenus*

Oedipus, 78
orientalism, 158
ornateness, 31
　as simplicity, 34

Ossian, 103
Ovid, 20, 22, 39, 40, 161, 179, 200 nn. 12, 13, 202 n. 6–8, 204 n. 15
　see also ethical form; place description, ethical

Pan, 37
paragone, 200–01 n. 2
Parry, Adam, 36, 200 n. 10
pathetic fallacy, 36, 195
Patillon, Michel, 25, 34, 199 n. 6 (intro.)
Patterson, Annabel, 126
Patterson, Dudley, 194
Percy, Victoria, 102
Perkell, Christine, 77
Petrarch, 93
phantasia, 20, 28–30
Phidias, 46, 201 n. 4
Philips, Ambrose, 125
Philomela, 200 n. 12
Philostratus, 20, 23
Phorcys, harbor sacred to, 69–70, 75, 201 n. 1
picturesque aesthetics, 84, 85, 90, 97–123, 203–04 n. 18
　and the grotesque, 90–91
　and the protoartificial in nature, 15, 105–06, 112
　schemata in, 15, 111–14, 123, 202 n. 2
　compare nature as protoartificial, in Virgil
picturesque tourism, 15, 97–98, 99, 101–11, 126, 128, 133, 153
Piehler, Paul, 10, 39, 54, 60, 93, 127, 200 nn. 9, 11, 205 n. 8
Piggott, Stuart, 102, 103, 126
Pindar, 40, 200 n. 13
Piper, H. W., 114–16, 154, 156, 202 n. 14, 204 n. 19

place description(s), xii, 11–17
  in Aphthonius, 39–42
  as emblems of mind, 12–13, 14, 16, 38–39, 48, 93, 97–98, 125–27, 129, 156–60, 170, 179, 185, 190–92, 294–97: *see also* place description(s), ethical
  ethical, 14, 36–42, 153, 161, 175, 177, 179, 184, 190, 195: *see also* ethical form; *locus amoenus*; Ovid; place description(s) as emblems of mind; Plato, *Phaedrus*
  see also Achilles at Patroclus-s funeral pyre; Alpinism; Alps; Anglo-saxon verse; Apuleius; *Being John Malkovich*; Cacus; Carthaginian harbor; caves; Cleopatra; Coliseum; Dante; Dido-s temple; Diodorus; Disneyland; Eden; Egeria; Favorinus; Florus; landscape and dialogue; London; Lucan; Mount Snowdon; Narnia; Ovid; Phorcys; picturesque tourism; Rome; ruins; Saint Anthony; Scotland; Serapium; Servius Sulpicius; Shakespeare; theater; Thomson; Tiberianus; Tolkien; *topographia*; *topothesia*; Virgil, *Eclogues*; Westin Bonaventure Hotel
Plato
  Critias, 43
  Phaedrus, 36–38, 66
  Republic, 46–49
  see also Socrates
Plutarch, 40, 200 n. 13
polysemantic fictions, in Virgil, 75–76
  see also allegory; retrospective form
Pompey's theater, 79, 202 n. 5 (ch. 3)
Pope, Alexander
  The Iliad of Homer, 23, 26, 32
  "Summer," 84

Porphyry, 201 n. 1
Porter, Charles A., 9
Portman, John, 190
Pöschl, Viktor, 74–75
postmodernity, 5, 17, 98, 106, 190–94
pragmata (things done or made)
  as ecphrastic subject matter, 23
  split into objects and actions, 49–50
  see also Lessing
Praz, Mario, 204 n. 1 (ch. 6)
Price, Martin, 99
Price, Uvedale, 99
progressive form, 45–46, 51–52
progymnasmata, 2–4, 20–27, 53, 72, 75
  see also Aphthonius; Hermogenes; Nicolaus; Theon
Prometheus, 162, 165, 166, 178, 180–81, 182
Proust, Marcel, 189
psychodrama
  and allegory, 127, 159
  and rhetoric, 164–65, 174: *see also* Byron, dialectical image patterns in
psychology, Gestalt, 50, 52
Punic wars, 76–77
purple prose, origin of phrase, 44
Putnam, Michael C. J., 4, 11, 71–72, 74–75, 76, 199 n. 2 (intro.), 201–02 n. 2

Quilligan, Maureen, 201 n. 9
Quintilian, 17, 19, 20, 28, 29–30, 31–33, 34, 56–57, 61, 65, 138–39, 196, 201 n. 9, 206 n. 2
  on allegory, 59–64
  on *descriptio* and *narratio*, 26–27, 31

Race, William H., 27–28, 35, 120, 203 n. 17
radiance, 31–32
  see also immediacy; vividness
Ramsay, Alan, *Tea-Table Miscellany*, 102

Randel, Don Michael, 74
Ray, John, 93–94
reading, as animating force, 138–43, 149–50
 see also logos; Wordsworth on education
reality effect, 11, 55, 64
Renaissance, 67, 200 n. 12, 202 n. 5 (ch. 3)
 progymnasmata in, 20–24, 39–42: *see also* Aphthonius; Lorich
repraesentatio, 20
representation of representation, 5, 16–17, 192–94, 196–97
 compare immediacy; vividness
 see also mimesis
repression, 16
retrospective form, 45, 51–54, 64–68, 75–77
Richards, I. A., 57–58, 60, 61
Richardson, Alan, 163–64, 167, 205 n. 9
 see also psychodrama
Robinet, Jean Baptiste René, 203 n. 14
Roger, Jacques, 203 n. 14
romance, conventions in, 65–67
 see also description, hermeneutic
Rome, 11, 15, 76, 81, 91, 104, 159, 162, 165, 178, 179, 195
 see also Coliseum
Rudy, John G., 133
ruins, 136, 140, 144, 150, 153, 157, 159, 161, 178, 184–87, 195, 205, n. 5
Ruskin, John, 36, 195, 200 n. 8
Russell, J. Stephen, 201 n. 8

Saint Anthony, home of, 41–42
 see also place descriptions in Aphthonius
Satan (Miltonic), 86–87, 88–89, 122, 145, 162, 177, 190
 compare creative perception
Scarry, Elaine, 195–96
scene, scenery (*scaena*), and theater, 77–95, 103, 183, 190
 see also Carthaginian harbor; Eden

Scotland, 102–03
Scott, Grant F., 19, 24–25, 162, 199 n. 2 (intro.)
Scott, Sir Walter, 85, 162
self-delusion, 16, 127, 157
Seneca, 93, 97
Serapium, 40–41
serial form, 49–53, 201 n. 3
 compare ethical form
 see also configural understanding; progressive form; retrospective form
Servius Sulpicius, 178, 184
Shakespeare, William, 67
 Hamlet, 169
 Titus Andronicus, 200 n. 12
Shelley, Percy Bysshe, 126, 154, 168–69, 185–86, 203 n. 17
Shulman, David, 196–97
Shumaker, Wayne, 203 n. 7
Sidney, Sir Philip, 67
Simonides, 45
Socrates, 36–38, 46–49, 142–43, 153, 200 n. 9
Sophocles, 78
Spenser, Edmund, 14
Spengel, Leonard von, 199 n. 4 (intro.)
Spitzer, Leo, 1–2, 5, 8, 13
Stephen, Leslie, 128
Stevens, Wallace, 12, 189
stoicism, 115, 178
sublime, 98–100, 107–10, 62, 177, 203 n. 18
 see also aesthetic categories, eighteenth-century; picturesque aesthetics

Tanit (Carthaginian goddess), *see* Juno
tenorless vehicle, *see* allegory; metaphor
theater
 and landscape, 69–95
 Roman, 79–80
Theon, 2, 3, 20, 22–23, 25, 33, 34, 199 n. 4, 199 n. 6 (intro.)
 see also progymnasmata
Thomson, James, 102, 103, 125, 126

Thoreau, Henry David, 12
Thorvaldsen, Bertel, 104
Thucydides, 4
Tiberianus, 38, 88
Tobin, James, 131
Tolkien, J. R. R., 14
topographia, 41
topothesia, 41
Trimpi, Wesley, 200 n. 1
Trojan war, 30–31, 76
  see also ecphrasis of battle; Dido's temple
Trott, Nicola, 14
Tullia (Cicero's daughter), 178
Tuve, Rosamond, 60

Uncommon, as aesthetic category, 98
  see also Addison; Burke; Gilpin
unity, 43–68, 189–90
  of individual work, 43, 44, 190
  of mimetic arts, 44, 47, 190: *see also* Halliwell
  psychic, 163–70, 190
  and vividness, 43–44
ut pictura poesis, 1, 43–45

vacancy, as spiritual openness, 111, 121–22
Valéry, Paul, 6
Virgil, 15, 90, 92, 103, 183, 190, 201 n. 1, 202 n. 6
  Aeneid, xi, xii, 1, 4, 10–11, 13, 14, 24, 32, 40, 46, 68, 194, 195, 200 n. 9, 13, 202 n. 7
  Aeneid 1, 69–85, 201–02 n. 2, 202 n. 11
  Eclogues, 14, 63–64, 135–37, 153
  Georgics, 14
Viscomi, Joseph S., 203 n. 6
vision, optical and imaginative, 15, 92–93, 125–54, 136, 141
  see also fancy; creative perception; imagination; landscape; Melancholy; picturesque aesthetics

Vitruvius Pollio, 80
vividness (*enargeia*), xi, 2, 19–20, 23, 27–36, 57, 189, 192
  and *energeia*, 33
  and wonder, 98
  see also immediacy; radiance

Wagner, Richard, 75
Walpole, Horace, 108–09
Webb, Ruth, xi, 2, 4, 5, 23, 24, 30, 102, 193
Weller, Philip, 102
Western Apache, language and landscape in, 194–95
Westin Bonaventure Hotel, 190–92, 196–97
Whitman, Jon, 202 n. 9
Williams, Gordon, 69, 80, 86, 202 n. 3 (ch. 3)
Williams, R. D., 75, 201 n. 2
Willis, Peter, 79
Wilson, John, 132
Wimsatt, W. K., 205 n. 13
Wolff, Samuel Lee, 66–67
Woodring, Carl, 120, 126–27, 128
Woolf, Virginia, 189, 190, 192
Wordsworth, Jonathan, 128–29
Wordsworth, William, 12–13, 14–15, 16, 21, 42, 70, 83, 85, 98, 99, 100–01, 169, 172, 190, 203 n. 11, 204 nn. 6, 7, 9
  backlash against the picturesque, 111–17, 125–54
  and Christianity, 128
  on education, 131–33, 140, 122–43
  fancy in, 110, 116–23: *see also* creative perception; fancy; imagination; *phantasia*
  forms in, 15, 115, 127, 151, 154
  imagination in, 110, 114–17, 153–54; *see also* creative perception; fancy; imagination; *phantasia*; vision, optical and imaginative
  on industrialization, 112

Wordsworth, William, (*Continued*)
  power in, 15, 115
  rhetoric of *philosophes* in, 115
  works:
    "The Baker's Cart," 116
    The Borderers, 157, 204 n. 2
      (ch. 6)
    "The Brothers," 139
    "Description of the Scenery of the Lakes," 97, 103, 111–12
    Descriptive Sketches, 111–13, 203 n. 12
    "Elegaic Stanzas," 118–20
    "Essay, Supplementary to the Preface," 141
    "Essays Upon Epitaphs," 49
    An Evening Walk, 115
    The Excursion (1850), 152, 204 n. 4
    The Excursion (1814), 15, 19, 92, 116, 125–54, 155–57, 162, 163, 178, 186, 187, 190, 194, 195, 199 n. 2 (ch. 1), 204 n. 4: reception of, 128–31; tale of Margaret in, 145–50; as therapeutic psychodrama, 127–34, 145–46; Wanderer's biography in, 134–45
    "Lines Left upon a Seat in a Yew-tree," 121–23, 147, 150
    Lyrical Ballads, 138
    "Michael," 139
    "Ode: Intimations of Immortality," 129, 149
    "The Pedlar," 204 n. 5
    Preface to *The Excursion* (1814), 129, 131–32
    Preface to *Lyrical Ballads*, 17, 113, 129
    Preface to *Poems* (1815), 17, 125, 203 nn. 13, 15
    The Prelude, 93, 114, 128, 129, 133, 153
    "Prospectus," 127, 129
    The Recluse, as Gothic church, 131
    "Reply to Mathetes," 132
    "The Ruined Cottage," 204 n. 5
    "The Sublime and the Beautiful," 113–114, 118
    "The Tables Turned," 139
    "There Was a Boy," 94
    "Tintern Abbey," 118, 203 n. 16
    "To M. H.," 117–18
    "Translation of Virgil's *Aeneid*," 85
Wu, Duncan, 14
Wye river, 108–09
  see also Gilpin; Wordsworth, "Tintern Abbey"

Young, Edward, 125

Zerner, Henri, 200 n. 2
Zoroastrianism, in *Manfred*, 167–68
  see also Astoreth